THE HEALER-PROPHET
IN AFRO-CHRISTIAN CHURCHES

STUDIES IN CHRISTIAN MISSION

VOLUME 3

THE HEALER-PROPHET
IN AFRO-CHRISTIAN CHURCHES

BY

GERHARDUS C. OOSTHUIZEN

E.J. BRILL
LEIDEN • NEW YORK • KÖLN
1992

This series offers a forum for scholarship on the history of Christian missionary movements world-wide, the dynamics of Christian witness and service in new surrounds, the transition from movements to churches, and the areas of cultural initiative or involvement of Christian bodies and individuals, such as education, health, community development, press, literature and art. Special attention is given to local initiative and leadership and to Christian missions from the Third World. Studies in the theories and paradigms of mission in their respective contexts and contributions to missiology as a theological discipline is a second focus of the series. Occasionally volumes will contain selected papers from outstanding missiologists and proceedings of significant conferences related to the themes of the series.

Enquiries regarding the submission of works for publication in the series may be directed to Professor Marc R. Spindler, IIMO, University of Leiden, Rapenburg 61, 2311 GJ Leiden, The Netherlands.

The paper in this book meets the guidelines for permanence and durability of the Committee on Production Guidelines for Book Longevity of the Council on Library Resources.

Library of Congress Cataloging-in-Publication Data

Oosthuizen, G. C. (Gerhardus Cornelis)
    The healer-prophet in Afro-Christian churches / by Gerhardus C. Oosthuizen.
        p.   cm.—(Studies in Christian mission, ISSN 0924-9389; v. 3)
    Includes bibliographical references and index.
    ISBN 9004094687 (alk. paper)
    1. South Africa—Religious life and customs. 2. Nativistic movements—South Africa. 3. Healers—South Africa. 4. Healing—South Africa—Religious aspects. I. Title. II. Series.
    BR1450.O56   1992
    262'.1—dc20   92-15125
                                                          CIP

ISSN   0924-9389
ISBN   90 04 09468 7

CONTENTS

PREFACE

This study concentrated on prophets and their activities without any regard for their affiliation to any ethnic group. It concentrated mainly on metropolitan Durban and surrounding areas and on the Rand, especially Soweto, but a number of prophets from the Transkei, the Free State, Lesotho, Swaziland, Bophuthatswana and other parts of Natal were also interviewed. Many of these prophets were contacted at the beaches, especially Durban's North Beach, where adherents of indigenous churches come from many parts of the country to 'baptise' which implies exorcism, spiritual renewal, healing, restoration of relationships within the family, in the churchcontext, and in society.

The role of the prayer healers is a vital one in many of the indigenous churches. Some make a distinction between the ordinary prayer healer and the prophet. This study concentrates on the prophet. Although most of the prophets are not leaders of the churches in which they are active, the office is considered to be vital to the well-being of the church. During the last two decades especially it has gained in stature because of the turmoil that exists in the minds of many blacks who have to move culturally and physically out of the microcosmic, tradition-orientated world to the macrocosmic modern world. This involves much tension and insecurity, especially within the South African context where the office of prophet has expanded in many indigenous churches. Nowhere has this office become so typical of the Indigenous/Independent Churches in Africa (AIC) as in South Africa. The tension and insecurity that change brings, the political turmoil in the black townships and even in the rural areas (in spite of the fact that most of the AIC avoid getting too involved in the political arena), calls for the counterpart of the diviner, who was for the traditional community the guide against the adverse forces which are responsible for ill-health, sickness, mal-relationships, misfortune and that which beclouds the future. The diviners have also become a more familiar phenomenon in the townships than was the case two decades ago. Hardly any stigma is attached to them or those visiting them. The same is the case with prophets who also act as diviners.

The works of Martin West and Jim Kiernan (included in the bibliography) are the most important on the contemporary position of the prophet in the AIC in Southern Africa. The present study, however, attempts to give special attention to the relationships of the prophets to the forces of the metaphysical world and their treatment of indigenous cultural diseases. The traditional influences are still much stronger with some of the prophets than is usually admitted.

The author wishes to express his special appreciation for the assistance received from various field workers who interviewed prophets, often in difficult circumstances during times of extreme turmoil in most of the black townships, and even in some rural areas. It has been a privilege for the author to have been able to meet many leaders, diviners, prophets/prayer healers, those in other offices and members of the AIC, in their homes, as families and during services held in their homes and churches in the townships. Furthermore, the visits to the sea, where many prophetic activities are encountered, have been of special significance in making contact with the AIC as a movement in Southern Africa.

The interest and assistance of the Centre for Science Development within the Human Sciences Research Council has always been an inspiration. A special word of appreciation to Ms. A.A. Clifford-Vaughan, for editing the manuscript.

ILLUSTRATIONS

Note: All photographs were taken on Durban beaches, and, except where otherwise stated, by the author.

Fig. 1. A prophet with her holy staff, thick cords around the waist and beads around the neck.

Fig. 2. From left to right: A prophet and leader of the women in the church; her husband, the minister; a prayer healer and diviner; a prophet; a lay preacher. All wear the typical waist cords.

Fig. 3. Three AIC groups appear on this photograph. The small group in the distance is proceeding into the water. The middle group and the group in the foreground are preparing themselves for entry into the water.

Fig. 4. Preparation is made by means of prayer, confession, singing (with rhythmic movements) and often Bible reading. Most groups have attended an all-night service before coming to the beach on Sunday morning, and some come on a Saturday evening for purification.

Fig. 5. The leader, "mother", of this group of three Zionist prophets and diviners lights the seven candles symbolising the presence of "the Holy Spirit" and the ancestors assisting and guiding them in their healings and couselling activities.

Fig. 6. The prophet faces the group as they engage in earnest prayer before entering the sea.

Fig. 7. The prophet is praying for the woman with the white fowl, which she has brought with her at the request of her deceased grandmother (her guiding ancestral spirit). The prophet belongs to The Christian Church in Zion, the patient to an established church.

Fig. 8. Healing procedures include the laying-on of hands.

Fig. 9. The officiant – in this case prophet-cum-diviner – with arms raised "opens up" the water, i.e. blesses it for the exorcism procedures. Photo by Dr H.-J. Becken.

Fig. 10. Removing the evil forces in a "struggle".

Fig. 11. The patient (also a prophet-cum-diviner) experiences the departure of the evil spirit(s). Photo by Dr H.-J. Becken.

Fig. 12. Calmness comes over the patient. After the exorcism they return to the place where candles were lit and prayers said. Photo by Dr H.-J. Becken.

INTRODUCTION

This study on the healer prophet has led to the conclusion that there are various ecclesiastical levels within the African Independent/Indigenous Churches (AIC). The following different types are to be discerned:

1) those who follow the established approach and the doctrinal norms which the so-called established churches[*] uphold;

2) those who have established pentecostal church approaches but, nevertheless, with minor differences when it comes to the ministry and the interpretation of the sacraments, especially baptism;

3) those who follow the original tenets of the Christian Catholic Church in Zion and remain consistent with its teachings and administration as well as such as the Ethiopian Churches and some with the Apostolic Faith Mission background;

4) those who are no longer original Ethiopian, Zionist or Apostolic, but who have departed to a limited extent only, from the mainline churches;

5) those who are marginal, and who are often treated by the above-mentioned categories as apostate because they are deeply embedded in the traditional world view and its metaphysical forces. Here is no distinction between Ethiopian, Apostolic and Zionist and many have the word "Zion" added to their names as well as "of South Africa". Although in all the categories mentioned above the African world view comes through, especially with regard to the emphasis on the symbolic union with the traditional metaphysical forces, this view is strongest in this category.

The sudden growth of Christianity among the African population has brought into the Christian orbit a stream of traditionalists who have not received the thorough catechetical instruction which was especially characteristic of the missionary founded churches. Many of these Christians have had hardly any catechetical instruction.

Christianity among Africans in South Africa is still not much older than one-and-a-half centuries. The largest sections, however, have been

---

[*] The adjective "established" is used here to designate the western, historic churches, formerly referred to as "mainline". The latter is no longer an appropriate description since the largest church among blacks in South Africa is now the Zion Christian Church, one of the African Independent Churches (AIC).

in the Christian fold no longer than a few decades. It is a mass movement
which has brought with it many traditional emphases.

The wish to go back to the roots of traditional Africa, the emphasis
on black consciousness and the self-discovery of the African heritage,
its wisdom and world view, have given rise to criticism among many in
the established (so-called mainline) churches, founded and influenced
by missionary colonialism, against the foreignness of these churches. In
these churches, ministers often emulated their missionary masters, but
a change has taken place. Even in these churches traditional approaches,
with regard to liturgy, communication, composition of indigenous choruses and hymns, are studied and many of their members seek healing
with the AIC. They also harbour beliefs which accept the existence of
traditional metaphysical adversaries and the pollution which is directed
to many of their flock and which accounts for many of the cultural
diseases (*Ukufa kwaBantu*).

These traditional influences have come much more from the bottom
up than from the top down. Thus, the fifth category of churches mentioned previously exerts the greatest influence on the other churches
above them in spite of attitudes towards them. There is a tremendous
variety of approaches and interpretations of practically every doctrine,
object, ceremony, ritual, office in the church, even with regard to the
sacraments. 'Baptism', particularly, could imply exorcism, healing,
receiving 'the Spirit', purification, spiritual power, wellbeing, establishing good relationships, etc.

General trends can be indicated but nobody should be misled into
thinking that he or she has discussed this movement exhaustively—no
one has, and no one will ever be able to do this. All who have made close
contact realize that this tremendous movement is fed by a rich tradition
which is deeply held by many of those who hail from it and who have
entered a Christianity which is, in many respects, richer than the
streamlined type of Christianity, which is poor in liturgy, in the exposition of the faith, in the holistic approach to man's body, soul and spirit,
with regard to man's whole existence in the socio-economic and political
sphere. This dynamic movement has no stale, set type of services,
methods of communication, types of ministry or even theology. Its
archbishops, presidents, bishops, ministers, evangelists, lay preachers,
prophets, prayer healers, deacons and guardians account for the movement of the church.

The whole movement is related to the self-discovery of the African
in a situation which has looked down (and still does to a great extent)

upon what he is, and what he has to offer. He started to do his own ecclesiastical thing. He had to adapt to the modern situation, and did it through his own method of bringing two worlds together. Through this adaption he adjusted to a new structure of authority, not necessarily based on age; and to a new concept of time with a locus in the future rather than in the past. This involved a creative approach to his own structures, rather than simple acceptance of those given to him by the churches or the political milieu. The emphasis was now on individual responsibility rather than on dependence on the community, but there was still protection by the community without financial dependence on any established white churches or other church organizations. There was a reappraisal of traditional holistic healing processes—a reappraisal which ran counter to mechanistic, impersonal and physically centred healing processes associated with modern medical approaches. These were seen to provide impersonal treatment in hospitals with a "cold" individualistic atmosphere.

The AIC movement is concerned mainly with a tradition in transition. The tradition is sometimes in conflict with, and sometimes reconciled to, the new. Certain aspects of the old (such as the ancestor) still have a tremendous hold on people. The old constitutes a real, dynamic, meta-physical world for them, a world in which age-old adverse forces continue to play the negative roles of making people weak and ill, and of destroying life. The evil spirits and demons are still real for many.

The matter-of-fact world of the secularised environment, with its harsh and unsympathetic institutions—including the established churches and medicine—has been less helpful than the ages old tradition which kept them going. In this traditional stage everything is fluid. It is sometimes impossible to define the diviner and the prophet; to state precisely what the different attitudes are to dreams, to visions; to define the task of the ancestors and the demons, or precisely who they are. This difficulty is mainly due to the fact that the situation is so dynamic and fluid that words used cannot adequately describe what is meant because their meanings change and are differently interpreted. Differences are detected also among the many denominations which constitute the AIC movement. In the transition of traditions, words change and lose much of their original meaning in the process. With a specific word certain basic connotations may remain but one is continuously surprised by how fluid everything becomes. Even the word "Zion" in the Zionist indig-enous churches has many connotations.

In this book, many of the activities of the prophet are related to the forces of evil, which play a vital role in the traditional context. There is a transition process at work here, as was the case especially during the first six centuries of Christianity, when many aspects of the traditional religions still influenced the Christians at the time. This was true of many situations where there was dynamic growth of Christianity. The New Testament gave the impression that the Christian mission's main aim would be exorcism. The "saint" opposing the "forces of evil" occupied the scene. This is evident in Paul's words in *Ephesians* 6:11 and 12, where he refers to "the whole armor of God... against the wiles of the devil. For we are not contending against flesh and blood, but against the principalities, against the powers, against the world rulers of this present darkness, against the spiritual hosts of wickedness in the heavenly places". The Christian communities as "the bearers of the Holy Spirit" became in the earlier centuries a force confronting the powers of evil, to which Paul refers. Through martyrdom and asceticism, the demons, these forces of evil, were overcome. During those early days of Christianity, full membership by baptism "was preceded by drastic exorcisms. Once inside the Christian Church, the Christian enjoyed ... the millenial sensations of a modern anti-sorcery cult" (cf. Brown, P., "Sorcery, demons, and the rise of Christianity in the Middle Ages", in Douglas, M. (ed), *Witchcraft, confessions and accusations*, London, Tavistock Publications, 1970, p. 31). It will be evident from this book that the AIC are also considered to be an "anti-sorcery cult", where established church members also find relief.

The proliferation of Christian communities during the third and fourth centuries took place among rootless people who came from the country to the Mediterranean cities and who lived in uncertainty (Dodds, E.R., *Pagan and Christian in an age of anxiety*, Cambridge, Cambridge University Press, 1965, p. 78, pp. 137-138). On the other hand, there were also Christians who were attached to the government service and scattered in various parts of the Roman Empire; as there were those who followed a monastic life, so that Christians were described as a "race of strangers" (Brown, P., *Augustine of Hippo*, London, Faber, 1967, pp. 323-324). This designation could also be applied to the African in the cities of South Africa, whether Christian or non-Christian. Here the small-scale churches became societies in miniature, just as was the case in the Mediterranean cities during the 3rd and 4th centuries; they were also "people of God" with a strong sense of cohesion.

Much of this book relates to the irrational in society which needs close attention. The belief in sorcery, witchcraft, demons and evil spirits cannot merely be circumscribed by "intellectualist" interpretations, but goes much deeper. There are sociological and other factors involved. Do witch beliefs have a normative effect on behaviour; do they assist in keeping the community intact? Can sorcery merely be treated in isolation—does it not conceptualize aspects of a community's social relationship and does it not assist them to relate to the problem of evil? Does the preoccupation with evil forces in small-scale churches serve as a means to bind them together against these forces? Or is much of this preoccupation due to the fact that Christianity evokes a stronger guilt orientation among people who hail from a primal or traditional religious background, so that they react against evil much more intensely than before? The tremendous emphasis on exorcism was characteristic of so-called primitive and early Christianity; it is evident again in the first and second century of Afro-Christianity in the southern part of this continent, as reflected in the AIC. This phenomenon is a major concern of the healer in Afro-Christianity.

During the downward trend of the Later Roman Empire, there was an increase in sorcery beliefs, which were ascribed to insecurity and the general misery that prevailed at the time, mainly because of the decay of traditional religions which could not give direction in the prevailing confusion. This was especially the case in the fourth century AD when there arose a class of so-called 'semi-Christians' whose "new faith in Christ was over-shadowed by a superstititious fear of demons" (cf. Brown, 1970, p. 19; Momigliano, A.D. (ed), *The conflict between paganism and Christianity in the Fourth Century*, London, OUP, p. 9 63). The term 'semi-Christians' refers to a syncretised type of Christianity in which the beliefs in adverse metaphysical forces, sorcery and magic still have an influence in the daily lives of people, albeit by reaction. This is the case with many in the AIC in contemporary Africa. The primal religion does not give an answer to the modern problems, so that large numbers of traditionalists enter the AIC, bringing with them the superstititious fear of demons, evil spirits and the negative forces at work, such as sorcerers.

The fourth century AD was the age of bitter doctrinal disputations and upheavals which led to much discordance and hatred, not only among people but between them and the supernatural forces, which also accounts for the insecurity and confusion that prevailed. Superstition was rife, sorcery increased as a result of the increase in insecurity among a large section of the urban population who were strangers to one another. This is the case today with many Africans in the urban areas. With the chaotic breaking up of old traditions, an atmosphere of betrayal reigns in relation to the ancestors, and what they stand for. This contributes greatly to the insecurities and fears of adverse forces, to which much attention is given in the AIC. One of the great problems among the less privileged classes is the little hope of personal advancement.

The emphasis in early Christian circles, was upon "pagans" who, because they "worshipped demons", would conveniently manipulate them in sorcery. This has repeated itself on the African continent. The main aspect of phenomena such as witchcraft, sorcery and spirit posses-sion, is their explanation in the context of misfortune (cf. Evans-Pritchard, E.E., *Witchcraft, oracles and magic among the Azande*, Ox-ford, Clarendon Press, 1937; Evans-Pritchard, E.E., "Witchcraft", *Africa*, 8(4) : 417-422).

Much of the religious literature of Late Antiquity deals directly with the problem of evil. During its time of rapid growth, Christianity was forced to consider its relationship to sorcery beliefs, witchcraft, magic and spirit possession. This same situation developed in Africa and is obvious among the African indigenous churches, especially in Southern Africa, which have to deal with destruction of the centuries-old tradi-tional explanations of misfortune, such as the anger of the ancestors, sorcery and witchcraft accusations, and the transfer of evil forces on people. In today's destruction of the accepted explanatory system, in a situation where the intimate family-related community life has been broken down and a developing individualism has come to the fore, human mystical agents with their negative acts of sorcery and witchcraft are considered to be the sources of misfortune.

In the Southern African context, components of the urbanisation process, such as the tremendous disruption it brings to practically every family, living alongside strangers, the breaking up of family life, the negative systems of "native control", the struggle to survive, are all factors which contribute to the disruption of the old roots and also to the rise of a type of Christianity that gives attention to this situation and provides explanations for misfortune. In a legal context, for example, the acceptable modern approach is that a person can only be sued if he has harmed another in some overt manner, but in a society which believes in witchcraft, misfortune is ascribed to someone who harbours ill-feeling against a person, his family or others near to him. Witchcraft attacks without moral considerations, while ancestors in general attack what is undesirable, wicked and evil. The belief in the malice of witchcraft as well as the wrath of the ancestors affirms the possibility of misfortune if one's relationships are not in order. Mystical danger looms and in African society, which is organised in groupings of kin or small communities with close, face-to-face relations, good interrelationships are of primary significance (cf. Gluckman, M., *Custom and conflict in Africa*, Oxford, Blackwell, 1963, pp. 94-95). In the small-scale indigenous church denominations, continuous reaction against witchcraft, sorcery and evil spirit possession should be seen against the background of the deep seated traditional desire to give expression to the strong sense of community. This makes members pre-occupied with those forces of evil which want to destroy their community.

The same emphasis prevailed in fourth century Christianity with the mass disruption of traditional societies at that time. In that era, as is the case now among a disrupted African community, misfortune was for "pagan and Christian ... unambiguously the work of superhuman agents, the daemones ... demons were the effective agents of all misfortune. The sorcerer caused misfortune only by manipulating the demons, the curser, by 'delivering over' his victim to their hostility" (Brown, 1967, p. 28). Among AIC, at the special places where exorcism is effected, it seems as if the "demon-hosts" have taken over in their attacks on individuals in these churches in the same manner as is described in Late Antiquity literature, as referred to by Dawes and Baynes: "If we believe that the myriad bacilli about us were each and all inspired by a conscious will to injure man, we might then gain a realisation of the constant menace that broods over human life in the biographies of Byzantine Saints" (cf. Dawes, E. and Baynes, E.H., *Three Byzantine Saints*, Oxford, Blackwell, 1948, p. xii). Attending the services of many of the AIC, one would immediately understand how "the constant menace that broods over human life" is an aspect of these churches' existence and why they concentrate so much on exorcism, with prayer healers and especially prophets as special offices to 'heal' victims from this pollution (cf. Brown, 1967, p. 28 and Momigliano, A.D. (ed.), *The conflict between Paganism and Christianity in the Fourth Century*, London, Oxford University Press, 1963).

As already indicated, during the 3rd and 4th centuries in Christian literature, the superhuman agents of evil were "humanized" in the form of the sorcerer who reflected the negative attributes and motives of the somewhat faceless demons in which the traditionalists ie. the non-christians of the time believed. The church's officialdom, however, desired that misfortune should be ascribed to the activities of the dead. They maintained that the misfortunes which afflicted their congregations had a purely demonic nature. The Church Fathers, such as Jerome, regularly applied exorcism to Christians who experienced "demon possession".

Of great significance is the statement by Peter Brown that the rise of Christianity during the 4th and 5th centuries is due to misfortune being divorced from a human reference; that the blame should be put firmly in the context of "spiritual powers of evil" and, he adds, "Hence, perhaps, the snowball effect of the rapid rise of Christianity. Men joined the new community to be delivered from demons, and the new community, in turn, resolved its tensions by projecting them in the form of an even greater demonic menace from outside" (Brown, 1967, 33). The "rapid rise" of the AIC is related to the ability to deliver a person from the effects of the demons, who are the servants of the sorcerer, but who is outside their fold. The saint in the early Christian centuries had effective vested power to counteract the effects of the sorcerer whose powers were unreliable.

The situation changed in the Christian church in the late fourth/ beginning of the fifth century, when Augustine (371-430) emphasized that the church had an explanation of misfortune which transcended traditional explanations. Augustine emphasized that demons were only permitted to act as a result of Adam's sin, ie. as punishment for sins. Augustine saw the human race as the "plaything of demons" (Augustine, *Contra Julianum*, VI, XXI, 67 referred to in Brown, 1967, p. 28). Those misfortunes, previously ascribed to the sorcerers, were now ascribed by Augustine to God's abiding anger sent because of His indignation. These misfortunes included the possession by evil spirits. Dreams were considered to carry messages of misfortune. Misfortune became closely associated with demonic possession, as is evident during the time of Gregory the Great at the end of the 6th century. About this time the witch, a person born with or who acquired an inherent character of evil, came to the fore. The witch's character was not an unconscious mystical quality, as in the case of the genuine African diviner (whose acts are often irresponsibly referred to as "witchcraft"), but was consciously gained by a specific act in conjunction with Satan, and once the evil character had been acquired by such a person, recantation of the "new-style witch" in the Christian Church was hardly possible. The sorcerer who acted in the Christian Church was now no longer tolerated—if such a person were still active he was considered as having denied his baptism and was not part of the Christian community.

Brown states that by the end of the sixth century "the image of the divine world had become exceedingly stable. Angels were the courtiers and bureaucrats of a remote Heavenly Emperor and the saints—the patrons, the 'protectors', whose efficacious interventions at court channelled the benefits of a just autocrat to individuals and loyalties ... a well-regimented celestial society. We have entered the tidy world of the Middle Ages" (Brown, 1967, p. 36).

This "tidy world", with its "well-regimented celestial society" has not as yet been reached in Africa. The celestial forces are still too complex, and many too ambivalent, to make such an evaluation of the world in which Afro-Christianity finds itself, but this may come. However, is there not the possibility that the "tidy world" is unreal, and that more should be done to understand the forces with which Afro-Christianity wrestles? Much of the struggling with these forces, as is evident in this book, seems to be one not against fiction but against "the principalities, against the powers, against the world rulers of this present darkness, against the spiritual hosts of wickedness in the heavenly places" (*Eph.* 6: 11-12). Many of these powers are socio-economic and politically orientated—they are related to the very existence of people who look for a place of security, peace, humanity and mutual respect.

CHAPTER ONE

BACKGROUND TO THIS THEME

The healing ministry of the Church has been neglected in the "historic" Churches. It has become central in the African Independent/Indigenous Churches (AIC).*

Healing activities have been based by AIC on charismatic church and indigenous related procedures. The activities of the *abathandazi* (prayer healers—literally, those who pray) and *abaprofeti* (prophets) are highlighted. The office of prophet is found in most of the Zionist Churches. Some churches (not all) make a distinction between prayer healers and prophets—both categories are healers but the prophet is often considered to be more senior than the *umthandazi* (the one who prays). While the prophet works mainly through visions, the prayer healer operates mainly through the injunction of dreams. Three main groups constitute the AIC, namely, the Ethiopian Churches (*Amatopi*), the Zionist Churches (*Amazioni*) and the Apostolics (*Abapostoli*). They have, however, different approaches but many of the denominations which originated from them have more or less similar characteristics. There were, in 1913, 32 denominations (the Ethiopian leadership played a role in the event which led to the formation of what was then the SANNC (since 1925 African National Congress)); in 1948 there were 800 denominations with 800,000 adherents, 9% of the African population; in 1960 2,000 denominations, with 2,100,000 adherents, 18% of the African population; in 1980 3,270 denominations, 5,953,000 adherents, 29,3% of the African population. It is estimated that there are now, in 1990, more than 4,000 denominations, 8 million adherents, ± 35% of the African population. This is the fastest growing church movement in Southern Africa.

The established church rejected the office of prophet and prophecy within it. Now and then, there is a controversy about the prophet and his/her prophecy outside the established church. Nowhere, however, has the role of the prophet in the Church become so prominent as in the AIC, especially in South Africa. As was the case in the first and second century

---

* The designation "independent" is often used for churches outside the established churches but the reaction against this holds that "independent" has a stigma attached to it, a split-off connotation. Most of these churches have not seceded from so-called historic or established churches, but are spontaneous indigenous developments.

of Christianity in the Middle East, Europe and North Africa, the prophet again gained prominence in first- and second-century Christianity in Southern Africa, but not in the historic churches. Never was the role of prophet so widely associated with healing as in Southern Africa.

Basically, the power with which a prophet works in the AIC is not derived from the community, but from his/her relationship to the supernatural forces.

The reappearance of the prophet in Africa's first- and second-century indigenous Christianity is mainly due to the fact that healing has so often been pushed out of the Churches into the cold atmosphere of western orientated individualistic hospitalisation. Healing in Africa has basically a religious connotation, in spite of being associated with magical acts. Unfortunately it was the priest, the repeater of rituals and of the liturgy, who predominated in the Church, and not the prophet, the analyser, seer, the visionary. Priests, pastors, ministers of the word of God should also be prophets, but in some churches this prophetic aspect of their ministry is subdued. The prophet is a reformer who needs a religious disposition that takes note of contemporary human need. Sundkler states "the prophet is the revolutionary element in the Independent Church" (Sundkler, B.G.M., *Bantu prophets in South Africa*, OUP, 1961, p. 115).

John Alexander Dowie, the father of Christian Zionism, founder of the *Christian Catholic Church in Zion* on 22 February 1896, emphasized abstinence from tobacco and alcohol, and strongly upheld the principle of faith healing. This Zion influence came from Zion City Illinois, USA, to South Africa as early as 1897, and the influence of the *Apostolic Faith Church* was brought by Elder John Lake and Thomas Hezmalhalch after they had visited the Church in Azusa Street, Los Angeles, where the outpouring of the Holy Spirit—it is maintained—took place, and which introduced the era of pentecostalism. They founded the Apostolic Faith Mission (cf. Oosthuizen , G.C., *The birth of Christian Zionism in South Africa*, Publication Series, University of Zululand, 1987; also, Mahon, E.H., "The formation of the Christian Catholic Church in Zion and its earliest contacts with South Africa" in *Religion Alive: Studies in New movements and indigenous churches in Southern Africa*, Hodder and Stoughton, 1986, pp. 167-174). Nehemia Tile, the father of the independent/indigenous church movement, who had already established an independent church in the early eighties of the last century, inspired the formation of the Ethiopian movement—*Ethiopian* referring to the only remaining black African independent state after Africa was cut up and distributed among western colonial powers at the Berlin Convention of 1884-5. Ethiopia became the symbol of liberation and *Psalm* 68:31 focused further attention on this symbol. It reads "let Ethiopia hasten to stretch out her hands to God." Ethiopian church leaders took part in 1912 in the formation of the African National Congress. It is of significance that there are many churches which combine "Ethiopian" and "Apostolic" with Zion so that "Zion" appears in over eighty percent of the masses of the indigenous churches. "Zion" stands for faith healing, prophecy, abstinence from tobacco and alcohol, and it is in this context that the office of prophet operates in the AIC.

There are some historical prophets who initiated world religions; there are others who initiated large indigenous church movements. The concern, here, is mainly with those in the AIC who concentrate specifically on the healing ministry. The contention is that traditional Africa had no prophets, and yet this continent has given back to the Church the office of the prophet, which it had lost during the third century. The prophet in the AIC is not concerned with the coming kingdom of political charismatic figures, such as Nkrumah and others who were mainly concerned with liberation. The Zionist prophet is usually not a messianic figure, not the founder of a new religion, not a political messiah, but a healer—in many ways a substitute for the traditional diviner and also the herbalist. There is also the John-the-Baptist-type prophet who is called by an angel, and who is a church leader *cum* prophet.

A) DEFINITION OF THE PROPHET

It is necessary to enter into the question of what is actually understood by the designation 'prophet'. As the AIC prophets work mainly in the Christian context, the understanding of this office in the Old and New Testaments is of major importance.

In the Old Testament a prophet is someone who announces the Word of God; he receives divine revelation which he has to convey to others and is actually a medium of revelation. The Old Testament *nabi* is from the Akkadic word *nabû* which means to call, proclaim or communicate. The *nabi* communicated the will of Jahweh to the people. The prophet played a great role in the Old Testament history but after the Exile, when Israel was in Babylon, the prophet no longer played such a significant role. The prophets understood themselves to be messengers of Jahweh. The prophet was conscious of the fact that the revelation he received came directly from God and that it had not originated from his own consciousness. This is referred to in *Jeremiah* 14:14 "And the Lord said to me: 'The prophets are prophesying lies in my name; I did not send them, nor did I command them or speak to them. They are prophesying a lying vision, worthless divination, and the deceit of their own minds'." Prophetic deceit is strongly confronted also in *Ezekiel* 13:2, 3, 5, 6: "Son of man, prophesy against the prophets of Israel, prophesy and say to those who prophesy out of their own minds; 'Hear the word of the Lord!... Woe to the foolish prophets who follow their own spirit, and have seen nothing!... You have not... built up a wall for the house of Israel, that it might stand in battle in the day of the Lord. They have spoken falsehood and divided a lie; they say, 'Says the Lord', when the Lord has not sent them, and yet they expect him to fulfil their word..'."

The prophet thus distinguished between his word and that of God, as is evident in the dialogue he had with God. The credibility of the prophetic self witness cannot be proved scientifically, neither can it be disproved on scientific grounds.

The prophet had a specific function of announcing the will and decisions of God which he received, often accompanied by unusual psychic experiences such as ecstasy, visions and dreams. The prophet was often called through a vision as were Isaiah, Jeremiah and Ezekiel. A person called to prophethood was called for life. One could speak of the office of prophet; they belonged to a specific class. Initially only a few were designated prophets, such as Moses, Miriam and Deborah, and two unnamed (*Judges* 6:8 and 1 *Sam.* 2:27). During the time of Samuel prophets increased.

The prophets often lived together (2 *Kings* 4:38; 6:1f) and were, as a rule, married and had children. False prophets came to the fore because of disobedience of the divine calling. After the exile there were only a few prophets until it came to an end in the days of Israel, and during the time of the Maccabees there were no longer any prophets.

In the New Testament the prophet had the same meaning as in the Old Testament. But the word "prophet" also included the special gift of the Holy Spirit, the charismata which was given by God to the first Christians. When the church did not yet have a New Testament, the prophets had to express the will of God in specific circumstances, or tell what future lay ahead of the churches. They made a few clearly comprehensible pronouncements but these were of passing significance. As with *glossolalia*, abuses came to the fore with the result that the prophets had to check each others' pronouncements (1 *Cor.* 14:32,37). Later, efforts were made to resuscitate artificially the office of prophet. Montanism is an example of this, when Montanus and his assistants were guilty of excesses. It was during this time that the church became conscious of the fact it had a New Testament. This meant the end of the New Testament prophet. They were no longer necessary. With both the Old and New Testament prophets it was a matter of speaking the Word of God with authority.

There is a distinction between the priest or minister and the prophet. The priest/minister is a functionary of a specific community out of whose religious tradition his office is derived—he is the protector of this tradition and a conservative religious leader. In contrast to this is the prophet with his dynamic piety, conveying a message which often confronts the *status quo*, reacting against the office of the priest. For this reason, the priest questions or rejects the legitimacy of the prophet. The opposition of the prophet to the priest is due to tradition. The priest protects the cult, the doctrine and scriptural tradition, while the prophet has a critical, individualistic stance against this and attacks the very essence of traditional religious expression. The priest sees him as having deviated from the original tradition: a heretic. The prophet shares the protesting character of the reformer. Both react against circumstances and what they see. However, the prophet receives a personal revelation from which his accusations are launched; the reformer bases his prophecy on fixed revelation in order to reform the circumstances and outlook of his time.

The prophet in the religions

In the religions, the prophet has a special relationship with supernatural forces. It is important to assess the distinctive qualities of the prophet which put him in such a special relationship—one which is of basic significance. In the various religions the calling of the prophet by the deity (deities) or ancestors is vital. No one can appoint himself to the office. Through visions and auditions, which often have an ecstatic character, the prophet receives the message or instructions from the unseen spiritual word and has to act in obedience.

The prophet grasps visibly, or through hearing, the reality and will of the deity or the ancestor or some or other trusted supernatural entity, and has to announce or proclaim what he sees and hears. The prophet experiences this relationship with the diety and/or ancestor(s) as being filled or inspired by this contact—which in the case of the Old Testament refers to the "spirit of God". The spirit takes hold of a person, who becomes possessed and then a direct mouthpiece of the deity or ancestor(s). This taking possession by the deity and/or ancestor can be affected also through the co-operation of those surrounding the prophet with dance or music, or by being spontaneously, completely overwhelmed by the supernatural forces. Such contact is accompanied by miracles which prove the integrity of the prophet, the genuineness of his preaching.

As in the case of the soothsayer, the prophet combines the visionary aspect in his activities. Much of the preaching of the prophets, especially those in the Old Testament, had to do with the future. Future events of a political and cosmic nature are 'predicted', as is the appearance of specific religious figures such as the Messiah of the Old Testament, the Mahdi in Islam.

With the Greeks the prophet had a middle role—he/she was the mouthpiece of the deity for the people and also the mouthpiece of the people to the deity. Dependence on prophecy is important—it finds its strongest expression in inspiration. Nowhere up to the second century does the prefix *pro-* in prophets imply future. Only later does it convey, under Christian influence, the modern meaning of proclaimer of the future.

The appearance and function of prophets is the clearest in those religions which have been founded through the lives and proclamations of historical prophets. Such an historical prophet was Zarathustra, the Persian prophet who confronted the priests of the old religion and announced the future coming of the Kingdom of Ahura Mazda. Mari, who founded Manicheism in the 3rd century AD, was, according to his style no prophet, but his actions had prophetic aspects. This was evident when, in 242, he stood before the Persian Great King Schapur I to proclaim his message. Buddha also was a mystic. What is described in connection with the prophet as a *calling*, was for the mystic *enlightenment*. He did not wish to proclaim his doctrine after his enlightenment, but like a prophet, he highlighted aspects of his insight into a dark world. He was a mixture of mystic and prophet. Prophetism clearly expressed in the prophetic context is found with Muhammad and with the Old Testament prophets. Called from the business world, he was carried to the desert where he received his calling to proclaim the will of Allah, a message which brought him into conflict with his people.

B) The role of the prophet in the Old and New Testament

The oldest phase of Israelite prophecy up to Amos included in the concept "prophet" the designations "seer" and "Man of God" (cf. 1 *Sam.* 9:9: "Formerly in Israel, when a man went to inquire of God, he said, 'Come, let us go to the seer'; for he who is now called a prophet was formerly called a seer"). In *Sam.* 10:10 the designation became a general term which included the seer. In contrast, this "man of God" referred to the "seer" (1 *Sam.* 9:6: "all that he says comes true") as well as to the individual prophet (1 *Kings* 17:18; 2 *Kings* 4:7) and this could also be applied to Moses (*Deut.* 33:1). The "man of God" who functioned as seer brought what was obscure into the present and the future and "heard" the divine Word. The "seer" had close contact with the priest, at the time of Bileam (cf. *Num.* 24:3f).

The *dream* was also a form of revelation (1 *Sam.* 3:10ff). Jahweh also communicated his message to the seer in his ears (1 *Sam.* 9:15). This is also evident in *Is.* 5:9: "The Lord of hosts has sworn in my hearing". The seer was approached when important decisions had to be made and was *paid* for advice (1 *Sam.* 9:7ff). He could appear unexpectedly to be with a specific individual or a community or as a blessing or a disturbance, or as a threat when he brought a disturbing message. There are those in the Old Testament who were partly prophet and partly seer, such as Gad (1 *Sam* 22:5). Here God is referred to as prophet, and in 1 *Chr.* 29:29 as seer, namely, "Now the acts of King David, from first to last, are written in the Chronicles of Samuel the seer, and in the chronicles of Nathan the prophet, and in the Chronicles of God the seer."

The word *nabi* (prophet) is related to the Akkadic nabu- (call) and could mean call and being called. The seer in the Old Testament is as charismatic (*Num* 24:2) as the prophet but the latter is the possessed one who withdraws from his environment. The prophet operates under the power of the Spirit, called the Spirit of God, which "jumps" on him like a wild animal on its prey and changes him into a different person (cf. 1 *Sam.* 10:6,10: "Then the spirit of the Lord will come mightily upon you, and you shall prophesy with them and be turned into another man... the spirit of God came mightily upon him, and he prophesied among them.") It is the hand of Jahweh who grasps the prophet (2 *Kings* 3:15). The prophet becomes powerful and often his possession gives the impression that he is mentally ill because "the Spirit" makes him unpredictable (2 *Kings* 9:11).

"The Spirit" was thus a power which came from the outside. It could manifest itself through individual and group ecstasy; there were prophet guilds brought about by dance, rhythmic movements which had therapeutic value. An enraptured group of prophets could not be easily imagined without dancing (1 *Sam*. 19:20; 1 *Kings* 22:10). Music accompanied this (1 *Sam* 10:5) and, as a preparation for ecstasy, as seen in Elisha—when music was played, "the power of the Lord" came upon him (2 *Kings* 3:15). Music assisted in getting the evil spirit away (1 *Sam* 16:16). Getting wounded was important for a prophet (cf. 1 *Kings* 20:35ff : "And a certain man of the Lord said "Strike me, I pray". But the man refused... a lion met him and killed him. Then he found another man... and the man struck him, smiting and wounding him...").

The culmination of the old prophecy came with Elijah who is clearly designated as a prophet. According to 1 *Sam*. 19:24, ecstatic culmination led to bodily nakedness without the inner life influencing the outward life. There was a time when the cultic dance, meditation and the prophetic tradition did not serve merely the person of the prophet or the closed community of prophets, but reached the people in their need. Elisha revealed what he had "heard" in audition and what he had been "shown" in a vision. He could even see the enemy through a closed door (2 *Kings* 6:32). Symbols were utilised to strengthen the dynamic effect of the message (1 *Kings* 22:1 : "Thus says the Lord, 'with these you shall push the Syrians until they are destroyed'." Magic could be attached to the remains of a prophet (1 *Kings* 13:21 : "and as soon as the man touched the bones of Elisha, he revived, and stood on his feet.") (*RGG*. p. 618; Robinson, T.H., *Prophecy and the prophets of ancient Israel*, (1923, 1948)).

The above prophet situation prevailed up to Amos. During the time of Amos the prophet's message was still delivered orally. The question of false prophets was associated with cult prophets who posed as salvation prophets.

The calling to prophethood and the task of the prophet

The prophet was sure that he was called by God (*Is*. 42:1ff). Vision and audition were vital. In *Is*. 5:22:14 and *Ezekiel* 9:1, 5, the word of the "Lord" came to their "hearing" or "ears" and *Ezekiel* 9:5 adds "with a loud voice" (Mowinckel, S., *Die Erkenntnis Gottes bei den alten testamentische Propheten*, 1941). Ecstasy was not considered constitutive for calling and receiving the Word. The prophets acted without any special consciousness about their acts. In itself prophethood was considered to be a *sui generis* phenomenon in which the Word of God was received. Constitutive for the prophethood was the experience of being overwhelmed by God (cf. *Amos* 3:8: "The lion has roared... The Lord has spoken; who can but prophesy?"; also *Ez.* 3:14: "The Spirit lifted me up and took me away... the hand of the Lord being strong upon me." The prophet was equipped as messenger to be the mouthpiece to individuals or the people. What the prophet heard in audition and saw in a vision he preached as a "message" from Jahweh (*Is.* 6). These words were not empty words but had an effect. They had to bring the messages pertaining to the social and political situation also, as seen in Amos, Hosea and Isaiah. Sometimes it was God's judgement on Israel's own political situation (cf. Albright, W.F., *Studies in the Old Testament prophecy*, Edinburgh, 1950; Rowley, H.H., (ed), *Studies in Old Testament prophecy*, 1950).

The main task of the prophet in Israel was the call to obedience to Jahweh. They had to bring the message of God to Israel and the peoples. They spoke (and wrote) with reference to a specific period and especially to where specific decisions were made. The various dimensions of Israel's existence, and those of the people around them, came under scrutiny. The core of the prophetic message was that the God who acts in history is the one who comes to judge but He is a merciful God. The community and humanity are always before God because man stands in the stream of God's history and humanity (Vriezen, Th. C., Prophecy and Eschatology, *Vetus Testamentum* 1, 1953, 199-299).

Prophets in Christianity

In the New Testament the noun *prophe-tē-s* appears 144 times. Here, the office of prophet is understood as proclaimer of the divinely inspired word of God. The prophet had certain specific abilities such as being able to see through a person. For example, the Pharisee who invited Jesus reacted as follows against the woman who anointed his feet, "If this man were a prophet, he would have known who and what sort of woman this is who is touching him, for she is a sinner." (*Luke* 7:39). The New Testament prophet had also a special knowledge of the future.

Not much is said in the New Testament about Jesus as a prophet. He is, however, referred to by this designation and sometimes compared with the Old Testament prophets. Jesus also had visions, auditions and even ecstatic experiences. He was taken by the Spirit so that his words were inspired by the Spirit. Jesus had prophetic knowledge and saw through human plans, he could read the thoughts of people. He knew the future. Jesus nowhere expressly said that he was a prophet. His healing ministry was however not associated with the prophetic side of his ministry.

The New Testament pictures the prophets as a closed "class", a familiar circle of capable persons with a specific office in the congregation. Paul states in 1 *Cor.* 12:28, "And God has appointed in the church first apostles, second prophets, third teachers, helpers, administrators, speakers in various kinds of tongues..." The apostles and prophets are often mentioned together (cf. *Eph.* 2:20; *Eph.* 3:5; *Rev.* 18:20). In *Acts* 13:1 Luke states that in the church of Antioch there were prophets and "teachers". The prophets were between the apostles and teachers in status and operated within a specific congregation. Nevertheless, for Paul, prophecy was the most important charisma of the church, as is evident in 1 *Cor.* 14:1, "Make love your aim, and earnestly desire the spiritual gifts, especially that you may prophesy." They had their function in the service (1 *Cor.* 11:5). Of special significance here is the reference to women, namely, "any woman who prays or prophesies..." Thus far, references to prophets were mainly in the male gender but there were also women, although only a few in the Old Testament. This has led, in some AIC, to a distinction between prayer healers and prophets— the prayer healers are juniors and can only pray and lay hands on a patient, while the prophets can predict, give advice in general matters and are considered to be seniors.

Paul emphasizes that prophetic powers need love (1 *Cor.* 13); that these powers are based on inspiration (1 *Cor.* 12:11) which is not ecstatically and emotionally expressed but with knowledge, in wisdom. This is also stated in 1 *Cor.* 14:15 : "I will pray with the spirit and I will pray with the mind also; I will sing with the spirit and I will sing with the mind also."

Prophecy also has the character of revelation, which tradition-bound doctrine does not have. The prophets also came with eschatological pronouncements (*Rom.* 11:26): "The Deliverer will come from Zion, he will banish ungodliness from Jacob." (See also 1 *Cor.* 15:51f; *Gal.* 5:21). Their task was the building up of the congregation, the giving of encouragement and consolation.

The prophets were under *control* ie. the subjectivism of some led other prophets to "test the spirits" (1 *Cor.* 14:29-33). The criterion of faith was vital (*Rom.* 12:6). The "holy apostles and prophets" were, however, something of the greatness of the past, the "foundation" of the church, to be replaced by other offices. In *Revelations* the prophets were seen as important successors to the apostles who disappeared. The word of prophecy was then vital (*Rev.* 22:18ff). Revelation came through ecstatic vision; they were either "in the Spirit" (*Rev.* 1:10) or "carried away in the Spirit" (*Rev.* 17:3; 21:10). The main emphasis in *Revelations* is on the eschatological future and the present is secondary.

The Christian prophets in Palestine and Syria brought back earlier aspects associated with the prophets, such as clairvoyance (*Acts* 11:28; 21:10).

The synoptic Gospels warned against false prophets (*MK* 13:22). The authority and role of these prophets were helpful to the congregation.

There are only two prophetesses in the New Testament. Although women in the early Christian congregation had the spirit of prophecy, they were not honoured with the title, except the Jewess Hannah.

"To prophesy" has a number of connotations in the New Testament— the noun is used more in the Gospels while the verb is used more in the Letters—namely:

a) proclaiming the message;
b) because the prophet knows the future, "to prophesy" implies wisdom;
c) it could also mean to reveal something obscure, to communicate to others that which is outside the realm of natural possibilities;
d) it could be of an ethical nature—teaching, warning, counselling—it leads to realisation of guilt and dependence upon God;
e) it is associated with speaking in tongues;
f) to work as a prophet in full dependence.

C) THE ROLE OF THE PROPHET IN THE PRIMITIVE CHRISTIAN CHURCH

The three offices of Apostle, Prophet and Teacher occurred in the earliest Christian church —however, they gradually disappeared. The Apostle died out and had no successor; the Prophet was still present in the church up to the beginning of the 3rd century. The Teacher remained indispensable in the church and, in line with his predecessor, the rabbi, concentrated on the exposition of Scripture and the doctrinal tradition. Apostle and Prophet were still mentioned together according to the injunctions of the Gospel (*RGG.*, p. 634). The question asked in practice was whether an Apostle was a false prophet (the term false apostles was not used).

In the early Church of the first and second century, the prophet was seen as the inspired charismatic proclaimer through whom God's plan for salvation of the world and the congregation became known to the individual person. The main task was proclamation, including proclamation on eschatological events. Although prophecy was held in high esteem in the primitive church, it was passing away, according to the apostle Paul, who also valued it highly (1 *Cor.* 13:8f, 12). It was stated that at the end of the world the congregation would not be dependent upon prophecy—it would not be in need of its service.

There was no sharp distinction between ecstasy, inspiration through spirit possession and prophetic revelation. In the New Testament the prophet was not possessed by God in such a way that he was not in charge of his senses and forced to do what was commanded. The prophet of early Christianity had a clear mind and consciousness. The distinction was made between prophecy and speaking in tongues—the first for the congregation, the latter for the individual; prophecy with the mind, speaking in tongues with the emotions—and Paul pleaded for levelheadedness (1 *Cor.* 14:2f).

With regard to the prayer life of the prophets: they were seen in the Old Testament as great men of prayer. This was also the case in the New Testament—ie. men and women of prayer.

Prophecy was seen by the apostle Paul as the highest gift of grace, not *gnosis* (knowledge). The prophet got his/her information directly. In the AIC the prophet emphasizes this direct information through vision. Prophecy is, in a sense, the same as proclamation of the gospel message but, while prophecy was mainly addressed to believers in early Christianity, proclamation was mainly directed to those who were not Christians.

During this period the prophets were still mobile preachers and could stay for longer periods in a congregation, which was not the case with the apostles. What the prophets had to say was respected and accepted as from "the Spirit". Its importance lay in the fact that it was an important factor for the building up of the congregation, its worship service and its spiritual life. Even though what they did was not seen as officially part of the church's activities, it was considered important. Paul wrote to Timothy: "This charge I commit to you, Timothy, my son, in accordance with the prophetic utterances which pointed to you, that inspired by them you may wage the good warfare" (1 *Tim* 1:18). This Paul repeated later in the letter: "Do not neglect the gift you have, which was given you by prophetic utterance when the elders laid their hands upon you" (1 *Tim* 4:14).

Those prophets who played to the tune of the people were considered to be false. The true prophets spoke only in the power of God out of personal conviction, not influenced by the likes and dislikes of people. Justin was one of the outstanding apologists from the post-apostolic era. Born round 100 AD, his *Great and Small Apologia* are still in existence. In them he defends Christianity against false accusations, and in the Dialogue with Trypho the Jew, he tries to indicate the limitations of Judaism and poses Christianity as the only true religion. Justin referred to false prophets (*Dialogue* 35:3; 51:2) and stated that the gifts of the prophet were still working in the church during his time (*Dialogue* 82:1).

Eusebius of Caesarea (±265-399), indicated that there were extensive discussions on true and false prophets. He himself, although not a prophet, was excommunicated because he refused to confront the Arian heresy which emphasized the humanity of Jesus to the detriment of his divinity. Montanism emphasized genuine prophecy. Montanists were followers of Montanus, from Phrygia in Asia Minor. He was active during the second half of the second century, with two women prophets whose preaching was ecstatic, emphasising the imminent Second coming of Christ, and that the era of the Spirit was at hand. His influence was so great that even the church fathers, such as Tertullian, who later joined Montanism, and even Irenaeus, initially refused to counteract Montanus' heretical preaching. Montanists went from Asia Minor, to South Galasia, Rome and Africa. They were excommunicated and persecuted and this was the main reason for the disappearance of the prophets from the church. Montanus came with his own Scriptures and a collection of new prophetic decrees which threatened the Scripture tradition of the Church.

The early Church set up against the false prophets a series of genuine prophets, starting with Agabus, already mentioned in *Acts* 11, and ending with Quadratus, the oldest apologist known by name. He probably stayed in Asia Minor and lived during the first half of the second century. There were those in the church who were against prophets speaking in a state of ecstasy, as the gift of prophecy, according to apostolic doctrine, had to remain in the church until the Parousia (1 *Cor.* 1:7 and *Eph.* 4:11ff) "And his gifts were that some should be apostles, some prophets, some evangelists, some pastors and teachers, for the equipment of the saints, for the work of the ministry for building up the body of Christ."

It was already stated by authors in the second century that prophets could disappear in the congregations. The author of 2 *Peter* emphasized, in chapter 2, the negative role of prophets, and accepted only the prophets of the Old Testament. Origen also stated that they would disappear from the congregations. In their place came the teachers, according to Clemens Alexandrinus. In his *Protreptikos* and *Paidagogos*, he accepted the infallibility of Scripture which consisted of Law, Prophecy and Gospel, a tradition which had been mediated by the prophets of the Old Testament, the Gospel and the Apostles. Behind this stood the Lord, as original source of all doctrine and its understanding, until the end when this assured position for the refutation of heresy and false prophets would be occupied by a teacher who upholds the tradition, and thus the congregational prophet would become obsolete.

Prophets disappeared for several reasons due to false prophets, according to some of the early church fathers, such as Hermas. He saw the true prophet as gentle, modest, calm, keeping himself away from every evil desire. The false prophet was arrogant, lying, seeking his own honour, unashamed... not waiting upon what was revealed but acting as if he knew everything. He acted as a soothsayer, only interested in remuneration. If he did not receive remuneration, he did not prophesy. There were also reactions against the ecstatic emphases of false prophets.

Prophetic announcements

In spite of the individual variety, the words of prophets had a common basic form. The basic form of the prophet's announcement was a single saying:

1. The formula of the prophetic message started: "So says Jahweh".
2. The prophet announced a coming event.
3. Most of the prophet's announcements had to do with events pertaining to disaster, calamities and destruction.
4. Accusations against Israel, for example, were conveyed through the corpse song by Amos (5:1f); by Isaiah through a love song (5:1ff); by Jeremiah through a song of lamentation.
5. The messages of the prophets came most often to individuals and, as a rule, to the King.
6. The method of bringing his message was to announce firstly the ill done and then the judgement of Jahweh. The first was the basis for the judgement; the second the announcement of the judgement (1 *Kings* 20:42; 2 *Kings* 1:3f).
7. Messages of positive announcements of welfare and well-being were sometimes interspersed with warnings (*Is.* 1:17; *Amos* 5:4-6).
8. Usually the prophecy came through a vision (cf. Rendtorff, R. *Prophetenspruch, Religion in Geschichte und Gegenwart*, Tübingen, Mohr, 1961, pp. 635-638).

D) The African prophet (healer)

In Africa, the 'prophet' designation is used in a wider context than is the case in the Old and New Testament, although the prophet includes many of the aspects discussed in the previous section. In this it is like "baptism", which is used much more widely in the African context than in the established churches, namely as a purification rite associated with healing, with exorcism, and with receiving the Holy Spirit. Thus the designation 'prophet' has become closely associated with healing. The designation 'prophet' could also imply that a person has charismatic qualities as a leader of the people and such a person could become a messianic figure (cf. Margull, H.J., *Aufbruch zur Zukunft,* München, Kaiser, 1966).

The diviners in the traditional African context were always respected, not only for their healing, but also for their prophetic qualities. Islam had its prophetic figures and strong African personalities came to the fore as prophetic figures. These prophet figures were often elevated to the messianic redeemers. Such figures were William Wade Harris from Liberia, who made an impact in various countries in West Africa; Simon Kimbangu of the former Belgian Congo (Zaire), who spent the largest part of his life in a colonial jail. Many saw him as their messiah who would free them from Belgian colonial rule. Although Kwame Nkrumah (Osagyefo) of Ghana was not a spiritual Messiah, he was nevertheless a trained minister of the church and became the redeemer of Ghana, giving strong impetus to the movement for the liberation of the whole of Africa from colonial rule. There have also been women founders of churches, such as Alice Mulenga Lenshina of the former Northern Rhodesia (Zambia).

In South Africa, as in many other parts of Africa, especially Zimbabwe, John the Baptist figures came to the fore. There were also those such as the Ethiopian movement, which reacted against white overrule in South Africa and played a role in the formation of the ANC in 1912. Among the Zulus there were Isiah Shembe, founder of the Church of the Nazarites, and Egenas Lekgenyane, the founder of the Zion Christian Church which operates especially in the Transvaal and has expanded to Zimbabwe.

Although the prophets mentioned above acted also as healers, the healing prophet has become part and parcel of many of the AIC. In most Zionist churches especially among the AIC there are the offices of prayer healer (*umthandazi*) and prophet (*umprofeti*).

The former is considered in most of these churches to be junior to the prophet.

The prophets in the ancient Greek context, with their special relationships to the deities, with their special visions which brought them into a state of ecstasy, and who had contact with the supernatural forces through "seeing" and listening, are much nearer in this regard to the prophets of the AIC. While the Old Testament prophet concentrated on proclamation concerning the future with negative overtones, such as the judgement and later the end of the world, and the New Testament concentrated on the eschatological future with an emphasis on deliverance, the AIC prophet directs his/her attention mainly towards healing in a holistic sense ie. opening up for the person the way to self-fulfilment. Coming from a cyclically orientated culture, the AIC prophet would not be as concerned with the future as those nurtured in a linear orientated culture, in spite of the New Testament emphasis on the future dimension of time. The New Testament prophet was considered to have a special knowledge of the future, and understood his task as preaching the divine word of God. This is not the emphasis with the AIC prophet—in the AIC, proclamation is done by the ministers, evangelists and lay preachers (*shumayela*)—but the emphasis is on healing. This is very much a Christian concern based on the activities of Jesus in this regard, but the AIC prophet links physical healing to social healing ie. the restoration of disturbed relationships, which implies those relationships which destroy socio-economic well-being. In the AIC, women prophets have greater scope for the utilisation of their gifts than in any other office in these churches. In the traditional context they predominate as diviners; in the AIC, women predominate especially as prayer healers, but also act as prophets.

E) The need for contextual healing

The office of the prophet in the AIC fulfils a specific need. A vacuum exists in the historic churches because of their emphasis on the individual aspect of sin—sin in these churches is basically seen as a wrong relationship between God and the individual, who could make amends without further considerations. It is here that diseases based on the traditional African world view, as due to malicious external factors or the victim's own doings, neglect or attitudes, have to be taken into consideration—much more carefully and sensitively than many of the missionaries have done thus far. Here sorcery, witchcraft, spirit possession, pollution, neglect of one's ancestors, relatives, community and environment, are the main causes. Maintaining the equilibrium in social relationships, which could be disturbed in so many ways, is of utmost importance. In order to restore the equilibrium, a holistic approach to the whole situation affecting the person is necessary, and herein the supernatural forces play a vital role. The bad and negative influences have to be detected and removed from the situation and from the person, and only then can normal health be restored.

In this context, not only the western medical profession, but also those churches established and directed by western missionaries, have little to say. Sorcery, witchcraft and spirit possession are realities for many Christians in the established churches and the AIC. In some cases it was even taboo to mention such diseases in the presence of a missionary. There are some churches which consider the rituals used in indigenous healing processes, with regard to typical African types of diseases, as effective, and believe they should receive sympathetic attention rather than condemnation.

There are many factors which contribute to insecurity in the African community. The transition to the new cultural environment brings forth many tensions as does the socio-economic and political situation, with its discrepancies and blatant injustices. It is in such circumstances that the assistance of the prophet, who compensates for the role of the diviners, is found in the AIC. The AIC stress the healing aspects of Jesus and as the diviner is both seer and healer, the prophet in the AIC fills the vacuum which the loss of the diviner has left. The AIC prophet is much more a substitute for the diviner than for the herbalist.

It is important that the established churches make closer contact with the indigenous healing systems where diseases are related to the African cosmology. The great emphasis is on restoration of relationships, on purification, on cleansing and the means used to obtain this; and these need discussion. Sickness and sin are related in this context. The individualistic concept of sin, often with exclusion of sin in the relational context, needs attention, especially when the office of the prophet receives attention. Witchcraft and sorcery were, up to the middle of the 18th century, rife in Europe and England. They were made taboo only in the latter part of that century.

The problem is that the world view, from which missionaries started, was not that with which Africa concerned itself. Thus no serious attention had been given to the realities of Africa ie. the missionaries generally did not step into the depths of the African world view. Even the Jesus presented was often presented as a foreigner. This does not imply that everything which is designated as the realities of Africa should be accepted, but Christianity should operate with an awareness of the African context and of how to address this situation with its message. Theological problems in this connection do not imply that African approaches should be rejected, rather that they be utilised in a meaningful way.

The only way to do something within the existential context, is to take these forces seriously. This is what happens in the AIC, and they attract people by the thousands—not because it is an easy way out, but because they receive help. Bewitchment, sorcery and spirit possession are realities. Anti-social evils are attended to by the prayer healers and the prophets and many do find relief. It is a question of reconciliation, and with their assistance people find help. Prayer plays an important part in such a situation, but for many it has to be supplemented by other visible ritual acts. There is hardly any sickness treated in the African context where a fellow human being is not seen, in some sense, as the cause of the ailment. Sickness and disturbed social relationships are bound together. The main task of the diviner in the African society is to restore relationships—he/she is such a restorer. The midnight revival services of the AIC, the washing with holy water, or at the sea, the attention of the prayer healer and the prophet is related to this. When these issues become substitutes for a living faith, the scriptural norms are affected. Through the work of the prophet, the equilibrium in these small house congregations, of which there are at least one hundred and fifty thousand in South Africa, remains intact or, where disturbed, the processes of reconciliation are put into action. Here people feel protected and fortified against all the adversities that surround them whether it be sickness, the socio-economic and political situation, or whatever. For this, a variety of rituals and objects are prescribed. Those who wish to see a living faith and hope without these rituals and objects should realise that it is not merely a question of destroying or "christianizing" such rituals and objects. Much could be learned from the AIC and its prayer healers/ prophets, who act with a modesty and sensitivity that make an impression on those who witness their activities. There are of course, in some cases, theological problems, but these difficulties should not lead to an attitude of rejection and destruction of what is basically genuine in their activities, and meaningful to those who receive such treatment.

It is clear from the above that the prophet, in various religions, had a specific relationship with the metaphysical forces ie. ancestors, deity or deities. This special relationship is of basic significance. The prophet had a specific function—that of revealing the will and decisions of these forces, often accompanied by ecstasy, visions and dreams. The phenomena also accompanied the call to prophethood. With both the Old and New Testament prophets, it was a matter of speaking the word of God with authority. The prophet was distinguished from the priest or minister in the sense that the latter was a functionary of a specific community and upholder of the tradition, while the former often came with a message which confronted the status quo, and even became a problem to the priest. The priest, with his protection of the cult and scriptural tradition, often had to bear the critical individualistic stance of the prophet over this.

The AIC prophet is usually not a preacher—this is done by the minister (*umfundisi*), the evangelist (probationer who may 'put hands' on people) and the more junior preacher (*shumayela*) is only allowed to preach and nothing else. The function of the AIC prophet is to help people in their need by solving conflicts, taking personal interest in the sick, especially those who have problems with illnesses related to the African cosmology like sorcery and witchcraft—diseases which are associated with the activities of evil spirits. This development is not only due to Alexander Dowie's emphasis on faith healing in the Christian Catholic Church, which he founded on 29 February 1896 at Zion City near Chicago (and which greatly influenced the African), but because of the vacuum Africans felt in the mission churches, where the specific African diseases (*Ukufa kwaBantu*) had been merely ascribed to superstition and ignored, or those who believed in them were censured.

With the AIC, prophet healing is thus not merely a physical issue, but is also closely related to the human beings' psychical existence. The socio-economic and political situation of blacks in South Africa is also a major factor of insecurity in the black community in which the prophet has a role to play. Being individualistic, the prophet is a symbol of reaction against the missionary-orientated attitudes to the contextualisation of healing processes which the missionaries and the western orientated medical profession rejected until recently. A change of attitude is to be discerned, even in the above-mentioned medical profession. The prophet is also the symbol of a holistic approach to life—although healing has become the major activity of the prophet, many other issues, such as those related to socio-economic and political deprivation, also receive attention. Basically, the power from which the prophet works is not derived from the community, but has as its source a metaphysical force(s).

F) A DESCRIPTION OF THE SURVEY ON THE WITWATERSRAND AND IN THE GREATER DURBAN AREA

An investigation into the role of the prophet was launched in Greater Durban's African townships and those on the Rand, especially Soweto. The first part of this empirical study concentrates on one of three sections of the interviews held. In this section, which consisted of twenty five prophets from the Rand (mainly Soweto) and fifteen from Greater Durban and surrounding areas, half of those from the Rand were prophets who ministered in churches with "Zion" in their name, with the rest, except one, having "Apostolic" in the name. Most of the prophets have been in the churches for some time—one on the Rand has been a prophet for thirty-seven years.

Of those on the Rand, half have always been in their present churches, while the rest have changed from other churches—a few, several times. Of those in the Greater Durban area, only one is still in the church he started from, while the rest changed churches—here also, a few have done so several times. There has thus been a greater mobility among the prophets in the Greater Durban area, as far as church affiliation is concerned, than on the Rand, especially Soweto. The prophets referred to in the Greater Durban area do not include the respondents approached at the Durban beaches, those who were active in the healing services recorded, nor many who were met casually on numerous occasions and interviewed.

The aims of this investigation were twofold, namely:
1. to analyse the preparation and role of the prophet as a prayer healer within the context of the AIC, to discern various healing procedures and what aspects of traditional healing methods are utilised by the prophets;
2. to focus on the prophet's own perception of this.

Interviews with prophets were held by field workers in the Witwatersrand area, mainly Soweto, and in the Greater Durban area in the townships. They were based on an extensive questionnaire consisting of eighty-seven questions. Interviews were held by the author mainly at the Durban beach where leaders, prophets, prayer healers, members and potential members of the independent/indigenous churches come for "baptism". This does not necessarily imply only initiation into the church but also purification, exorcism, contact with the Holy Spirit, healing, getting power and for well-being.

Prophets had been elected on the basis that their specific churches accepted them as prophets. After having been contacted at services, the respondents were interviewed at their homes on the basis of the question-naire, by qualified field-workers mostly. Others were contacted by the author in the townships around Durban and at the beach, where healing services are regularly held. Healing services were also recorded on casettes by fieldworkers and translated. The fieldworkers conducted interviews mainly in the Zulu language in Greater Durban, and in Zulu and Sotho on the Witwatersrand. The interviewees usually first assessed the motives of the interviews and when they concluded the motives were genuine, they opened up and co-operated in a wonderful manner. The author, who has visited the places of "baptism" at the Durban beaches during more than sixty percent of the Sundays during the last three years, and who is regularly in the African townships at homes and services, did not find a single person uncooperative when he approached them for information. Those contacted at the beaches came from many parts of South Africa, such as the Transvaal, Free State, Bophuthatswana, Transkei, even Venda, Lesotho and Swaziland, and of course, Natal. The sea is a most effective venue for healing purposes with the result that many prayer healers and prophets were encountered there. This was also the experience of the fieldworkers. The limitation of such a study is perhaps the problem of not being able to stay with prophets and record their activities during a reasonably long period. Nevertheless, the large number of prophets contacted during more than three years of intensive research activities, related to a number of different projects, and the close relationships established with prophets as well as prayer healers and diviners have provided significant insights into this important development in the AIC.

CHAPTER TWO

THE CALL OF THE AIC HEALER

It should be stated at the outset that there is a difference between the types of leadership within those AIC which hail from the Ethiopian church movement, and have remained closely associated with its structure, theology and kingship pattern, and those which are Zionist. The latter includes the Zionist-influenced Ethiopian and Apostolic AIC which have a more pentecostal type of leadership but with the leader often acting as a prophet as well, although in a large number of this category of AIC the prophet has become a separate type of ministry. Referring to the "Kingship pattern" of the Ethiopian churches, Sundkler refers to Zionist churches in which there is a combination of this type of leadership "with another strong leadership pattern within Zulu society; that of the diviner or witchfinder (*isangoma*). The outcome of this development is the Zionist *prophet*... There is an obvious parallel between the Zulu diviner and the Zionist prophet... (i) The initial call to become a diviner or to join a Zionist church and become a prophet. (ii) General appearance, behaviour and activities, the Zionists being a modern movement of witchfinders..." (Sundkler, p. 109). Since these words were written, the healing ministry of the prophet has become a central issue in most Zionist churches with less emphasis on leadership aspects associated with this office. Their healing activities are mainly associated with "pollution" ie. those diseases which fall within the context of the traditional African cosmology and which are due to evil metaphysical forces, as will be indicated later.

Various aspects recur when the influences, which have had a bearing on those who became prophets, are analysed. The following outline based on the surveys, gives an insight into those recurring aspects.

A) DREAMS

All emphasised that they were called through a supernatural force—either an ancestor(s) and/or the Holy Spirit ("the Spirit") in a dream. A few stated that their "grandmother" told them to become a prophet. Such dreams are checked and evaluated in the church by a prophet or prophets, and when the prophet(s) decides that the dreams are genuine the calling is accepted as official. One prophet saw white pigeons flying over her and then her grandmother ("ancestor") called her to be a prophet. "Grandmothers", as ancestors, feature with quite a few in their calling— this could also be seen in the *isangoma* (diviner) background where maternal grandmothers play a central role in the calling of women to the office of diviner. Furthermore, the grandmother was the main educator in Zulu society where she had a prominent status in this role and also in that of ancestor.

B) Illness

All the prophets went through an experience of being ill or seriously ill, as was the case with the traditional diviner when he/she was called to be a diviner ie. the *ukuthwasa* experience. This condition is ascribed to the intervention of an ancestor who wishes a person to become a diviner. Such contact by the ancestor, referred to as "being called", results in a painful feeling on the left shoulder. If a person agrees to accept the call then the whole procedure of becoming a diviner is initiated. If, however, the person does not wish to become a diviner then he/she has to slaughter a goat in order to appease ("apologise" to) the ancestor(s) for not accepting the call, which could have serious consequences as such a call comes with the authority of a highly respected ancestor(s). Disobedience, without making amends, could lead to malfunctioning relationships in the family, or some or other disaster. If such a person called decides to become a prophet rather than a diviner, it is a more serious affront if the ancestor passed away still adhering to the traditional religion of his ancestors.

The majority of the Greater Durban and Rand prophets were ill before they became prophets. One stated "Yes, I was ill until I became a prophet". Another who was not ill stated "but I lost many of my children which was said to be related to my refusal to accept the call as a prophet." Becoming paralysed was often referred to as an experience during the illness stage of those who were called to prophethood. A woman respondent was promised total healing if she obeyed the call to prophethood, which she did, and she stated that she was immediately healed.

One prophet related how other prophets could not diagnose her illness. During this period, which lasted a year, she was blind, but then "lightning came into my house and I started to speak in tongues; then I saw in a vision, something which looked like a small baby passing by next to me. I tried to get hold of him but failed—*Ngase ngibona imibono* (and thereafter I saw visions). After this experience I started to act as a prophet".

The majority of the respondents in the Greater Durban area, before being initiated as prophets, went to another prophet who told them that, if they gave heed to the call, their illness would subside. This happened also with half of the respondents on the Rand. The sicknesses in the case of these respondents were caused *inter alia* by "very strong" ancestors who wanted them to be prophets. They thus received the injunctions to accept the office of prophet from their ancestors. All, except one of the prophets of the Greater Durban area, were directly called to be prophets. The one exception received the calling to be a diviner, but chose to become a prophet. After a goat was slaughtered in order to "apologise" to the ancestors who wanted her to become a diviner, she was allowed to accept the prophethood. Of those on the Rand, sixty percent were called directly as prophets; twenty percent of the women respondents were first called to be diviners, and one male respondent to be a herbalist, but all became prophets. One later also became a diviner and acted in the capacity of both prophet and diviner. A number of these doubly qualified diviner/prophets were observed at the beaches—as Zionist prophets, who also train to be diviners, have increased during the last few years.

It is significant to see how the *ukuthwasa* phenomenon in the traditional context is interpreted within the indigenous church situation. One prophet stated "A person feels something on the shoulder. Jesus spoke about this. Many will be prophets but won't be able to prophesy. If you say you have contact with an *idlozi* (ancestor) the people bring goats and listen to what you say". This prophet wishes to emphasize that he works through the mediatorship of an ancestor but does not exclude his approaches to Jesus.

Another prophet, also founder and leader of a church, described *ukuthwasa* in the context of his church as follows: "*Ukuthwasa* is caused by an ancestor. The diviner, herbalist or prophet can treat it. The prophet can do it if he is trained to do it. I do not chase the diviners away if they work in conjunction with the ancestors (ie. if they do the *amadlozi* thing). If they do not want to become diviners they come to our church. There I give them water that has been prayed over, take them to the sea and baptise them and the ancestor does not 'worry' the person any more. They then decide not to be a diviner. I had four diviners at the sea this morning—one old lady, two younger girls and a young male. I put them into the water, call out their names, baptise them in Jesus' name. They removed all the skins ('fetishes') from their arms and body, put it down at the beach before they entered the sea; after I have baptised them I say to them that they can put it on again. Some of them put it on after they have been baptised but these four refused—they asked the address of the church. When I baptised them they then *see* (ie. 'have visions') as a result of the Spirit of God working in them. I go to the sea again next week and if they are there, I will put them again into the water. They sometimes come to the church with a goat which I am asked to bless. I do not chase them away. I want them to stop if they do the *amadlozi* thing".

This same very well known prophet and healer of his church in the Durban area had a vision that he should take the diviners and others, *inter alia* a teacher, seven successive Sundays to the sea to dip them in the water in order to cleanse them from all evil, which they did. They were at the beach for seven Sundays at 4h15, first singing, then entering the sea and while singing, handclapping and rhythmic movements take place, the baptism procedures were effected. After this the crowd followed their prophet singing "Eshisa eZion" ("it burns in Zion")— repeating these two words for about twenty minutes while they were rhythmically moving and clapping hands, following the prophet who leads them in the procession on the beach.

Another prophet maintained that only a diviner can treat *ukuthwasa* and added that "a person who disobeys her ancestors always has bad luck—sometimes such a person even loses her job. Some become seriously ill when they go to hospital and doctors are unable to find out what disease such a person is suffering from. Such a person has dreams in which she sees all her dead relatives (ancestors). The cause of this is that the ancestors want her to work for them and heal people. The diviners know about this because they experienced it before they became diviners and they have undergone the training". Her reference to "bad luck" relates to the reaction of the ancestor(s) if they are not obeyed when they call a person to be a diviner. A number of the prophets have first been called to be diviners and they had to sacrifice a goat especially for the ancestor(s) in order to apologise to them for not fulfilling their wishes. Prophets relate that the act of disobedience to the wishes of the ancestors could be traumatic. For example, a prophet said that he dreamt about other diviners and saw himself dancing among them, and that he also dreamt of himself sitting among snakes or staying with them in the river. River snakes are considered to be very strong and dangerous. "The power of the ancestors", he further stated, "take hold of you and you want to become a diviner".

Most prophets saw themselves as being called by the ancestors and some did not distance themselves from diviners. They also had a kind of *ukuthwasa* experience before becoming prophets. Christian diviners, ie. those who trained both as prophets and diviners, are regularly encountered today where indigenous churches operate. To become a Christian diviner, a prophet can only be trained by a diviner: "Only diviners can create diviners", said one prophet, who then elaborated on how the diviners are trained. "Ancestors work with a person, who then sees visions, and also sees through a vision the house where they have to go for training. A person starts by foretelling things. She develops an interest in weighing up the good and bad sides of people. She stares fixedly at one person and tells him his problems, which have never been told to him by any human being but which are the naked truth.

This is a gift from an ancestor, a member of her family, who enters her and guides her in seeing the future. Such a person is best helped by a diviner to become an *ithwasa*, a student diviner, an initiant. It is through a dream that she is told who is going to treat her. She feels pain on her shoulder, she does not like meat, neither noise nor to stay with people. Such a person is always quick in walking and conscientious in what she does. She often does not wish to wear shoes; does not eat pork or mutton—only goat's meat. She does not eat eggs and uses no oil, except cooking oil, in order to cook her food. *Ukutwasa* is not a disease. It is the initial stage of becoming a diviner under an experienced diviner, when the initiant is given magical herbs and the rituals are observed, such as announcing her to the ancestors through the slaughtering of a goat(s). Some persons have ancestors 'on them' who want these relatives to work for them. This is treated by *amagobongo* and *impepho* is burned and you talk to the ancestor on its smoke.

The ancestors come to you when they want you to become a diviner, herbalist or prayer healer. If you don't want to be any of these you request them to excuse you for not accepting their call. The ancestors call you to become a prayer healer. If you do not want to become a diviner or herbalist you slaughter a white goat ie. if you want to go in the way of the Holy Spirit. The senior prophet is of a higher rank than the diviner".

Another prophet emphasized that the senior prophet prays for the person who does not wish to become a diviner, but who wishes to be a prayer healer or prophet. Such a person is "given ropes to wear which give power to prophesy". In this case *isiwasho* is used to purify the person through vomiting, steaming and purging, and the body is bathed without soap.

There is thus an affinity between the diviners' experience, concerning *ukuthwasa*, and that of some of the respondents when they were called to be prophets. The prophets who are unable to resist the call of their ancestors to become diviners accept the call, and go through the various stages in the training process. These prophets apply the various ritual procedures more comprehensively with regard to traditional healing than do those prophets who did not go through such a course. Prophets who did not have a thorough training with respected diviners have no standing with them. A few well-known diviners were Christians before but now show no affinity with the churches to which they belonged, although they speak with appreciation about the experiences there. One well-known woman diviner is married to a bishop of an indigenous church.

C) Visions and dreams

One of the main aims of the training of prophets is the acquisition of the ability to experience visions. Emphasis is on the illness stage and, later, on the acquisition of visions stage. One stated, "I saw visions at night when I was half asleep. They prayed for me and used *amagobongo*—this is the diviners' *muti* (medicine) used during training". Another related the following experience: "I felt something and I could scream. I had a vision and then I started to predict about my people who were with me. This is how I started to be a prophet. I was then enabled to pray over water for healing." It is as if the problem of the patient is " whispered into my ears" said one prophet. Having visions does not mean the prophet ignores the dreams of patients, but these are interpreted to them especially "if the Spirit so leads". This is why dream interpretation is one of the aspects receiving attention during the training period of prophets. Visions, however, take precedence with the prophets—they "see" the disease and the cure "as if watching from a video or TV"; others "see it through visions as in a mirror". As the Holy Spirit and/or ancestors are the sources of these visions, special attention is given in their training to the contact procedures.

Because dreams and visions play a vital role in the healing procedures, they receive close attention during training—especially how to interpret them. Usually the *umthandazi* (the prayer healer) receives in a dream, the night before the visit of the patient, the diagnosis of the disease and the healing procedures, from an ancestor(s) or the Holy Spirit. The prophet receives this in a vision when the patient appears before him/her. The ancestors also operate through visions. All the prophets from Greater Durban and the Rand, except one, stated they receive assistance in their work from *abathandazi* (prayer healers), mainly women. Such prayer healers pray for the sick and are especially active with healing sessions on Sundays, as many of them are working women. They usually give individual attention for long periods to their patients. In some of the churches no distinction is made between prayer healers and prophets, while in others they are treated as junior healers, prophets being the seniors, as indicated earlier.

Isiah Shembe, the founder of the largest AIC in Natal—*iBandla lamaNazaretha*—had, at his calling, witnessed the presence of angels in the form of white doves, circling above him at the sea. Some of these prophets also had such an experience: "I saw an angel opening its wings when I was asleep, but the voice of that angel was like the voice of my grandfather who said I should wake up. Immediately after that I saw many of my relatives who had long ago passed away from the earth. They told me to be a prophet". Here the chief ancestor (grandfather) is referred to as an angel and the family "in the beyond" were actively involved in the calling of this prophet as is the case also with the other respondents.

Fasting (*bopha*) is also a prerequisite for obtaining the ability to have visions and to explain them. Each initiate has to learn the art of fasting during the training period. Some of the prophets maintained that they were fasting either in the mountains or in one or other lonely place, remaining without food for a week. Usually fasting does not last for more than a week, more often for three days. The prophets, prayer healers and ministers usually fast longer than the church members, especially when approaching revival and healing services.

D) The role of the Holy Spirit and/or ancestors in the calling of a prophet

Called by ancestors only

Reference has already been made to the definite role that ancestors have in the calling of most prophets. Refusing such a call by an ancestor or ancestors could result in grave consequences, not only for the one called, but also for his/her relatives. One prophet who initially resisted the call by a grandmother (ancestor) maintained that many of her children consequently died. She had to heed the call.

The ancestors may call a person to be a prophet and subsequently to be a diviner. The illness is again experienced (*ukuthwasa*) and the various rituals are observed at the house of the diviner.

Only four of the respondents—only one in Greater Durban—maintained that they were called by an ancestor alone.

Called by 'the Spirit' through an ancestor

The ancestor acts as mediator for the Holy Spirit to call a person to the office of prophet—a prophet could thus be called by 'the Spirit' through the ancestor(s). More than half of the prophets had this experience.

A young man who was called by his ancestors to be a prophet, and who did not heed the call, became paralysed. Being informed that his ancestors were angry, he heeded the call by 'the Spirit' to be a prophet. Most of the prophets maintained that the ancestors had to agree whether they should accept the call by the Holy Spirit to become prophets. In spite of this, the Holy Spirit nevertheless plays a vital role in their calling and activities.

Called by the Holy Spirit alone

One of the male prophets felt that "something heavy was laid upon his shoulders" during singing and praying in a church service. This brings to mind the *ukuthawasa* experience of a person called to be a diviner when pain is felt on the left shoulder. After this experience he started to speak in tongues and adds, "while this happened the Holy Spirit said to me that I was going to be a prophet. Immediately after this I could see things regarding people as if I was viewing a TV screen and it was as if someone was talking in my ear". Here, the Holy Spirit made direct contact without the intervention of ancestors. The church in which this prophet serves is known as the *Sardis Church of the Holy Spirit in Zion*.

There were a few others also who had the experience of being called directly by the Holy Spirit. A prophet of the *United Holy Messenger Church in Zion* relates: "I was asleep and the Holy Spirit came to me and held me on my legs and hit me on my head very hard while I was on the floor... I was unable to walk straight; then I bent my knees and prayed... while I was praying I heard the "voice" speaking to me and I saw some visions... which enabled me to "predict" the sickness of other people. Then I started to be a prophet". "Predict" means being enabled to diagnose sickness. The diagnosis actually comes either from the Holy Spirit or the ancestors. Hearing "the voice" refers to the injunctions of the Holy Spirit or ancestor. The prophet's ears are often shouted into by the leader who baptises his flock at the sea in order to open his/her ears, so that he/she will be able to hear "the voice" more clearly.

Another prophet's direct call by the Holy Spirit, in a dream to be a prophet, was confirmed by the prophets at the church service. There they told her to buy a blue uniform, as one of them had dreamt that she should wear a blue uniform. When she obtained it, they prayed over the uniform. She was then "gowned" to be a prophet and able to prophesy and heal patients/victims. She was a prophet in the *Bantu Independent Ethiopian Apostolic Church of South Africa* and was previously a member of the *Christian Catholic Church in Zion*.

While there are those who have been directly called only by the Holy Spirit, the largest majority of prophets have ancestral experiences in their calling, which is reminiscent of the experiences of the diviner. Sickness, ancestors, angels, dreams, visions, fasting, the Holy Spirit— and in one instance the name of God were all mentioned. None mentioned the name of Jesus in their calling as prophets in the AIC. This does not imply that Jesus is unimportant, but that in their calling "the Spirit" and/or ancestor spirits predominate. They are associated with "power" and it is "power" that overcomes the weakness brought by illness, especially "pollution".

E) Purification in order to qualify for prophethood

In order to be receptive for messages from the metaphysical world, prophets need to be "pure" ie. cleansed from all the pollution that could affect their ability to have visions (and dreams) and to interpret them. Purification is effected through "bathing, vomiting and divining out evil spirits" ie. casting them out.

The Rand prophets were much more specific as to how they were purified to be prophets: "We bathed and were taken to the river to be immersed and we also vomited, we prayed hard and fasted for many days", another went on her own to the river "where the Spirit gradually taught me how to drive out evil spirits"—the river is the place of cleansing; "I was bathed, vomited, given enema. I was taught how to interpret dreams; I slaughtered a goat to thank and celebrate the fact that I had now become a qualified prophet"; another was not ritually purified but found himself speaking in tongues and receiving information through dreams and then he realised that God wanted him to be a prophet—he added "maybe like Daniel in the Bible".

The prophets consistently referred to having been immersed in the river, made to vomit (the evil out), taught how to drive out evil spirits and how to interpret dreams. A goat-slaughtering (a thanks-giving) ceremony, ended the procedure, thanking God and their ancestors for healing them and allowing them to qualify as prophets. Some had to go to the graves of their guiding ancestors, for example, that of their grandfather or grandmother. One stated, "I had to be prayed for at several occasions to prepare my messenger (ancestor) to perform the work". Being taught to cast out evil spirits is a significant part of the training. Another vomited, after which his deceased grandmother (ancestor) instructed him and gave him the secret of interpreting dreams.

Those few who rely fully on the Holy Spirit did not go through a purification ritual—the 'Spirit' teaches them how to drive out demons or evil spirits without such rituals.

Purification rituals, however, play a significant role with most candidates to prophethood.

F) STATUS OF THE PROPHETS

A number of churches had only one prophet but the number increases as the membership grows. The 'Correntian' Church in Zion has seven (six female and one male), the Apostolic Zion Church has three, while most of the others had one or two prophets. Only one in this sample had no prophets, namely the Swaziland Church of Christ in Zion.

Distinction on the basis of gender

In most of the AIC a distinction is made between the abathandazi (prayer healers) and the abaprofeti (prophets)—the former has a lesser status. In a few churches the former were only women and the latter only men. Where such a distinction is made, the former obtain their information mainly through dreams, the latter mainly through visions. The abathandazi concentrate mainly on healing activities, while the prophet attends to misfortune. Usually the prophet has knowledge of the rituals to be used with regard to diseases that are based on the African cosmology. Some prophets, especially women, are also trained as diviners. Women had a significant position in healing practices as prayer healers. While women in the main line churches are limited to their specific denominations, women who act as prayer healers in the AIC come into continuous contact with people of other churches, and people in general, because of the consulting, praying and healing role they play—services which are available to everyone who wishes to make use of them. The prayer women and prophetesses have a respected status and influence recognised by many in the 'historic' churches and by traditionalists. Because of the status acquired through their talents and personality, women acquire leadership roles in the AIC far more frequently than in the 'historic' churches. The position as healers which women had in traditional society has not been lessened in the AIC. In traditional society, healing in a holistic sense takes precedence with regard to the activities of diviners, who are mostly women. Healing remains in close association with the supernatural forces and herein women play a significant role as they are the 'bridges'. The 'historic' churches neglected such healing activities and stultified an important function of women in the religious context. As prayer healers and prophetesses, women have the same status as men who are prayer healers and prophets.

Distinction on the basis of age and experience

The senior prophets are the more experienced ones who have built up a reputation for special gifts, while the junior prophets are considered to be unable to operate independently due to lack of experience. It was also maintained that the lesser prophets are working through dreams most of the time, not visions, while senior prophets only work through visions. A senior prophet of the *Foundation Divine Christian Catholic Church* stated: "I hear words from the Holy Spirit in a sort of vision and I am able to heal, but the lesser prophets are predicting by feeling with their nerves or body what is wrong on a patient." One method of diagnosis of an illness by the prayer healer is to experience in his own body the same discomfort of the illness as experienced by the patient, ie. the prayer healer then has a clear picture of what is wrong with the patient or victim. The lesser prophets rely more on dreams than on experiencing the discomfort of the illness from which the patient suffers. The lesser prophets are still under instruction from senior prophets and thus under probation.

Distinction on the basis of gifts

Sixty percent of the prophets interviewed base seniority not on the number of years a person practised as a prophet, or how active he/she is, but on the "gifts bestowed on a person by the Spirit". The distinction is, in some cases, not overtly made, but the people know, on the basis of performance, that a specific prophet in the church is more powerful and effective than others. These gifts depend on "the working of the Spirit and God", according to one respondent while the others who emphasized gifts referred to the contact a prophet has with powerful ancestors and "the Spirit".

The need for a prophet in the church

This is a question that has already received some attention by implication. Judging by the numbers of people from various denominations who consult prayer healers/prophets, one concludes that the need is being felt by many. The prophets themselves maintain that their task is to help people positively and actively. Their concern to help people "through the traditional ways" and to help them to establish harmonious relationships among themselves and with others, and with the supernatural forces, which for many also include the ancestors, do account for their impact. They are people "who are able to speak with 'the Spirit' and who for most, have close contact with their ancestors who are in a position to assist them".

Prophets advise people on the various forces that influence their lives, how to avoid bad luck and misfortune. Through their work they "develop and build up people in the church"; they assist those who are affected by sorcery and witchcraft; "they 'see' the secrets of people—even the unknown they know"; they work for the well-being of almost every church member. Through visions most of the prophets 'see' conflicts in families and sin in persons. They 'see' these things more clearly when they have been fasting.

Prophets readily related how, for example, through "prophecy", they detected money which disappeared, how they knew about the forced settlement of people in certain areas before anyone else; that a specific AIC would cease and that a new one would be established; how they prophesied barrenness and how they received through visions the procedures to be followed so that a certain woman could conceive. One prophetess claims that she even resuscitated ("woke up a person who was dead for 21 hours") through prayer; another indicated where a baby who was lost for seven days, could be found; another prophesied that her client's neighbour "is using witchcraft in the house during the night and that this is the cause of her sickness. Then I went into that house and made that house strong by using *muti* (medicine). When the diviner (*isangoma*) went to the house he was unable to move away from the house after I had confronted his bad deeds with prayers and medicine. So he was caught on the spot in the morning."

The prophets on the Rand related some of their acts of prophecy or pre-knowledge as prophets: they knew who would be killed by lightning, what caused the malrelationships between husbands and wives and vice versa, who would be stabbed to death (a few referred to this, which is endemic in Soweto), who poisoned a person (sorcery). One prophesied that a child would die after birth, that a bishop would have an accident, that a bishop's son would die, that lightning would "attack" a house, that a child would be killed by a car, a drowning, death before marriage, that a daughter would get lost. A number referred to having prophesied who would die, that insanity would be experienced by persons who had been bewitched, that a pregnancy would end in the death of a woman. Another prophesied an unnatural pregnancy. Thus, a number prophesied accidents, stabbings, deaths, pregnancies and divorce.

The prophecies about the future are usually of a sombre nature—accidents, stabbings, death, divorce. This could be a projection of a state of mind as a result of the circumstances in which people find themselves in Soweto. Prophecy in connection with sickness is much more relevant as it often leads to the restoration of health. Issues on which the prophets are consulted were enumerated by them. Examples are: days for special services and for healing services, services for school children before examinations, assessing of candidates for leadership positions. They are consulted on women's gatherings, choosing of the vestment colours of new members and they tie a person with cords ("ropes") when prescribed by the Holy Spirit and/or ancestors. They are consulted on marriages, problems, family conflicts and marriage plans, by people who want promotion in their churches or work, on having children, on problems at the work place, on winning the favour of employers, on bewitchment and sorcery and how to be relieved of it, on how to let a girl or boy fall in love with a specific person, on a person on trial for theft, assault or murder, on financial issues, on future events, how to become a prophet, how to appease the ancestors, but mostly on illnesses and how to cure these. One stated: "If ever I am consulted by whites it would be mostly about the proper development and success of the business. The coloureds come for their smoking, drinking and family problems".

All these issues, and many more, receive the attention of the prophets. Patients/victims often keep contact with the prophets after they have been healed. Some of these join the church of the prophets who helped them.

The prophet's position in the church

Only one prophet in the sample of the Greater Durban area maintained she had no authority in the church, while others stated they had some say in their church's procedures. The lady prophet ministers, preaches and gives instructions to officials in the church, while another female prophet plays a special role in her church when enquiries on the conduct of members and the general problems of the church are on the agenda, because of her "deeper insight".

Most of the bishops and presidents of the AIC of the Rand/Soweto sample are also prophets; ordinary ministers could also be prophets, and a leader without a specific title could also act as a prophet. A few maintained that they had authority in the church because they were prophets. They are revered because they are "seers" and healers, revealers and guides. They fill the vacuum which resulted when the diviner, who always had a unique position in the traditional society, was discarded for accepted Christianity. The prayer women (*abathandazi*) are also respected, but they do not enjoy the same status in some churches as prophets.

The prophets who are not church ministers, presidents or bishops, do not take part in the administration of the church in the same manner as church leaders who are prophets. In both Greater Durban and in the Rand/Soweto area, a large section of the leaders also have a prophetical standing.

With regard to their self-evaluation: only a few prophets thought that they did not have a strong position in their churches and these were mainly from the Greater Durban area. None of those on the Rand/Soweto area thought they had a minor position. A lady prophet from Greater Durban thought she had a strong position "because I am a priestess" and another "because people trust me as most of my prophecies are true". Most of the members value the "spirit of prophecy" of the prophets highly, and consider this to be an important asset in the Churches.

Some of the prophets are also church leaders such as ministers, bishops, presidents. A few of the prophets maintained that they had more influence in their churches than the bishop or leader. A male prophet stated "Yes—I am always next to the bishop and president and I am their minister; so they respect me". A lady prophet stated with confidence that "the leaders are guided by me on what to do because I am next to them". Women leaders are not an exception in the AIC and there are women bishops and presidents who lead their churches with efficiency.

In most AIC however, the functions of the minister and prophet are clearly demarcated. While the prophet may have excellent successes in his activities, the opposite may also befall him. If the latter happens to a minister the stability of the group is at stake and it could lead to secession(s). Thus, the minister has to act more carefully when it comes to retaining the *esprit de corps* of the group. An experienced prophet, however, commands respect and his successes lead to more power and recognition for his special charismatic gifts and his divining and prophecy. His anti-sorcery successes against the hostile forces in the urban and socio-economic spheres are not, in the first place, to confront these forces but to strengthen the group inwardly, in order that they act as a repelling force, corporately united against the onslaughts which would weaken the position of their group.

On the question of why some prophets are more effective than others, various significant answers were given such as "it depends on your (sic) Holy Spirit how powerful you are"; on faithfulness in following the instructions concerning fasting and the avoidance of what is evil; the God-given gifts differ; it depends on talents which are not the same; on subjection to the power of the Holy Spirit and not a person's own efforts; on how gifted a prophet is in a specific area; God gives different gifts for different tasks at different stages. Others ascribed it to the power of the specific messenger(s) (ancestor(s)) with whom he/she as a prophet had contact; another ascribed the difference between prophets as due to "the striving for prominence with some in spite of the fact that the working of the Spirit is the same".

The differences are thus ascribed to:
a) differences in gifts, talents given by God;
b) faithfulness concerning instructions relating to fasting;
c) some strive to do their healing in their own power and consequently have less success;
d) some are gifted in specific areas of healing and not in others, for example, some handle *ufufunyane* (possessed by foreign spirits) and other typical African diseases better than others who have more success with regard to physical ailments;
e) ancestors account for the differences in success—if they co-operate with the prophet success is certain, if not, the prophet is handicapped—this applies to those who work through specific ancestors;
f) those who rely on the Holy Spirit alone are considered by some to be specially effective in their churches.

Prophets and marriage

All the respondents agreed that a prophet should be married (because God appreciates the fact that a man and woman are married, God has commanded people to get married). "Of course it is good to be a father of your own children from your own wife" says the male prophet from the *Nazareth Church of God in Zion*. Another prophet stated "every man must have his own wife... there may be *two* or *more* but he must be married". "Even a woman prophetess can get married" said a female prophet. The male prophet of the *Sardis Church of the Holy Spirit in Zion* maintains that prophets should get married, "so that they won't cause trouble by lusting for other peoples' wives". This aspect applies also to women prophetesses: "if she is unmarried she could be betrayed and find herself in love with another wife's husband which would lower her dignity". Another stated an unmarried prophetess "will not be respected and will not be accepted as a prophetess". The "guidance to get married should come from the Holy Spirit" emphasized a lady prophet, and added that if this does not happen, she should not get married.

Prophets are not only allowed to get married—it is important that he/she should be married. In African society a married person is considered to have more wisdom, dignity, understanding, maturity and authority than an unmarried person.

G) Training

Twelve of the respondents were trained by the prophet who cured him/her, others not. One stated: "No one trained me except the Holy Spirit", while another respondent in the Greater Durban area related how the prophetess prayed for her "until the Holy Spirit and ancestors spoke to me in a sort of dream".

Among the prophets interviewed on the Rand were (i) those who were cured by a prophet but not trained by that prophet, (ii) those who were trained by the prophet who cured them and (iii) one who stated the prophet neither cured nor trained her "for God communicated with me directly". A male prophet had the experience of being called directly by the Holy Spirit—such a call implies that the person concerned need not undergo special training: "Training happened on its own. You just believe in God and accept what you see in a vision is true and that it comes from the Holy Spirit". One respondent fasted for three days, the prophet prayed for her and took her to the river to be "strengthened" in the water. Thereafter they had a service lasting the whole night at which she started to speak in tongues, a sign that she received "the Spirit of prophecy".

Training was not an issue with a number of the prophets—"only you must be able to pray and know how to make *isiwasho*", said one. "*Isiwasho*" is a combination of water and ash which has been prayed over and is used as an expellent.

A lady prophet "was called by the ancestors and through dreaming at night, different types of medicine were revealed to her and how to use them." Training, as in the case of early pentecostalism, is not necessary because the work is done through injunctions received by 'the Spirit' or ancestors. The training of healers within the indigenous church contact is not as thorough as the training of traditional healers. The former is based on the assumption that 'the Spirit' type churches rely heavily on the injunctions of the metaphysical forces without the intense emphasis on ritual, although ritual does play a role.

The respondents from the Rand were in close contact with their ancestors and some with the Holy Spirit. A female prophet was instructed in the interpretation of dreams and then taken to a river to be bathed; another called by the "messenger of God" was taken to a river, immersed, bathed, given water mixed with ash to vomit (*palaza*) and given an enema. Others were told to interpret dreams and visions and relate these to a prophet, were then taken to a river, made to vomit and received advice on various diseases and their treatment. Some related that after they were cured of their illnesses, they were bathed, made to vomit and given an enema. There were those who spoke in tongues after this, saw visions and could then interpret certain dreams. The ancestors seemed to be more active in telling them what to do, such as fasting for a few days, even telling them to pray for an initiant and see that the bathing, immersion at the river and the vomiting took place.

Nocturnal services are also held in connection with the training of a prophet. These are revival services at which the prophet-to-be is put into office as the spiritual guardian of the house congregation of the church.

All the respondents from the Greater Durban area maintained that training was free of charge, while sixty percent had to pay for their training in the Rand/Soweto area.

CHAPTER THREE

HEALING METHODS OF THE PROPHET

The healing ministry of the prophet is his/her most significant activity and is sought after by members and adherents in the mainline churches. This is, in fact, the main reason why many members in the mainline churches are regularly to be found at the healing sessions—especially the nocturnal services of the AIC. There are many from these mainline churches who became members of the AIC because they have been healed as a result of healing sessions, and because of the personal attention they received during the time of their illness.

The importance of the prophet is highlighted by the study of West (cf. West, M., *Bishops and prophets in a black city: African independent churches in Soweto*, Johannesburg, Cape Town, David Philip, 1975). In most of the churches he contacted, a double hierarchy exists, namely, that of the administrative authority which is headed by an archbishop, bishop or president, and that of prophet, healer and prayer woman. West came to the conclusion that in all the Zionist type of churches "prophets are extremely important. Very often they stand outside the established hierarchy, although their actual authority may be considerable." (*Ibid.*, p. 24). The prophet, in particular the senior prophet, not only takes precedence with healing sessions but when evil which disturbs relationships has to be removed, does so. Prophets have varying powers and receive them from God or from guiding shades (West, p. 98). The methods of the prophets vary in detail but there is considerable uniformity (West, p. 104). Prophets are successful because they claim supernatural power and sanction for their activities, and they understand the nature of the complaints of their patients better. They tell their patients not only how a disease happened , but also why it happened, and this is extremely important in the African context. They are more convincing in their diagnosis, from the patients' point of view, than the western trained doctor. Fear is often replaced by understanding. Their treatment, within the context of African cosmology, is vital. In the AIC, healing is integrated with worship, which is also of primary significance.

According to the AIC, healing is not the prerogative of scientific medical practice, and cannot be limited to this in the African context as it is more a religious matter (cf. Becken, H.-J., *Theologie der Heilung*:

Das Heilen in den Afrikanischen unabhängigen Kirchen in Südafrika, Hermannsburg, Verlag Missionshandlung, 1972, p. 22). The use of 'western' medicine is rejected by the majority of the prophets and if some type of medicine is used it is usually *muti*. This could be herbs, roots, leaves from trees, bushes and plants, sometimes mixed with treated parts of animals and ordinary ingredients, such as salt, blue stone, white wash, sea water, vaseline, methylated spirits, bicarbonate of soda, vaseline and sulphur, sugar, ash. Water—various types of water as indicated—plays a vital role.

Apart from the psycho-somatic aspects of sickness, social malrelationships and their negative effects are described as sickness. Sickness is due to the decrease of life force (*Zulu: amandla* or *umoya*), of numinous power which is ascribed to the intervention of adversaries. This leads to physical, psychical and spiritual injury. It can be affected by socio-economic circumstances such as unemployment, hunger, injustices, deprivation in various spheres including the political situation, struggle, fear, infertility or catastrophes in nature. Sickness has to do with some or other adverse or dangerous situation. Sickness is due to *umnyama* (blackness, darkness), an inexplicable, brooding, negative power which confronts everyone; a source of a feeling of uncertainty in life which cannot be counteracted by a person through his own power.

Healing is thus not merely a physical or even psychical issue in which process the medical practitioner and patient are involved, but it is a complex interaction between the patient, the healer and the congregation. Illness is also a religious matter in the traditional religion and in the AIC—not often a religious matter alone. When the prophet scrutinizes the background of the patient in order to establish the source for the illness, hatred, jealousy, some moral misdemeanour or disobedience to the injunctions of the ancestors are indicated as being the cause.

Sickness could be from God, the ancestors, witches or evil spirits, also referred to as "spirits of sickness" (*imimoya yesifo*). Even the forces in the universe could have an influence on a person. The moon could be responsible for heart or mental diseases; the new moon could be responsible for epilepsy (*isithutwane*); the 'growing' of the moon could lead to the increase of illness among people and to heavenly disease (*isifo sezulu*), while with the full moon, people become better because they receive power (Becken, p. 35). People are born good and evil, healthy and sick; it "lies in the blood" (Becken, p. 36). Sin and guilt lead to sickness as sin and guilt are life destroying powers. Sickness is an evil as it comes from evil forces and results in an evil heart.

Health is seldom circumscribed. Health, life (*impilo*) implies that there are no malrelationships, no disturbances in the body, mind and soul. In the AIC this condition is described as purity (*ubumhlophe*), the opposite of blackness/darkness (*ubumnyama*), and as *inhlahla* which literally means "luck" but has a much deeper meaning, that of inner well-being. Both these positive concepts describe the opposite of "blackness" (Becken, p. 39). Whiteness in healing medicines is of special significance. The full life force is described by "blessing" (*isibusiso*). Blessing counteracts the forces contrary to health and the negative consequences of the acts of such forces.

Health is not a personal matter but is related to the well-being of the whole community. The right relationship with God and with the whole community gives peace (Zulu: *ukuthula*; Sotho and Tswana: *kgotso*; Becken, p. 40). Real health is to be found only in the community, in the congregation. It is to be found in a balanced relationship between one's body, soul and spirit, between those around one, such as a harmonious relationship with the congregation and with the metaphysical forces of which God is the highest. Healing thus concerns the whole person in his individuality and communality. For healing, a healer is required, and such a healer in the traditional and AIC context should be in close contact with the metaphysical forces from whom healing comes. To be redeemed implies a right relationship not only with the metaphysical forces, but also with those in the community, in the congregation.

The "medicines" used, such as water and various ingredients, are symbolic acts, taking away the evil symbolically. Health means that one is able to continue with one's existence undisturbed as a human being, without any adverse circumstances putting obstacles in the way, and this implies harmonious relationships in all spheres of one's existence.

Purity of the healer

It is important that the healer should be pure before any act of healing can be successful. This includes praying and fasting. The prophet gives much time to his/her own relationship to 'the Spirit'. Those who live in symbiotic union with the ancestors ie. who mediate through the ancestors, regard the undisturbed relationship with them to be of vital importance. An intimate relationship with the metaphysical forces enhances the effectiveness of the healing activities of the prophet. Ngubane refers to this as another form of possession and states "a Prophet (or Prophetess) in such sects may be thought of as being in continuous contact with the Spirit. In that case his role is seen as more or less identical with that of a diviner..." (Ngubane, H., *Body and mind in Zulu medicine; An ethnography of health and disease in Nyuswa—Zulu thought and practice,* London, Academic Press, 1977, p. 148).

The diviner's training, with its ascetic disposition to avoidance of certain foods, alcohol and tobacco, withdrawal from society, and emphasis on what is pure and ritually clean, is not different from the prophet in this regard. Prophets however spend much time in prayer and fasting.

A) SYMBOLS (OR MEANS) OF HEALING

Kiernan, calls the Zionists "small-scale curing communities in which reserves of spiritual power, called *umoya*, are ritually built up and expended to offset the effects of human mystical agents which afflict the individual" (Kiernan, J.P., 'The weapons of Zion', *Journal of Religion in Africa*, Vol. X, fasc. 1, 1979, p. 13). He further refers to 'powers' and 'specifics' utilised in these churches, stating that, "'specifics' are contingent infusions of spiritual power designed to cope with particular problems, eg. drinking a portion of water and ashes, which has been blessed for this purpose, transmits sufficient power to alleviate stomach pains. While 'specifics' are exhausted in their application and are thus renewable, powers are permanent and lasting endowments. Some belong personally to gifted individuals such as prophets; others are attached to the functions of membership or of office within the community; what all conferred powers have in common, however, is that they are employed in the manner of weapons" (*Ibid.*). The traditional cosmology is based on an all-pervading mysterious force and there are malevolent forces which have to be confronted continuously. This explains the emphasis on "weapons" which are to be utilised in this struggle.

Colour, vestments, cords, staves

The Spirit or ancestors prescribe which vestments should be worn during the healing process. The prophets have vestments with different colours. In the Greater Durban area, only one prophetess did not have the experience that special vestments are prescribed by the supernatural forces in connection with healing. Nearly all the prophets from the Rand/ Soweto area maintained that such vestments are prescribed, although a few stated that it does not happen often; only one said it never happened in his case.

The colours of the vestment used by the prophet in healing sessions have special value and a bearing on the outcome of the treatment. The role of colours in the healing procedure is explained as follows: "White for visions and blue for healing". The colour (whatever is prescribed) gives the prophet " strength and power". A female prophet stated that the colour is "needed by the Holy Spirit and when I wear it I become more powerful". A few prophets said the colour is required by the Holy Spirit.

The colour thus gives "more power" to do the work properly, more successfully... "it gives me power and makes the evil spirits flee from me"; "the colours make communication between myself and the 'messenger' strong, effective and clear".

Only three respondents stated that colours are not very important, and a male prophet of the *Sardis Church of the Holy Spirit* maintained they have no significance for him "but for others".

Thus, the colour of the uniform in which the prophet does his/her healing practices is of significance. The colours used are usually white, which symbolises purity, blue which symbolises love, and green which symbolises faithfulness. One or all of these colours could be used on a vestment. White, the colour of wholeness, is usually the basic colour. Traditional colour symbolism has always played a significant role in healing practices.

Red as a colour for the uniform has made its appearance more often lately among some Zionist groups who have a diviner-cum-prophet as a healer. The red is the symbolic colour of traditional diviners. Many Zionists, however, have a red cord or red string in the cord, or red crosses made out of red cloth on their uniforms. This signifies contact with non-christian ancestors.

The following qualities were ascribed by the respondents to the cords that Zionists wear:

a) they fortify a person against diseases and evil forces;
b) they enable a person to clarify what is being conveyed (in *glossolalia*; it helps the person "to follow all the Holy Spirit languages";
c) the colours of the cords are significant—different colours are used for different illnesses;
d) they give power to the prayer healer to heal; they make healing more effective;
e) only when prophets prophesy "do they use cords to get more spirit".

A prophet from the *Nazareth Church of God in Zion* does not rely on cords but "instead on prayer and even on pure water which has been prayed over". None of the respondents rejected the cords, not even the prophets who relied solely on the Holy Spirit. Cords are used even by some of the established church members, among Africans. The main emphasis is on fortification against the forces of evil.

The cords, which are substitutes for the traditional amulets (around the neck or wrists), and the ropes round the waist or across the shoulders, emphasize fortification against witchcraft, sorcery and the evil forces. The cords, the traditional amulets and the ropes fulfil the same function and have the same aim. But the cords appear within a new context, in which Christianity also has a role to play.

The cords are regularly dipped in water mixed with salt or in sea water, or in the sea itself. Some of the prophets have chains round their shoulders as is the case with some of the diviners. The overall emphasis remains a symbolic fortification against the forces of evil which are responsible for sickness.

Staves used at healing sessions are channels of mystical power, and are referred to as 'weapons' utilised to ward off evil forces. They are part of the armament of each full member in the Zionist Church context. Not all have their staves with them at the beach when they come for 'baptism', which includes exorcism, healing, getting more of 'the Spirit', to obtain spiritual and physical power and well-being. However, in some of the groups, each adult faithfully brings his stave and plants it in the sand while 'baptism' takes place. This, together with the flag planted alongside, is to ward off the evil while exorcism and the other activities take place. All these staves are then bundled together and, as in the case of the cords, are put into sea water. The sea water is powerful enough to get the evil out so the staves are not used while in the sea, but only when dancing, singing and drumming take place alongside the sea on the sand, with rejoicing in the victory obtained over malevolent forces. At healing sessions away from water the staves are pushed against the patient. There, no male can assist in healing without a staff—only women can—although males also have the right to carry a staff. In traditional society women were not allowed to carry a stick as it was a symbol of authority. In the AIC, the staff also emphasises the herding aspect—some staves are made like those of herdsmen—the taking care of one another.

Water (isiwasho)

Most of the prophets use *isiwasho*, usually tap water, river water, fresh water to which salt has been added, or sea water mixed with ashes (water is 'cool' and so is woodash—utilised to counteract the 'hot' problematic situation or condition). Some prefer rain water as it is stronger than the other types of water because it comes directly from heaven. Running water is more effective than static water. Patients are often put under a shower because of the effectiveness of running water. Rain water gathered during a storm, and during lightning, is considered to be especially effective in healing. All the prophets use some or other kind of water mixture as an expellant for cleansing. Sea water or water mixed with salt is also used for vomiting (*palaza*).

The *muti* (medicine) used by the prophets is associated with vomiting, steaming, bathing, enemas. Vomiting (*palaza*) is generally prescribed. For example, a prophet states that he boils the water and pours salt into it (if it is not sea water) and gives it to the patient to vomit ie. to remove the evil from inside. With steaming and bathing the evil is removed from the outside. In the traditional context evil is a negative entity on the body, which could be washed off, or within a person, which could be removed through vomiting (*palaza*) or emetics. Most of the prophets do not limit themselves to *isiwasho* (cleansing) but also use medicines. The sea, a river or a dam are the places where bathing takes place in order to wash the negative forces off the body. A specially potent place to remove evil forces, and to be strengthened, is the sea. It is stated that prophets do not discard traditional rituals for healing, especially in the case of *ukufa kwabantu* (diseases which fall into the context of African cosmology), as it is not easy to heal persons with these diseases by using *isiwasho* only. The few prophets who do not use divination stated that this is only done by diviners. These churches have less syncretistic tendencies in their healing processes. A lady prophet, whose father is a diviner, does not apply divination in her healing practices.

Only two AIC prophets, of the *Apostolic Church of Christ* and of *The Apostolic Zion Church*, maintained that divination is not practised in their churches.

Water plays a tremendously important role in the healing practices of the AIC, as was indicated above. The major emphasis is on purification: the water cleanses, it is an expellent. Purification belongs to the consciousness of the religious person who is disturbed, or whose position in relation to the community has become disturbed and who wishes to have this restored. Every cult has to do with purity. The impurity of the body— outside and inside—reflects the impurity of the soul or innermost being. Religious purity is restored through water cults. Water reflects impurity ie. the disturbance of the innermost being and relationships, and because it is found everywhere, it becomes an obvious purification ingredient.

This leads to purification cults. Purification is seldom effected with blood—mostly with water. Water is associated with the idea of a new birth, a rebirth, a change. From here the baptismal or water rituals develop, each having their symbolic power because of being associated with water. In the traditional context, evil is negative magic on a person or evil within a person. It should be ritually washed off or taken out of a person through emetics. Water on a person, especially running water (river, sea, showering are often prescribed by the prayer healers and prophets), still has the association with this traditional background. When mixed with ash, salt, etc, water then has the role of taking the evil out through vomiting.

The prayer healers and prophets in the AIC use water mixed with salt or sea water, for vomiting (*palaza*), as a purifier ie. cleansing the person from the inside, which implies that the evil has to be vomited out. It serves as an expellent. Reference has also been made to *isiwasho* (a mixture most often of ash and water although other ingredients could also be added, such as white wash (lime) and salt (if it is fresh water), which is also used for cleansing).

Ashes, lime, salt, impepho *etc.*

Except for a few prophets who said they do not believe in divination, all stated that they do heal through divination. The majority use ash and water which have been prayed over. Others referred to "ash of the diviners", to *impepho* (herbs burned as incense by the diviners in order to attract the attention of the ancestors), and *umcako* (white wash, lime). The latter is reminiscent of the traditional approach. Black and red ("hot") medicines, in traditional society, are cooked and this stops the disease. This is followed by white ("cool"), uncooked medicine which heals the person. The *umcako* purifies as white is the symbol of purity.

It is important that prayers be said "over" the mixture. The power of the word is important—it could substitute the spell—as the mixture is blessed and becomes 'holy' water. Ash, sugar, white wash, salt, *impepho* (a plant which gives off a scented smell, used by diviners to call up the ancestors) are used. Others also use blue stone, epsom salts, Sunlight or blue soap, vinegar, milk etc. Various mixtures are concocted from some of these ingredients.

All the prophets, including those who maintained they only relied on the Holy Spirit, used one or other kind of ingredient. The main emphasis is on inner cleansing and this cannot take place only by prayer, but certain rites have also to be performed. The fact that ingredients (*muti*) are used satisfies the mental disposition (with their emphasis on what is concrete) of many of the AIC members who hail from the traditional society, with its traditional medicines which are meticulously prepared and given to the patient/victim. Medicine has a specific potency, and in it lies healing power which becomes effective, either in an *opere operato* manner, or when prayers are said over it.

Some prophets, when treating a patient/victim, have specific vestments for healing. Others prescribe vestments with specific colours to their patients—the specific colour changes according to the revelation ("prediction") received about the patient ie. what colour vestment the patient has to wear when he/she goes to sleep.

Colour symbolism, as already indicated, plays a signficant role in traditional healing and also among the AIC with their uniforms, cords, medicines and candles.

Holy time and holy place

None of the prophets questioned in the Greater Durban area thought that healing required a special place or time, except one, who maintained that he heals only after 18h00. Except for two prophets from the Rand/Soweto area, none of the others thought that special places and times were any significance. Healing could thus be effected at any time and place for most of the prophets. Because water plays such an important part in healing, all agreed that, given the choice, they would appreciate the opportunity to be at a dam, river or, especially, the sea.

The male prophet from the *Itshe Legumbi Apostolic Church of South Africa*, for whom neither place nor time is important, nevertheless adds: "I prefer the night for it is silent and polite". By "polite" he meant that not much noise is made. The male prophet from the *Ararat Church of God in South Africa and Mozambique* prefers "to perform healing in the church or in a private room during the evenings or throughout the night".

The impression is left that the need to heal is greater than time and space.

Use of the Bible in healing sessions

All the prophets stated that they do not use the Bible when healing people. The New Testament, the book of healing, for in Jesus' ministry healing was a central function, is very seldom used at the healing sessions conducted at the sea. Usually a service precedes the healing session when it takes place in the house, in church or in the open spaces in urban areas, and here the Bible has a place. But it is not read during the healing sessions. Thus, the history of healing of centuries ago, even by Jesus, gets no precedence, but healing history is made in the here and now. Thus what is of importance in the AIC is, not what has been done at the sea of Galilee, but what is being done at their place of healing. It may seem strange that the name of Jesus comes so seldom to the fore in healing sessions while "the Spirit" and/or messenger(s) are so prominent, but in African cosmology, "power" is the main emphasis and "the Spirit" and "messengers" are associated with power as indicated earlier.

It would be a distortion to maintain that the Bible has no role to play at healing sessions. These sessions are usually the last part of a service where the Bible has been read—often several times—and the sections read contemplated upon. Many of the groups who come to the beach for exorcism or healing in general, bring a Bible with them, although they seldom read from it. It is nevertheless present during their healing activities.

Hospitals

Most of the prophets of metropolitan Durban maintained that they do not visit their patients in hospital—they either do not have the time, or their ancestors do not allow them to go there. If they do go to hospital, it is an indirect admission that they have failed. Most of the Rand/Soweto prophets do visit their patients in hospital while only two stated "not yet", and another said , "no, because I don't like to see them in a worse condition". Hospitals are thus less popular in metropolitan Durban, where many still have close connections with the rural areas, than is the case in the Rand/Soweto area. Hospitals are not unconditionally symbols of healing. Healing rather takes place at the church service, which is usually held in a private home, where the congregation take an active role with their singing, dancing and praying. Healing is thus practised in and outside the home, especially that of the leader or the prophet. One prophet stated that it takes place mainly in the church on Sundays, but from Monday until Saturday "privately at home".

All the prophets maintained that healing takes place in the church and privately—"people do come privately". They do not just come to the church service, which is often held in a house. Most of the indigenous churches have their services in homes, which often, but not always, belong to the leader, and in open spaces in the cities, or outside the huts in rural areas. Only a very small percentage have church buildings. Only about five percent of the ± eight million AIC, in over four thousand denominations, are housed in church buildings. This is practically a churchbuildingless christian movement—a movement of house congregations.

B) Rites of healing

Diagnosis

Prophets receive their information about a patient either through dreams and/or visions, but more often through visions. It is important to get the correct diagnosis of the illness ie. 'prediction'. This is given to the prophet through a vision by "the Spirit" or messenger(s) (ancestor(s)) or both; the medicine to be prescribed is also related to the prophet by the Holy Spirit or by an ancestor(s) or both. While the medicine or holy water is prepared, dancing and singing, accompanied by handclapping, take place in order to make it powerful. This is then given to the patient/victim who is informed about further treatment.

Firstly, the diagnosis takes place. This is why "prediction" takes precedence. In the traditional society the diviner is the "seer", the one who establishes what has gone wrong, what influences led to the patient's condition, and what should be done to eradicate or rectify this. The "prediction" is described as communication received from the Holy Spirit and/or ancestors. The patient/victim sometimes also informs the prophet about the specific illness he/she suffers from. Visions or "predictions" are also referred to as "the spirit of prophecy". Some prophets emphasize that they do not diagnose but are directly informed by the ancestor(s) or 'the Spirit'. This direct revelation is described as follows: "as if I am looking into the mirror and see the disease or sickness affecting the patient". Other means of diagnosis are, for example, "filling a bottle with water and as I look through the water I would get the message". In some cases they establish the type of illness by experiencing the same pains the patients experience. Another gets his information on the illness of a patient through feelings which radiate from the patient.

Dreams and visions are thus the main sources from which the prophets receive information concerning the patient/victim. Only one lady prophet, interviewed in the metropolitan Durban area from *The*

Bantu Independent Ethiopian Apostolic Church of South Africa, maintained she experiences only visions. A few prophets from Soweto give preference to dreams rather than visions, such as the prophets of *The Canaan Church of God in Zion* and the *Itshe Legumbi Apostolic Church of South Africa*. The largest majority receive information both through dreams and visions, but mainly through visions. When asleep they receive information about the person's illness through dreams and when the person is with them through visions (*imibono*). What has been dreamt at night often recurs in a vision during the day. Visions are experienced during the moment of healing while one's mind is awake. Dreams are problem indicators, and visions give information on how the problem can be solved or the illness healed. Dreams come when one is fast asleep, visions when one prays and is wide awake. When prophets heal they see the sickness or problems with their "inward eye"; visions give the prophet inward "images" ie. the diagnosis of the future, problems confronting the patient/victim, the sickness, how the problems can be avoided or solved, or the sickness healed. Visions are mainly obtained when in a 'state of prayer'.

Some make the distinction between dreams and visions on the basis of their *source*: dreams come through an angel, and visions through ancestors. A male prophet, from *The Nazareth Church of God in Zion*, does not experience visions, but relies on dreams. Instead of visions, he experiences the feelings to which the patient is subjected because the illness is rejected in his own body.

Thus, dreams at night reveal the type of sickness while, for most prophets, visions indicate the healing procedure to be followed, although diagnosis could also take place through visions. Dreams take place through the intervention of angels or ancestors, while visions take place only as a result of the intervention of ancestors and/or the Holy Spirit. Visions are not associated with angels.

After the "prediction" of the sickness, the medicine to be used is usually seen in a vision, which tells, for example, what type of *isiwasho*, (purification "medicine") is required.

The "Spirit of prophecy" also indicates the type of prescription to be used. For example, one of the respondents stated that, in her case, the following ingredients are usually prescribed by the "Spirit of prophecy", namely, "boiled milk, salt, vinegar, red pepper, epsom salt, blue stone, blue soap and, in most cases, the ropes".

Some prophets rely solely on "the Spirit" to give them the "method of healing". One respondent emphasized that "a person must be guided by the Spirit within him; otherwise he would do his own thing if he did not depend on the Holy Spirit". Another said: "In most cases the Spirit of prophecy would lead one in what to do for the patient such as telling me to make a rope for the patient, or give water mixed with ash to the patient".

Other prophets also depend on the prayers of the congregation in their healing procedures. Although vomiting, steaming and enemas have a prominent place in their procedure, the empathy, warmth and integrity of the prophet give confidence, and a relationship of trust is built up between the prophet and the patient. The medicinal mixtures which have been "prayed over" by such a prophet are considered to be especially effective. So too are the prayers that are said for the patient by such a prophet. The prescription in prayer is received. Although some prophets believe that the *isiwasho* and other ingredients used have the necessary effect, they do not stop praying for the patient.

Diagnosis is thus obtained by a prophet through a vision, in a dream, or by experiencing the ailments in his/her body from which the patient suffers. Some see the patient even a day before he/she comes for help—such information is received through dreams. One prophet maintained: "When a patient is in front of me I may receive visions, but if the message comes a day before his visit to me, it comes through dreams". This distinction between dreams being experienced the night before, and visions when the patient is present, has been made by several prophets. In visions, everything related to the life of the patient is revealed. Usually messages from the ancestors are heard; this is why reference is made to a "voice" being heard. Ancestors reveal the secrets through a "voice". This is why prophets' ears are shouted into at the sea to open them so that they will be able to hear the "voice" more clearly. A prophet from the *Ararat Church of God in South Africa and Mozambique*, maintains that "the ancestors may somehow bring a certain message and when I carefully listen to the message I would find that it is almost the same as the one coming from the Spirit". Thus 'the Spirit' and the ancestors do not contradict each other. For some this is so even if the ancestors died as non-Christians, because Jesus brought the message to them where they were in the underworld.

The types of medicines are also indicated through visions or dreams. Nearly all use something tangible apart from prayer ie. nearly all ritualise healing—only a few prophets concentrate only on prayer.

The prophets mainly associate prediction with the diagnosis of illnesses and how to heal them. 'Prediction' is also related to the detection of sorcery and witchcraft which are main sources of illness. As will be seen later, this is a major task for many prophets. 'Prediction' is also associated with seeing lost things and where these are to be found; predicting what is going to happen in future, such as an accident or misfortune; telling a person about her future life and the events or issues that will influence her life; predicting "bad luck", dangers and how to avoid jealousies, hatreds, deaths etc. predicting the progress and problems of the Church and what the eventual outcome of an action will be. All this depends on the enlightenment that comes from "the Spirit" and from the messengers (ancestors). In order to obtain this from the ancestors, certain rituals which will be described later, are observed.

There are those who concentrate on 'prediction' and healing ie. they inform people about what caused their misfortunes and diagnose their illnesses. The emphasis is on establishing the cause rather than the symptoms. They *see* what illness or discomfort plagues a person in a vision, ask this person whether the diagnosis is correct, and, if this is the case, "we pray together requesting the messengers (ancestors) to give us the prescription". There are those who, as is the case with prayer healers in general, get the diagnosis through dreams. This is described as a message which has been obtained through a dream when asleep, either from ancestors or the Spirit.

A prophet of the *Apostolic Christ Church of South Africa* stated that in "most cases the Holy Spirit would tell me about the sickness of people, their health or family problems and how they should be healed". "The Spirit guides and tells me the medicine to be used" said another. "The Spirit of prophecy" informs them of the medicines to be used. People are healed "if the Spirit leads". There are prophets who have the same pains as those experienced by the patient or victim and this enables them to diagnose and heal the patient. One prophet stated, "I first suffer from the sickness which the patient experiences—sometimes I suffer in my dreams". This "feeling" in one's own body of the illness somebody has or the destructive "medicines" some one has on his body, was an acceptable diagnosis in traditional society.

All the respondents, except one, use candles during these healing procedures. Candles are also used for various purposes by the prayer healers/prophets:

a) they help "to clarify the visions"; they shed light on visions; they assist in prophesying;

b) candles are used when "we make a light for the ancestors who bring the prediction and healing";

c) they are utilised by the Holy Spirit during the diagnosis of the illness of the patient and when the medicines have to be indicated through visions;

d) they shed light on the matter in question ie. they clarify those things about which the prophet prophesies and which lie in the future;

e) the candles "open the way for the messengers (ancestors) when God sends and throws light on the message or information with which they are coming";

f) "the candles light the way for my messengers to meet with the messengers of the patient". This procedure is often witnessed when attending the rituals with the candles; different colours represent the ancestors of the prophet and the patient who are brought in contact with each other "in order to get good results"; white candles are used by all during healing procedures—they represent the Holy Spirit and could also represent ancestors who died as Christians; blue and green candles (blue symbolises 'love' and green 'faithfulness') could also be used; yellow candles are also often used as they could represent the ancestors who died as Christians or they represent the ancestors of one of the parties in an act of reconciliation in order to restore relationships and thus result in healing. Red candles are used by some groups to represent the ancestors who died as non-Christians—red is often used by prophets-cum-diviners on their uniforms or headgear (during the last decade this colour has become more popular among the strongly syncretic section of the AIC);

g) "the candles light everything so that a prophet would see all the details about the problem which the patient may be experiencing";

h) "the candles act like a torch which lights the way for the messengers so that the patients' condition may be clear".

Only one respondent does not use candles in her healing procedures, but only as light in the house because she prefers them to paraffin lamps.

The main emphasis concerning candles is the light they bring to open up the way for the Holy Spirit and/or ancestors. Emphasis in this connection is put on the meeting of the ancestors of the prayer healer/ prophet and the patient in order to be "strong" against the adversary or the illness. They also enlighten visions and, through this, assist in indicating both the disease as well as the medicines to be used.

Why does an illness happen?

The reason why a person experiences an illness is of significance, but more so for the prophet or prayer healer than for the patient. The treatment depends upon the cause of the disease which is so often mysterious. It is important for the healer because the complexities surrounding the illness are often difficult to unravel. Much depends on revelation through visions. The cause, whether it is the ancestors, sorcery or witchcraft, is important for the prophet. Many of the causes can be traced back to jealousy, hatred or relationships which have gone sour. Most of the Rand/Soweto prophets stated that they can tell the cause of a disease and that it is important for the patient to know this. Most victims/patients want to know who the sorcerer is or who bewitched him/her. This is revealed through a dream or vision which comes mainly from ancestors, but also from the Holy Spirit.

The limitations of western medical care should be ascribed to its so often one-dimensional approach, in spite of the fact that many illnesses have their origin in the psychic sphere of human existence. This level of man's existence is often totally ignored in the western medical context. In many African countries the respected traditional healers receive recognition. Prayer healers/prophets today attract the attention of many in the mainline African churches because they meaningfully address the real adversaries against the health of people who still live, mentally and physically, in the context of the traditional world view.

Exorcism

Exorcism is one of the main activities within the indigenous churches, one in which the prayer healers play a major role. The prophets explain their hitting of the victim on the body, especially the shoulders, as follows:
a) "we are fighting the devil inside the person";
b) it is 'the Spirit' who "makes us do this hitting of the patient which is actually fighting the illness so that it can go away";
c) "if there is a need to hit a person especially on the shoulders, it is because the disease has to be pushed out";
d) "we don't actually mean to hit the patient but we hit the demons"; "we try to get rid of the evil spirit in the person";
e) "we chase the evil out of him or her. Those of us who hit the patient unite our ancestors with the ancestor of the patient and jointly the evil spirits are driven out".

A strong united force is thus built up against the forces of evil in order to overcome them and their evil effects. This will be discussed more extensively later.

Praying and dancing

Prayer does have a place in the healing process of the *abathandazi* and *abaprofeti*. When the illness is diagnosed the prophet prays for the patient/victim. Some of the prophets utilise prayer and divination in their healing procedures. There are a few who concentrate *only* on prayer and water that has been "prayed over"—29% of the respondents. One prophet stated that he uses medicines, but also prays for "almost all patients" who come to him. The way prayers are said often gives the impression that the words used should have a positive effect on the patient, and that the forces of evil responsible for the disease should be excommunicated. Prayers often give the impression that the words so forcefully expressed should exorcise the evil forces present in the patient.

Prayer plays an important part in healing sessions but much of the praying takes place while dancing. In traditional African society dancing took place when something was "asked" from the ancestors, as well as when gratitude was expressed to the ancestors for honouring their requests. In Africa, one does not remain static in the presence of the metaphysical forces, but makes contact with them mainly through rhythmic movements and singing.

Dancing, in traditional Africa, is not merely a way of relaxing, it is a way of obtaining power, of asking from the ancestors, and of expressing gratitude to them. During the first fruit festivals it was a way of opening up the new cycle. Dancing was central in the religious expression of Africans and also in their healing ceremonies.

In the AIC, dancing still retains its central role, while it has been largely stultified in the historic African churches. All the prophets interviewed from the Durban area dance around or with the patient in the circle, while sixty percent of the sample from the Rand/Soweto area dance around a patient. One of the prophets maintained: "I am told by the Holy Spirit when I should dance with the patient—sometimes the Holy Spirit tells me not to do it". Some of the prophets do not dance around the patient themselves, but let those present perform this ritual. There are prophets who prefer that no dancing take place around the patient because it might disturb the prophet's communication with the Holy Spirit and/or the 'messengers', a term often used for the ancestors.

The reasons given by the prophets for dancing around a patient are the following: a) The Holy Spirit tells them to dance; b) some dance because "we are calling the Holy Spirit to be among us"; c) there are those who dance because they "make the Holy Spirit more powerful, more effective"; d) dancing gives "power to a prophet to experience the vision more clearly"; e) dancing gives more power and makes the prophet totally committed to the Spirit; f) dancing prepares the prophet "to receive clearly the message from the messenger"; g) dancing empowers those who dance around the patient and this brings the prophet and the patient fully under the control of 'the Spirit'; h) one prophet stated "we dance if we feel that the sickness is very strong in the patient's body". Prophets from a few churches do not observe any such rhythmic practices during healing sessions. Dancing, chorus singing and handclapping in the indigenous churches recall what takes place in the Pentecostal Charismatic type of churches among other sections of the population. Most of the indigenous churches could be termed Africanised charismatic churches. There are different types of rhythmic dances—slow, fast, moving slow or fast around the circle, bending of the one knee while moving rhythmically, shuffling the feet while moving, turning the feet more to the inside of the circle while dancing around the circle, moving very fast, "like the wind", with long paces around the circle during exorcism sessions, while the victim is in the centre. Individuals are turned around and around very fast and this is considered to be a sign of receiving the Spirit. This is often seen at sea "baptisms" where baptism could be exorcism, getting the evil spirits out, getting more of the Spirit/Holy Spirit, coming in closer contact with the ancestors, healing, a request for inner power or for "luck", which implies well-being. These movements need further study.

Singing (hymns and choruses)

Various reasons are given for singing during healing procedures:
a) "Singing is important—they are just making my Holy Spirit more powerful" said a lady prophet from the *Apostolic Zion Church,* who implies that the Holy Spirit uses her more effectively when those present sing—mainly short choruses—because singing is also praying. They consider singing indispensable because it gives them "more power to perform the task of healing more effectively";
b) it helps everyone to be under the control of 'the Spirit';
c) those singing during healing procedures help the patient, the prophet

and the messenger (ancestor) "to give to me the whole message about the patient";

d) "it encourages the messenger (ancestor) to give to me the whole message about the patient";

e) "singing makes the patient more susceptible to my commanding and healing prayers". The "commanding prayers" referred to here are those prayers which command the evil spirits to leave the patient.

For most of the respondents, singing of those present at the healing session (which often takes place after the service) is indispensable for effective healing. This implies singing and handclapping. Different rhythmic movements are performed with the hands—sometimes fast, then slow.

Some AIC have their own specific type of handclapping, for example, at *The St John Apostolic Faith Mission*, this act is performed at a very fast pace. The clapping of hands "is an expression of being united in the act of healing with those who participate and with the metaphysical forces, and it allows the Holy Spirit to control everyone and to let them participate in what is being done. They come more readily under the influence of the Spirit", according to one respondent.

Singing thus has to do with the invocation of the Holy Spirit and the ancestors to strengthen the prophet, the patient or victim. The singers themselves also have to receive power which is transferred to the patient and keeps away the forces of evil. The main emphasis is on being fully under the control of the Holy Spirit and/or the ancestor(s). The patient/victim is in the centre and the indispensable activities, such as praying—which could become shouting in order to drive out evil spirits—laying on of hands, speaking in tongues, putting the holy staves (*izikhali*) against the patient, singing, dancing, handclapping, hitting a person on the body especially the back and on the shoulders, putting the patient in the water, vomiting, steaming and emetics, are all part of a healing session with many of the AIC. *Muti*, as indicated above, also plays a vital role.

What do they sing?

The bystanders may sing any hymn or chorus—usually it is a chorus they themselves have composed—preferably those hymns or choruses which will direct the thoughts and prayers of all present to the healing activity. Some of these choruses have only a few words which are endlessly repeated, such as *Woza Umoya* ("Come Spirit"), and which put them in the spiritual state of sharing the combined power they receive through the healer with the patient. Preference is thus given to hymns/choruses which are relevant to the occasion. Here "the Spirit should guide them" concerning the hymns/choruses, to be sung. There exist hymns/choruses especially composed for healing sessions—some AIC allow no others except these.

What they sing during the healing sessions was spelt out by some of the prophets.

Handclapping, singing and dancing put people more easily under the control of the Spirit. It gives the prophet "more power" because he/she receives it from the Holy Spirit and/or ancestors more readily in such a joint effort. It also helps the patient to be "in the Spirit" more quickly. These activities, said others, help the "messengers" (ancestors) to have more power and assist such that "our messengers should meet and unite with the messenger in the patients' life". Through a symbolic act, using candles with different colours, this unification, also referred to as reconciliation, is effected. When the different parties harmonise, the task of the prophet is made much easier. The white candle among these candles represents the Holy Spirit. The yellow candle, for example, represents the ancestor(s) of the prophet and the green the ancestor(s) of the victim. Yellow is considered to be the colour of the ancestors and green symbolises faithfulness. Their "reconciliation" is basic for effective healing sessions. This is a procedure followed by a number of the prophets.

The congregation have thus a special and dynamic task to perform during the healing sessions. While singing they "pray with their hearts" ie. pray silently. They often sing while the prophet prays. The praying function of the congregation is considered by some prophets to be more significant than singing. The congregation usually becomes silent when the prophet starts to talk and predict what is wrong with him/her to the patient. In some AIC, the *abathandazi* are expected to assist the prophet. The healing procedure is, in this case, one of joint action. There are other sessions in private homes in which only the prophet and patient are present and the healing procedures are performed.

The contribution of those present, the congregation, during healing sessions is a significant one as:
a) their activities in regard to singing, handclapping and dancing enable 'the Spirit' and/or ancestors to act powerfully;
b) they assist in subjecting the patient sooner and more fully to the work of the Holy Spirit and/or ancestors;

c) revelations through visions (predictions) come easier so that the illness can be more easily diagnosed and the remedy more clearly indicated;

d) they enable the ancestral spirits of the patient and the prophet to unite more readily in assisting to heal the patient. The whole procedure becomes a catharsis, not only for the patient, but also for those who take part in a most dynamic manner. This, for some, even leads to *glossolalia*.

The importance of the congregation during healing sessions does not, however, imply that no healing procedures could be effected without them. Much healing activity takes place when only the prayer healer (*umthandazi* or *umprofeti*) and the patient or victim are present. A few of the prophets did not consider the congregation to be of any special significance when healing sessions took place—this minority emphasized that the group is not essential in their healing procedures while others stated 'not readily' or 'not very much to me'. The general conviction however, is expressed in the words of two prophets: "when they are present they give me power"; "the group supports me in casting out demons or evil spirits—they make my task easier".

Cleansing/expelling (bathing, steaming, vomiting, emetics)

Different types of water are used or prescribed by the prophets for their patients, as has been indicated. These are water from a tap, running or river water, sea water, water mixed with salt, dam water, rain water ie. water directly obtained from rain in a bucket, water obtained in this manner during a storm and when lightning is severe. Water is generally mixed with ash, and is considered to be very effective during healing sessions. Also, water obtained from a thunderstorm when lightning was severe is most effective in warding off evil forces that attack a victim. Rain water is preferred by some because "it comes directly from heaven". Sea water is not only used for outward purification—patients being pushed underneath the waves, but it is also drunk in order to vomit the evil out.

Fresh water mixed with salt is also used for vomiting purposes. Steaming is also prescribed by the healers. Sea water, taken to far away places such as Soweto, is used with great discretion—a very small amount is thrown into the bath water, for example, from time to time. It is a most effective means of purification. Because running water is considered to be especially effective, the prophet and the prayer healer often prescribe showers to their patients. Various types of emetics are also used for inner cleansing. The prophets pray over the water in the bottles, whether taken from a river, the sea, a tap or directly preserved during rain. It is important that the bottle or container should not be closed when such prayers take place. The water is then more powerful and effective for the purpose used. Only one respondent maintained that he prays over the water whether it is opened or closed. One stated that "the bottle must be opened so that the angel may enter the bottle" while another associated the water with "prediction": "I open the container or bottle, as it makes it easier to see every secret".

Fasting

Most of the prophets fast before healing sessions. One who fasts sometimes, stated that "even the patient fasts because we want his heart totally directed to God so that he can have holy communion". Another stated that prophets fast only when they are going to the sea or river; "also when there is a person about whom there is to be prophesied". The prophet should also fast, "but you do that", said one, "if you are told by the Holy Spirit". Only a few prophets stated that they either do not fast at all, or fast very seldom. For them, fasting for their patients is optional. The prophets stated that:

a) fasting makes them more powerful, "easier for the Spirit to control and to guide us";
b) others again encourage the patients/victims to fast as often and as much as they can—fasting helps in conducting the healing session properly, assisting the person to be under the full control and guidance of the Spirit;
c) "whenever I fast it makes it easier for me to receive the message from the messenger";
d) the patient/victim may fast as long as the prophet so wishes and some prophets recommend it;
e) even the prophet who associates only with the Holy Spirit and not with the ancestors, fasts, because "it makes the Spirit more approachable and guides me more easily". In this case the fasting of the patient is not considered to be essential.

Fasting is essential for a number of the prophets. However, it is less so among those in Greater Durban than among the prophets in the Rand/ Soweto area. Where prophets demand fasting it is incumbent on them to fast longer than the patients.

Symbols of protection (staves, cords, flags)

The staves referred to as 'weapons' (*izikali*) are associated with Moses, and most of the prophets maintained that their staves were like the "stick of Moses which he always carried"—it was his "weapon" and with it he led the people of Israel out of Egypt performing various miracles, including healing.

The respondents explained the function of the staves as follows:

a) they are used "to fight the devil";

b) they are substitutes for laying on of hands ie. instead of putting hands on patients, they "rather use the sticks";

c) "they give the prophet power; they are like the staff of Moses which performed miracles";

d) "God said we should carry the staves as his whole armour"; "they are powerful weapons through which we cast out evil spirits—even the Bible says we must carry them and use them";

e) "the messengers work through them on the patient";

f) the woman prophet who did not utilise specific colour vestments nor candles in healing, carries a staff with her as "the whole armour of God". Only one prophet from the *New Holiness Christian Church of God in Zion* does not use it—"to me it has no significance". In some of the AIC, only the elders are allowed to carry the staff.

For most Zionists, staves are indispensable in their healing procedures. They are also "dipped" into the sea in order to remove any evil attached to them and in order to "strengthen" them for their task. Usually those present at the sea put their staves in a bundle and dip them as a bundle into the waves. This is a symbolic act of expressing the unity of the owners of these staves after they have performed the rituals at the sea. Some plant their staves in the sea where the waves can sweep through them. This purifies the staves from all evil forces which they have to confront. Staves have a definite task in exorcism as the patient/victim is hit with them in order to remove evil forces.

The staves can be straight or crooked at the top (like a Biblical shepherd's staff), or round, or have a small wheel, star or rooster in metal attached to them. Some prophets also use metal staves. Some cut them from a specific type of tree. Some staves are merely sticks made from special wood. Most, however, have a cross on top, or the end is folded into the form of a circle which signifies its complete effectiveness when used in healing. Some maintain it symbolises fertility. The staff symbolises its bearer; receiving a staff is like being "dressed" ie. receiving a uniform. It has great personal significance—one receives the special status of being a Zionist. Both his staff and uniform are often buried with the person (cf. Oosthuizen, G.C., *Afro-Christian Religions, Iconography of Religions* XXIV, 12, Leiden, Brill, 1979).

Flags are widely used by prayer healers/prophets:
a) to prevent any unseen danger, any form of disaster or death;
b) to prevent lightning;
c) to protect the one owning it from unseen evil forces;
d) to "apologise to the ancestors when they are angry";
e) "the Bible speaks about flags, therefore we must use them".

Only about twenty percent of the prophets do not use flags. The others ascribe great importance to the presence of flags at services, baptisms at the sea, and for personal protection against danger and evil forces which keep diseases and illness away. Flags are often observed on houses in urban areas and on huts in many parts of Southern Africa, mainly to ward off lightning, and also at open air services to ward off the evil forces while the service is in progress.

These flags are usually made of white, blue, green or yellow cloth and are assembled on shorter or longer sticks or poles.

The Cords are usually wrapped around the waist, across the shoulders, round the neck, ankles or wrists as protection against the forces of evil. (There are some in the mainline churches who use these cords.) Some have them around their uniforms or wrapped around their head like a band. These ropes and cords have also to be purified from evil spirits, and one often sees them being put or thrown into the sea and then taken out as a purified symbol of protection.

White stones can also be found around the houses for protection. During Easter and Christmas, especially, these stones are whitewashed.

C) Powers of healing

Spirit versus spirits

Spirit possession implies here that 'the Spirit' or Holy Spirit gets hold of a person(s) during healing sessions. Such possession by an ancestor(s) was not emphasized by any of the prophets; they were, however, emphatic about the "possession by the Spirit" ie., as they reiterated, "if we have the Spirit among us, we do get the Holy Spirit". Being possessed by the Holy Spirit means that the Holy Spirit "works" among them. Reference is made to the "automatic" act of possession by the Holy

Spirit, just as "when God was ascending he told his apostles to go and stay in a room and wait for the Holy Spirit and the people got the Holy Spirit".

It is also maintained that 'the Spirit' wants to "reveal the problems and illnesses of the patients so that they should be healed". Such possession by 'the Spirit' helps them to feel the problem or illness of the patient concerned; it makes the 'prediction' and healing procedures more successful. Most of the prophets emphasized that such possession, where the patient and bystanders sometimes faint, is a sign of the presence of 'the Spirit', and that at that moment he operates intensely among them. Furthermore, they then "feel the problem of the patient concerned".

"Spirit possession" is not in the least related to "demon possession", but to the presence of the Holy Spirit during healing procedures.

The emphasis on 'the Spirit' at healing sessions is due to the very clear association in Scripture of the Holy Spirit with power. The 'messengers' (ancestors) also plays a role with most of the prophets, as indicated earlier. This is especially so in diagnosing illnesses and in healing sessions where diseases which fall within the context of the traditional African cosmology are concerned. Jesus the prophet, continuously associated with healing sessions in the Gospels, is hardly mentioned in any of the AIC healing sessions. Healing needs "power" and the Holy Spirit is of the three Persons in the Trinity, the symbol of power. Hammond-Tooke states: "the concept 'power' resonates strongly with traditional African conceptions. It is the (unanalyzed) essence inherent in all medicines and in the symbols of 'magical' ritual. It is also the characteristic, *par excellence*, of ancestors, witches and alien spirits. The external manifestations of this power, apart from its effects on people and things, are typically seen in ecstatic behaviour, the bursting of the bonds of personal constraints and of normal reality, often expressed in trance, *glossolalia*, visions and healing. Much of this is also part of traditional religion, and Sundkler (1961) has pointed out the marked parallelisms between the Moya-theology of the Zionist Churches and the Zulu diviner. They are indeed striking" (Hammond-Tooke, W.D., "The aetiology of Spirit in Southern Africa", *African Studies*, 1988).

He rightly emphasizes that while the position of blacks in South Africa is one of powerlessness—socially, economically, politically— "the perception of their position must be that of impotence" and adds: "It is surely here that one must look for the great emphasis on the work of the Holy Spirit: the concept provides a potent counterbalance to the realities of the existential situation. But, paradoxically, it does this in a microcosmic mode... it does not provide a recipe for transforming society as a whole" (*Ibid*).

The emphasis on 'the Spirit', with Jesus receding into the background at healing sessions, has to be seen in the context of the African traditional outlook regarding vital force, or *numinous* power, which is the quality *par excellence* in everything. The supernatural forces have most of it at their disposal and among human beings its degree of intensity and effectiveness depends on the position of the person in the hierarchy. It is present in all organic and inorganic entities. Thus, 'the Spirit' is the Spirit of power, and the ancestors, as traditionally 'holy' (ie. loaded with mystical power), are the sources of this mystical power. Sickness means to be weak, and healing to obtain strength, and the source of power is, in the context of the African cosmology, the Spirits (the ancestors). In the Bible it is yet another Spirit, referred to as the Holy Spirit. This accounts for the tremendous role that the Spirit and the messengers (ancestors) play in healing, and the reason why the name of Jesus is hardly ever mentioned. His presence is, however, never doubted.

Confronting 'the Spirit' or Holy Spirit are the demons or evil spirits. Demons are seen as coming from jealous people who use these bad spirits to attack a person or persons who they want to suffer. Because harmonious inter-relationships carry with them a high premium, they remain a sensitive target. One prophet maintained that the demons are "seven spirits which I am not sure where they come from"; another stated that they are "thrown" on people by the diviners. The remedies prescribed by the prophets of Greater Durban are set out as follows:

a) "I pray for people who are suffering from it and I use white wash to make *isiwasho* to use in vomiting, enemas and emetics";

b) "demons are bad spirits which are working against God—I make them weak by keeping the sick person for a week without taking food and then I bath him in the river while I am praying and hitting him";

c) "I pray for that person and take my cord and tie it to his body and pray and then I give him *isiwasho* to vomit, for steaming and for enemas";

d) "people are instructed how to let other people have demons but I give them *isiwasho* and *muti* and pray for them so that they can get relieved of the demons".

The Rand/Soweto prophets stated *inter alia* that:

a) one can get rid of demons by joining the Church where prophets pray for the victim when this person follows God;

b) "they are brought upon people by other people who are jealous and to get rid of them a person should go to Jesus";

c) "to get rid of them one should come to God in faith and do good works in repentance";

d) "they are from Satan, they are his workers. To get rid of them the person must believe in God and His Son, Jesus, because demons do not like God and His Son, Jesus";

e) the diviner's approach with regard to demons was also noted: namely that they can call up demons through certain medicines and instruct them to harm specific people of which their client is jealous. This is why the prophet of *The Apostolic Church of Christ in South Africa* states: "they are made by people; they do it through medicines—they can even make the Tikoloshe and other evil things";

f) "they are the workers of the devil and a person can get rid of them by praying to God, Jesus Christ and the Holy Spirit";

g) "they are from the devil but demons are also made by witch doctors or wizards. To get rid of them one should not run away from them but believe in God and work for God";

h) "one gets rid of them by running to the Church";

i) "to get rid of them one must repent in his spirit and dedicate himself to the hope that is in God";

j) "they are servants of Satan who is a bad angel. Believe in God and He will protect you from demon possession".

Demons can be got rid of my joining the Church, by believing in the Triune God, by performing certain ritual acts such as *isiwasho*, by vomiting (*palaza*), through steaming and emetics, through being put in running water, especially river and sea water, through hitting a person on the body, putting the 'holy sticks' against the body, dancing and singing around a person with demons in order to strengthen those who are engaged in the ritual of exorcism, through prayers, especially those of the prophet, or by working for God and repenting.

Many of the activities of the prophets have to do with the problem of demon possession.

God versus Satan

The prophets firmly accept the existence of Satan: "There is a devil. He is responsible for illness and disease because every bad thing which is happening is part and parcel of the activities of the devil". One respondent was not sure whether the devil could be responsible for sickness because God limited ("has taken off") his power "when he chased him away". He is now "an evil angel who was one of the sons of God but who is now a bad son".

Most of the prophets saw evil in the devil and its activities, it being responsible for illness and all "bad things". The devil does not like a good thing; therefore he causes diseases". The devil is described as "one of the angels who opposes God and wants to fight God... he is responsible for illness while God is responsible for healing". The devil has his abode in the human heart "because the heart believes in evil things".

The devil is thus considered to be:
a) an evil or bad spirit;
b) an evil or bad angel;
c) one of the angels who opposed God and wanted to fight God;
d) one of God's bad sons;
e) Satan who wants to rule the human heart;
f) the one who is responsible for illness, disease and misfortune.

The Rand/Soweto, Greater Durban prophets and the metaphysical forces

Traditional African life has no meaning without ancestral presence and unusual power. Although ancestors were not worshipped, they had an extremely central position in traditional African societies because of their judicial, sociological and metaphysical significance. They do not merely survive, but take an active part in the affairs of their progeny. Their position and influence depend on the social status and influence they had in the community. They watch over and protect the living. They are, in the traditional context, also the actual owners of the lands, kraals and animals—from them come all life and possessions. They live with their descendants in a symbiotic union. This inter-relationship and interaction involves reciprocal behaviour and a concern which is expressed in various ceremonies and ritual. They are either 'underneath' or 'above', watching over their progeny. All ancestors are active and are described as guardians over the living. In the indigenous churches they are often seen as coming on the clouds as did Moses and Elijah. Through them an intimate contact is maintained, by those on earth, with the metaphysical forces. They have mysterious, numinous power which sustains those on earth.

Sixty percent of the prophets in the Greater Durban area maintained that they do not work *under* the power of the ancestors, but rather that the ancestors are mediators. Those on the Rand/Soweto work either under the power of the ancestors and/or in conjunction with the Holy Spirit. Only a few maintained they work only under the ancestor(s). They are consulted and advice is sought from them in spite of the fact that they "are traditional spirits" ie. pre-Christian spirits. Some maintain the ancestors are closer to them than Jesus—they are present all the time. The status of Jesus is not always clear. This is also reflected in Brandel-Syrier's study on indigenous church women and their relationship to the ancestors (cf. Brandel-Syrier, M., *Black woman in search of God*, London, Lutterworth, 1962, p. 149).

Those prophets on the Rand, mainly from Soweto, who stated the ancestors work under the power of 'the Spirit', emphasized that they are the "messengers" of God and they are acceptable to them because they know them, but they are foreign for the whites. The ancestors are considered to be "messengers whom God sends with His message". One finds here contrasting views on the role of the ancestors in the churches, although for the largest majority, contact with ancestors is of vital importance. The prophet of the *Nazareth Church of God in Zion*, from Soweto, stated, "I work under the power of the Holy Spirit. Truly speaking, my ancestors cannot give me power, but only God can give me power through His Spirit". This is in direct contrast with the attitude of the prophet of the *Apostolic Church of Christ in South Africa*, who "works under the power of the ancestors and of the Holy Spirit because I am both a prophet and diviner". With most of the prophets, the ancestors have a special place in their lives and activities as they are messengers sent by God, "and of course we know them since they once lived with us on earth". There are those who work under the ancestors because they were called by them to be a prophet and, as messengers from God, "they reveal His message regarding the problems people have".

In many cases the symbiotic relationship between the prophets and the ancestors is still alive, and for them, extremely meaningful. In the traditional society, the diviners are expected to retain a high moral code on the injunctions of the ancestors; if not, they lose their powers of clairvoyance.

Working through the ancestors under the Holy Spirit

Zionists emphasize that the source of their healing power is centred in *umoya* (the Spirit). This refers to the Holy Spirit and is interpreted as an all pervading spiritual force which is basic to well-being and health. It counteracts and neutralises the destructive forces associated especially with sorcery. This mystical power "represents an array of capacities, skills and instruments without which the work of Zion could not be accomplished" (cf. Kiernan, J.P., Saltwater and ashes: Instruments of curing among some Zulu Zionists, *Journal of Religion in Africa*, Vol. IX, fasc 1, Leiden, Brill, 1978, p. 28). For most of the prophets the ancestors fall within the orbit of *umoya* especially when healing sessions take place.

With some prophets the ancestors are actively involved in what they do, which is reminiscent of the role they have in the activities of the diviner in the traditional society. The emphasis is on the conviction: "we know the ancestors and they know us well". The word 'ancestor' however, is not often used, but rather messenger—"the Holy Spirit called me but He sends my ancestors as messengers". Another emphasized that he "works under the Holy Spirit with ancestor intervention who are messengers of the Holy Spirit". The spirit of the grandmother especially, or grandfather, features in their reference to the messenger. Subjection to the wisdom of the aged who are deceased, as well as to their authority, often features with the prophets. The very fact that the ancestors allow them to work as prophets in the Church, is given as reason for following their instructions.

Apart from the Biblical approach of a few prophets who believe that the Holy Spirit and other spirits are irreconcilable as co-workers in this life, one prophet works only under the Holy Spirit because "the Spirit and the ancestor quarrel". One often observes how candles with various colours are used to represent the ancestral parties (such as the patient's/victim's ancestors) in healing. When they are "reconciled", the healing ceremony can proceed—this gives much more potency to the procedure.

The role of the ancestors is dominant in healing procedures when it comes to diagnosis, especially of diseases that fall within the context of the African cosmology where numinous power is the antidote against these diseases. The majority of the prophets have a mediatory role between the patient/victim and the Holy Spirit.

'The Spirit', with the emphasis on power, is easily understood in the traditional African context. When it comes to healing, Jesus is seen within the context of the western doctor. This was more or less the position given to Jesus by the missionaries in the established/historic churches. The missionaries have not made Him part of the African world view, but have westernised the African to fit a westernised healing Jesus into the African world view. Jesus had "not stepped into" the depth of the African cosmology; 'the Spirit', the source of mystical power, as is the case with the ancestors, fits into the African cosmology in which ancestors (African holy spirits) play a decisive role.

This does not imply that every prophet accepts the ancestors plus 'the Spirit', although most do. One prophet clearly stated: "I believe that the Spirit which the Apostles used is the same one I should also use, but not my ancestors, for even the Apostles did not use their ancestors in healing". The few who do not consult the ancestors emphasized their calling by the Holy Spirit, and that the Holy Spirit and the ancestors "quarrel" because they have completely different backgrounds. However, none refuted the existence of the ancestors. They were "realities" which the prophets ignored in their capacity as Christians. The largest majority had no problems in consulting the ancestors as important sources of information, especially in the diagnosis of illnesses and what should be prescribed.

Messages from the ancestors

About twenty eight percent of the prophets consulted stated unambiguously that they *only* get messages through the Holy Spirit. One respondent stated: "The messages come through the Spirit; sometimes it would sound as if an angel is talking right in my ears". Those who referred only to the Holy Spirit are emphatic that the messages they receive do only come from the Holy Spirit.

The rest of the respondents ascribed the message either only to the ancestors, or to the ancestors and the Holy Spirit. Some of those who get their messages from the ancestors either referred to a grandfather, or especially the grandmother, from whom these messages come. A number subscribed to a statement of one of the prophets that "they are the ones who bring messages because God chose them as His messengers", in spite of the fact that a number of them died as adherents of the traditional religions of their forefathers.

The central role that the ancestors still occupy as communication media with the supernatural world, cannot be denied. They had this role for century upon century and continue with the task as revered beings, even in the churches. They have a concern for their progeny which is highly appreciated. These bonds remain very strong with a large section in the African community.

Messages from the Holy Spirit

Messages are regularly received by the prophets. Perhaps a few should be related here, firstly from the Greater Durban area:

i) "I tried to give up prophesying but the Holy Spirit sent the lightning which hit the tree near my house and burnt it. The Holy Spirit told me to resume prophesying if I do not want to be burnt like my tree";

ii) "I do receive messages from the Holy Spirit, for example, if lightning is going to come and destroy the house of somebody I wake up and go to that person to inform him and then I make a flag which is erected on a pole on the thatches or zinc roof of the house in order to prevent it from destruction". (Lightning is a great danger in Natal. Every year lightning kills a number of people especially in their huts. In the rural areas of Natal flags are seen attached to the roofs of huts or to high poles in order to ward off lightning. Flags in the AIC context ward off evil forces, including lightning.)

iii) "I receive messages from the Holy Spirit that a specific person has to slaughter an animal for his/her ancestors; that a person should fast for many days in order to allow the Holy Spirit to be with her/him";

iv) "The Holy Spirit indicates what the person is suffering from and what *muti* and *isiwasho* should be used in order for this person to recover".

The prophets in the Rand/Soweto area receive messages from the Holy Spirit and these are related to general misfortunes, the problems people encounter and their ailments. Most of these messages are related to the illness of the patient who "is standing or sitting in front of me". Most messages have to do with food poisoning, evil acts of people (sorcery), bewitchment, information about bad luck which has befallen or will be experienced by certain individuals and how it may be used or have them healed.

D) THE HEALER'S INFLUENCE

Established churches and healing sessions

During the day, and in conversation, many members of the 'historic' churches will dissociate themselves from the indigenous churches, but they are there at the nocturnal healing sessions. They simply arrive for healing, whether they are Methodist, Anglican, Roman Catholic, Lutheran, NGK of Africa, Congregational, Presbyterian or Assemblies of God, and with AIC members attend healing sessions where they feel they could receive help. Members of the established churches are even present at the sea sessions of the AIC.

Often the churches know about the visits of their members to these healing services, but they are not in a position to forbid them even if they wanted to. Some prophets receive regular visits from elderly people who are members of the established churches. The latter are no longer "mainline". The Church with the largest African membership in South Africa is the Zion Christian Church, an independent church with more than two million African members.

The understanding and mutual sharing in the plight of the patients are main attractions. There is the emphatic, warm and genuine disposition of the prayer healer and prophet who does not have the official type of approach of the average minister in the church service when it comes to healing. Concern about the patient's well-being is attractive, as is the attention given to healing as a central issue which includes restoration of relationships with God and fellow human beings. Many are convinced of the power of 'the Spirit' in those Churches and want to be close to the prayer healer. For others, the ancestors have a place in the healing process, as was the case in the traditional society. When reconciliation is effected with them and with fellow beings, a deep sense of well-being and satisfaction takes hold of the patient or victim. Here, the various diseases which were disregarded by the missionaries receive close attention. Many of the miracles that are experienced here have to do with the relief patients find from the burden of the typical African diseases such as possession by various types of evil spirits, sorcery and witch-craft. There is a dignified self-assurance in the disposition of the prophets which leaves the impression on others that they do have special charismata which are not found in the historic churches.

Members from the established churches regularly join the AIC where the requirement is not stringent catechetical instruction, but faith in the efficacy of the leader and the church as a whole. An exception is the *Apostolic Church of Christ of South Africa* which does not receive visits from members of the established churches, nor is it joined by members of Zionist Churches, because of the emphasis on strict catechetical instruction and a stringent baptismal policy. However, other churches' members do come to their services for healing. The importance is not in becoming a member, but in sharing in their healing sessions.

This chapter has dealt with the various methods and procedures used by prophets with regard to healing and what it encompasses in this context. The activities in this regard form a major part of their agenda.

The attraction these activities hold for many black people in the townships and rural areas points to a specific need, a need which has not been satisfactorily attended to by established churches. This explains, in part, the rapid growth of the AIC on the continent of Africa, and in particular, in South Africa.

Treatment and remuneration

Most of the prophets require a fee for their services. The prophets stated *inter alia* that people pay for 'prediction' and healing; the fee for 'prediction' is usually much less than for healing. One stated that she charges R1 for prediction and R10 to R50 for healing; it depends on the sickness. All the metropolitan Durban prophets charge fees.

Not all the prophets on the Rand/Soweto charge. However, out of those questioned, only three did not charge, although one said "not yet". The fee fluctuates from R1 upwards—payment is according to the disease, and victims affected by African cultural diseases are often charged more than those who come for the usual ailments.

Because many of the diviners in the urban areas are considered to be charlatans (with little or no training) who are involved in healing activities for the quick money they can get from unfortunate people, the prophets, who charge less and who are considered to be more reliable, have become more popular during the last decade. In a time of stress and strain, the demand for diviners' activities increases and so, too, does the number of practitioners. This has been the case during the last few years in the African townships, when charlatans have cashed in upon the insecurity that reigns. The insecure situation accounts for abuse by some of the diviners, which has resulted in the office of prophet (or prayer healer) becoming more acceptable. The healing aspects of the warm fellowship experienced within the congregation also shed more positive light on the work of the prayer healer/prophet than was the case in preceding years.

CHAPTER FOUR

TRADITIONAL AFRICAN EXPLANATION AND TREATMENT OF DISEASES

Africa has an age-old history in which its own approaches based on its own genius are reflected. What Africa has acquired through the centuries cannot possibly be discarded in a few decades and the bulk of Christian membership in Africa is not older than a few decades. This is especially true of the AIC. The African world view is still strong with many, and even more so as a result of the discovery that basically what is termed "modern" and "western" is extremely superficial. The African cosmology is organic, not mechanical; personal not impersonal. It is thus important to take the metaphysical world with its beneficial and adverse forces seriously. The biblical approaches also have to be taken seriously. The diagnosis of the diseases and its healing in many AIC's is thus effected in the context of both the traditional and biblical world views. The agents of healing in that context, namely the prayer healers and prophets, do not always consciously differentiate between traditional beliefs and treatment, self prepared medicines and new innovations regarding symbols and methods. With most of the prophets, prayer does play an important part in the healing process even though it is often accompanied with much singing and dancing.

There are three types of diseases to which the prophet (prayer healer) gives attention. These are the usual physical ailments, psychosomatic diseases and the diseases which resort under the African cosmology, or the African diseases (*Ukufa KwaBantu*).

A) Physical ailments

Ordinary physical ailments range from headaches and common colds to more severe types of illnesses. These illnesses are due either to somatic or to ecological factors and are classified as natural diseases, for which the Zulu term is *umkhuhlane*. For these diseases, medicine—referred to as *muti* in the traditional societies—is used. The word *muti* refers to a tree, or a shrub, or a herb. There are medicines for healing and for harming, or even killing a person. The intention behind the use of these medicines is important. The potency of such medicine is either inherent or is derived from ritual language used when it is administered. The medicine used for ordinary ailments is not ritualized. With regard to the natural diseases, the symptoms lead to their identification; with regard to the others, the nature of their causation predominates in the diagnosis.

In contrast to the physical ailments are the psychosomatic diseases, which fall into a different category because of the psychical aspect involved. But even more intensely different are the so-called African diseases based on African concepts. These concepts have various names in the different African cultures, but most of the concepts are used in these cultures. The AIC's, especially those which are Zionist, have the reputation of being able to exorcise the forces of evil, which are an incessant brooding danger (especially in the urban areas). The effect is to counter attacks from sorcerers and those forces which weaken their *umoya*, their inner strength, leading to illness, physical and spiritual weakness, and malrelationships. The latter break up the strong sense of community which AIC's try to protect at all cost. They are concerned about the quality of life of their group. When a prophet falls ill, his moral life could come under suspicion and his prophet powers be questioned. Health is an important norm for spiritual well-being, although it is accepted that illness is not always due to an individual's own limitations.

Most of the prophets have not alienated themselves from these concepts, although they have adapted them within their Christian context. They do not alienate themselves from the approaches of their people, but attempt to take these approaches seriously and to be of help in times of need. They take all three types of illness seriously. The ingredients they use are either potent in themselves or they are symbolic and are accompanied by specific rites which the prophets have adapted. The main concern is to restore the balance, the equilibrium, of the forces that control life. The family takes care of the sick person.

Colour symbolism plays a vital role in traditional medicine and it also plays a role with the prayer healers and prophets. In the Zulu context black and red medicines remove the disturbing negative substance. (These medicines are cooked.) The white (cool) medicine "puts" the health back. The prophets use black medicines more often than red, while white medicines are often used. Symbolic medicines have been adapted by the prophets in a great variety of ways. These are used to re-establish relationships, to remove evil substances, to restore the disturbed balance between the person and the environment, and to strengthen a person against future attacks.

Women in the AIC context are more susceptible to African cultural disease than men; they have great difficulty with attacks by adverse forces and thus with "pollution". They predominate at healing sessions, whether these take place in homes, at dams, beside rivers, or on beaches. They are probably more vulnerable to the attacks because they act as bridges between the metaphysical forces and those around them.

There are more prophets who use traditional and non-traditional ingredients in their healing procedures than there are those who use only *isiwasho* (holy wash). Water is nevertheless powerful and takes a pre-eminent position as a repellent. However, for most prophets, it has not replaced *umuthi* (traditional medicine), which is not merely traditionally utilized roots, herbs, etc. but a combination of these and other western ingredients.

In order to grasp the role of the prophet with regard to physical ailments, reference should be made to the ingredients they use. A prophet from the *Foundation Divine Christian Catholic Church* stated: "I use bicarbonate of soda, boil it with water and pour a little salt on it and I add a little alum and sheep dip, and then I pray for it. The patient uses it for steaming his body". Another prophet who also mixes non-traditional ingredients with traditional medicines said: "I mix them together with my *muti* (medicine) or *isiwasho* if the Holy Spirit informs me to do it like that".

Healing sessions within the context of the group or congregation are more effective because of the accompanying communal prayers, rhythmic movements and singing. The communal base is important.

Many of the prophets on the Rand and in Soweto combine western ingredients with traditional medicine, holy water and prayer. For a few, "the Spirit" has to indicate how the components should be combined. Other prophets do not mix western ingredients with traditional *muti* (medicine). They use only western ingredients such as vinegar, epsom salts and red pepper and mix them with water and ashes. One emphasized that "if ever a patient is going to use western medicines, I pray for the medicine to be effective". Another prophet takes a stand against any mixing with western medicines because "African herbs won't be mixed". Western medicines are "only used for colds and flu ... but not for serious sickness" according to another prophet.

There are those who consider the combination of western and traditional ingredients as specially effective, not because of any inherent strength in western medicine but because of the combination of what are considered to be powerful substances. This is sometimes added to the often used *isiwasho* ie. water and ash that has been prayed over: "I sometimes buy medicines from chemists, but the strong mixture would be from my medicine rather than from the western medicine".

It is interesting to see how ordinary ingredients are considered to be medicines: " I use blue stone, boiled vinegar and brown sugar. I may mix or combine the aforesaid medicines with what I might buy from the chemist". However, these ingredients have more of a symbolic value than anything else, reconciling the helpful metaphysical forces, or warding off the evil forces. When cents—it has to be cents—are thrown into the sea-water this symbolizes "luck" implying, according to Archbishop T. Shange of the *Free Holy Apostolic Church*, that the activities at the beach will be successful.

The more general diseases are thus treated with various types of ordinary ingredients which could be obtained in the shops or from pharmacists, and these are mixed with ordinary traditional medicines. However, the mixtures become more complex when the disease is considered to be of a specially hideous nature.

The staff, which conveys mystical powers and which wards off malevolent forces, is often used during healing sessions, as are emblems and uniforms with specific colours such as green, white and blue. These colours symbolize faithfulness, purity and love. The yellow and red colours signify the presence of ancestors who passed away as Christians and the red the non-christian ancestors, as well as the diviner practices in the healing procedures.

B) Psychosomatic diseases

Uhlanya

Traditional concept : Insanity
Psychiatric diagnosis : Schizophrenia*

Disturbance is ascribed to the disharmony that exists with the supernatural forces. The result is that evil spirits could take possession of a person. Among the prophets various approaches to the diagnosis of the causes and to the healing procedures concerning disturbances are discernible.

An influential leader-cum-prophet describes the cause of insanity as follows: "People take something from the skull of a person, mix it with all kinds of herbs (*maphipa, nogane, dagwa*) to get the person's brains

---

* For psychiatric diagnosis see Wessels, W.H., *Zulu folk healers and psychiatry*. Final Report supported by Nermic, 1990, 156pp.

off; they go through the person's nose and take his brains off; they take bones, pulverize and mix them and give the mixture to a person by putting it in his food, or in what he drinks such as tea and so on. There are many types of mixtures which can be used. For example, they get elephant or lion bones, pulverize them and give them to a person stealthily, and such a person should first be taken to a European doctor for an injection, given pills to sleep, and then be taken to an *inyanga* (herbalist). *The inyanga* gives the medicine which makes a person insane, but can also give the medicine to cure such a person. Powder is given as snuff to an affected person. He starts to sneeze. Water comes from his head—a lot of water. They take *ngwavuma* (herbs) and grind them and pour boiled water on them. The person drinks the mixture and he vomits. In this way the water on the brains is drained, and then the brains come back. The patient jumps up and down, wants to break everything, runs around, and after this calms down. This is a sign that the person is healed".

It is clear that the diagnosis of the victim's problem does not fall within the context of science, but rather within the context of mythology and magic. This is evident in many, though not all, of the expositions of the prophets who put mental (psychical) diseases within the primal or traditional framework, with its mythological interpretation of the causes of such diseases. Affliction by evil spirits is put forward as a major cause of insanity. The *inyanga* (herbalist) medicines bring "the *ufufunyane* to a person; this then moves through to the head and distorts brain functioning"; the evil spirits are "thrown" through perpetrating witchcraft on a person who is hated or through poisoning a person. Such a person becomes mentally disturbed if he walks over ground which the diviner has "treated" (*umeqo*), or when he eats food to which has been added "brain damaging herbs" mixed with animal oils and blood.

Only twenty percent of the prophets ascribed *uhlanya* to non-mythological factors, such as excessive use of *dagga*, and "straining of the brain".

During the summer, the victim is considered to be more insane because it is the time when the herbs that were used to bewitch are in bud. Jealousies, worries, alcohol and ancestors can cause a person to become insane. People could be jealous of the property of someone, which leads to tense relationships and sorcery practices, or a person becomes mentally disturbed when traditional practices are not observed. The ancestors become angry and punish the person with insanity by "disturbing his brains". A person's name could be called in conjunction with a specific medicine (*khafula*) which is mixed with animal fats and various types of herbs, so that "in summer" such a person becomes "very mad". A person could be poisoned with the soil taken from graves which is mixed with parts of a monkey, and also with *umthetha ngedwa* (speak-alone medicine) "which causes mad people to speak alone". Through visions the causes are detected.

Who should treat it?

Questions were put to the prophets about who should most appropriately treat insanity. Traditional doctors, western trained doctors, prayer healers and prophets were mentioned as possibilities.

Aside from themselves and the prayer healers, the prophets referred mainly to the herbalist, to treat the *uhlanya* patient/victim. Only one stated that a diviner should treat the patient/victim. This was because the diviner has ancestral contact and "knows different kinds of *muti* which are used to get rid of the bad actions of ancestors". The herbalists receive preference because they have expert knowledge of herbs and roots, while the diviner has to learn from them about the use of such medicines. A few of the prophets said they would refer a patient/victim to a western doctor first.

The prayer healer/prophet is the preferred treater because he/she predicts (or, in other words, diagnoses the diseases and "predicts the method to be used for healing". It is not merely diagnosis that is of issue, but also treatment, and the latter is achieved through communication with 'the Spirit' (a term used much more than Holy Spirit) and/or ancestors. The prophet/prayer healer has "holy power" and therefore God hears him/her. Because of this "holy power" he/she is able to communicate with God, who gives the prophet the method of curing the patient. The prophet is significant as healer because, through visions, the disease can be "seen". Furthermore, "prophets pray over the water, the pills, the injections and medicines which a person is going to take. The healers have the same power as Moses, when he changed the rod into a snake".

It is thought that diseases caused by forces operating in terms of the African world view should be treated within the context. All the prophets maintained that traditional healing methods, as distinct from western methods, are effective in treating mentally disturbed people. Water forms a significant part of the medicines prescribed, and although it is 'prayed over', such water is in itself often not "strong" enough to counteract the evil forces. Therefore ash, or salt (if the water is not sea water), or other ingredients are added, or dancing takes place round the water to make it strong. Water that has been static has lost some of its strength. Water mixed with ash (*isiwasho*) which has been prayed over is most commonly administered. When this water is used, cords are bound around the head and body of the patient/victim. Victims are thought to have been subjected to the forces of evil. This is why water, directly from heaven, or gathered during a thunderstorm, particularly when lightning occurred, is considered by some to be especially powerful. In the greater Durban area, *izinyamazane* (burned parts of wild animals, mainly antelope) are inhaled through the nose; *uvamqo*, which is used to provoke vomiting to cleanse the person internally is given and herbs (*acatshwa*) are put on the victim's head.

Nevertheless, prayers play an important role. These are said so that 'the Spirit' or 'messenger' (ancestor) reveals the causes of a sickness, and how to heal it. Prophets put cords around the heads of the patient/victim; the patient/victim is made to vomit, steamed, and given emetics; western and indigenous medicines are mixed; and incense (*impepho*) is burned to ensure the presence of the ancestors. One prophet even gets women and men to wear specially made headgear. Others tie cords, not only around the head and the waist of the patient/victim, but also around the ankles. Traditional medicines used by herbalists (but not those used by diviners) are given; immersion in the sea or in the rivers takes place; red pepper features in the medication of some prophets; and fasting and constant prayer is prescribed for both the prophet and the patient. Only a few of the prophets rely only on the Holy Spirit. If the treatment is not successful, the patient is sent to a hospital.

The *ritual procedures* for the treatment of insanity vary from one prophet to another. One senior prophet-cum-church leader gave an exposition of his own procedure: "You first speak to the ancestors of the person, and to your own ancestors. You are now given the 'way' to treat the person. If this person has bad forefathers, the prophet helps the person to get rid of them. A black fowl is slaughtered, prayers are said, and you talk to the fowl, saying 'This is a bad forefather (ancestor) to the person who is sick'. Then you kill and bury the fowl. The ancestor has now been changed ("made") into a good forefather. After this you slaughter a white fowl, and call the forefather back because he is now a good ancestor. This white fowl is taken to where the black fowl is buried. You talk to that black fowl which represents the bad ancestor, and tell him that he should now remain a good forefather to the person. Most often, the ancestor called is a male, but the ancestor could also be a female. The patient/victim now recovers because his/her ancestor is well disposed". The black fowl represents the forces of evil and destruction, and the white fowl represents restoration and purification. Sickness is seen as a conflictual relationship which has to be solved before a healing process can be effected. The prophet showed the author a girl of about 18 years old who had spent two weeks in hospital. She could not get rid of *ufufunyane* (evil spirits). He applied to her the above-mentioned procedure and, according to her own testimony, she recovered.

This same prophet emphasized that only the *umthandazi* ("prayer person") and the prophet could help in curing *uhlanya*, but the traditional procedures have to be followed. He explained another ritual procedure as follows: "First of all, slaughter a fowl which has been bought by the guardian of the mentally disturbed person. Take blood from the fowl and mix it with water which has been prayed over; talk to God to make the water holy; and then give it to the insane person. Then, take dry grass (*isiqunga*) from a place where people usually walk, especially from a place where paths meet. Then pray again, and after this, wash that person with the mentioned mixture. After this, dig a hole, and bury that grass. When all this is done and the person is on the road to recovery, his/her relatives have to buy a white goat. Then, pray again to the ancestors of the insane person and to your ancestors. Then the person recovers".

The herbalist, who uses traditional medicines, also advises the patient, when he recovers, to have a goat slaughtered. This is a sign of the completion of the work which is called in Zulu *ukuphotula*. The word conveys that the curative treatment has been finalized.

In the first case, described above, colour symbolism is significant, as is the restoration of relationships. Reconciliation leads to healing. In the second case, the water and blood mixed with the grass over which many people have walked, restore mental health. The strength of the medicine overcomes the disease which caused the victim to go astray, and lose his bearings. The victim finds the correct path again.

There is thus a variety of approaches to insanity among the prophets. Some of these are prayer in combination with certain ritual acts, such as administration of *isiwasho* (cleanser), fasting, burning of *impepho*, prayer over western medicines and tablets, and utilization of *isiwasho* for vomiting, steaming and purging. Some of the prophets rely heavily on traditional medicines and "contextualised" traditional rituals, as is evident in the use of fowls in the above-mentioned reconciliation ceremony. A black sheep may also be used in the traditional context. One prophet stated that he gave medicine to inhale, and that he used something else called *uDupha* for administering an enema (*Uchatha*).

Insanity is not merely a mental disease, but it is caused by disturbances in relationships with the ancestors or by disturbances in various social relationships. The treatments thus concentrate mainly on reconciliation, and on restoration of right relationships.

Isidalwa

Traditional concept: Retarded and/or deformed
Psychiatric diagnosis: Mental retardation and/or insanity

This condition, which is explained as being deformed rather than as being retarded, is ascribed to many causes. The following are typical explanations:

a) The condition is due to an act of God. One person said "it is not the sin of the father or the mother. You cannot blame anyone born with it. God made it. Only God creates cripples".

b) The condition is due to the actions of the *inyanga* (herbalist). The herbalists mix herbs (*ubulelo*) which they grind, and they see to it that a person gets it into his/her stomach and that he/she becomes crippled. According to one prophet, a "fish's bones could be mixed with other medicines, because the fish's eye gives a squint impression" or, the *inyanga* gets a crab "because it goes to the one side" and he grinds it and mixes it with medicine. This will make a person crippled.

c) The condition is due to an incident which occurred during the pregnancy of the victim's mother. The victim's mother may have walked over medicated ground (*umeqo*), or she may have walked over a snake or eaten bewitched food. Any of these incidents will cause the baby to be born a cripple. The condition is due to the failure of family members to obey ancestral rules;

e) This condition is due to laughing at handicapped people. This could result in the children of such a person being affected.

f) This condition is due to not following parents' instructions.

g) This condition is due to jealousy of others.

h) This condition is due to "the witch sending a familiar such as an animal, which hits a person hard and gives him a stroke";

i) This condition is due to a person not receiving all the required immunizations as a child.

Most of the prophets explained the condition within the context of the traditional African world view.

Who should treat it?

Thirty percent of those who were asked about treatment stated that western trained doctors should treat the condition. Forty percent said the herbalist should treat it. Twenty percent were in favour of treatment by the prayer healer/prophet, and ten percent felt the prayer healer/prophet together with the western doctor should treat it. The *inyanga* (herbalist) has the herbs and acquires the fish, crab, or other ingredients for the medicine. Those who were in favour of the western trained doctors maintained that these had the scientific 'know how' and various kinds of machines to treat the problem, and could prescribe various kinds of exercises.

Some respondents maintained that the prophets and prayer healers were God's messengers. One respondent said: "All their pleas are usually heard. The Bible says when you believe in God's helping power, you will be helped through prayer". Another maintained: "God has given the prophet powers to see what takes place in the lives of the people and in their futures. So, the prophet has this mighty power, which assists him/her in the healing task. He/she prays for a person until that person recovers".

How should it be treated?

The following procedures were proposed by the various prophets who were asked about treatment of the condition.
a) Physical exercises: It was said that: "all the veins must work".
b) The use of ingredients to counteract those which were utilized to bring about the physical deformity. Such ingredients are a fish's eye or a crab. These are used in conjunction with medicine (*muti*), vomit (*palaza*), and enemas.
c) The treatment of pregnant women with physical difficulties has to be taken to the herbalist "who will make her lick burnt herbs and drink boiled water with herbs. The intention is to clean her through getting her to vomit out the bad seed".
d) Some prophets pray for the person "all the time" until he/she is recovered. They give 'holy' water to cleanse the person inwardly and outwardly. They also give the person cords with different colours which have to be worn on the affected part of the body.
e) One prophet gives such patients a mixture called "Zulu mixture" which the person has to take every day. Holy water (*isiwasho*), which

is a mixture of sea water and ash to which white wash is added, is also given. Holy water is also used for vomiting, for steaming and for purging (*chatha*).

f) The use of prophets together with western doctors. One prophetess who proposed prophets/prayer healers maintained that "a cripple seldom recovers ... it is the work of God ... whether he has punished the cripple's parents for their evil deeds, God only knows, but nobody can cure that". She did not place the problem within the context of the traditional causes others put forward for its existence, although she made special mention of the cripple's ancestors. She gives the patient holy water which helps his "trusted messengers to heal him".

g) Western medicine. The western trained doctor was proposed by one respondent because he "bends and pulls bones and flesh into place". Western doctors give physical assistance such as special shoes, hearing aids, etc. In this case, such deformity was taken completely out of the mythological sphere, and the condition was thus perceived to be treatable at the physical level.

Isithuthwane

Traditional concept: Seizures
Psychiatric diagnosis: Epilepsy

According to some of the prophets, there are two distinct causes of this complaint:

a) Some people are born with it because the mother had "sickness of the blood". If the condition is caused in this way, it is the most difficult to cure.

b) In the case of other people it could be "brought on by means of witchcraft". A child, for example, will then "be full of worms".

The prophets stated that they see the cause of the condition in a vision when the person faints, and foam comes through the mouth and the body vibrates. The person's body becomes swollen and shakes, and the victim chews his tongue until he faints and goes limp. Only when this happens could it be said that a person is a victim. He/she falls on the ground "when it is very hot". Such a person shakes violently. Ninety percent of the prophets maintained that victims fall down. Forty percent maintained the victim's body shakes, and thirty percent said that foam comes from the mouth when an attack is experienced.

The causes of the disease

According to fifty percent of the respondents, the victims are born with the disease. Thirty percent of the respondents said it was due to an accident to the spine or the brain. Fifty percent put it in the African traditional context, saying that the problem is experienced as a result of the victim stepping over traditional *muti* (medicine).

The disease could be "thrown" on a person through the intervention of a diviner or herbalist. However, some people have it from birth (it is a "born-with" disease). Otherwise, it could be self-inflicted through "too much liquor" or due to the wrath of the ancestors, or to the jealousy of other people (often relatives). The latter may wish the person to become insane through the use of Zulu medicines. Sorcery plays its role since the disease is caused by stepping over *muti* (medicine) which has been poured on the ground where a person may walk. One respondent maintained that the *muti* is made "by mixing the bone of the snake with the flash of lighting of a snake" and that this *muti* "goes up to a person's brain and affects it". Those born with the disease received it when the mother stepped over *muti* which was specially deposited there for her. When the victim steps on or over the medicines of the herbalists and diviners, the poison runs through the veins to the brain. One informant said "it goes up your nerves until it reaches your brain". The heart will also be affected. An affected person will start falling down and will start shivering.

The snake features prominently as a cause—perhaps by analogy with the way epileptics fall down and writhe on the ground. Those who subjectify the world do not assume scientific interpretations and scientific solutions, but attempt to balance out mysterious forces. The diagnosis thus falls within the context of myth, which has nothing to do with scientific assessments of situations.

Treatment

Of the respondents who were questioned about treatment, forty percent thought the herbalist was the best person to treat the epileptic; thirty percent thought the prophet was best; ten percent felt that a combination of the diviner, the western doctor and the prophet/prayer healer would be best; and ten percent favoured the western trained doctor together with the prophet/prayer healer. The western trained doctor has a minor status as a healer in this context.

The consensus among the prophets was that the herbalists were very good at mixing *muti*. The herbalists know the different kinds of *muti* because herbal medicines used in sorcery are bought from them. Some maintained that the herbalists were the best at treating the disease because they were most effective in "creating" it. They were thus thought to be best able to restore the health of the victim.

The herbalist puts medicine on the forehead of the patient/victim and smears all the joints with fat; he also gives the patient/victim *muti* to inhale. As is the case with most of the prophets, the herbalist treats by *ukupalaza* (vomiting), *ukuqguma* (steaming) and *ukuchatha* (enemas). Some informants said that patients were given mixtures cooked in water, and that they had to avoid beer and smoking.

The *isangoma* (diviner) prescribes "medicine" mixed with ingredients from antelope (*izinyamazane*). The medicine is burned, and the patient inhales the smoke. The standard medicines used against enemies are also prescribed.

The prayer healers/prophets are high on the list of those able to heal the epileptics, because of the power of prayer and because of the powers given them by God. They do not act independently. "The Spirit" and/or ancestors tell them what they should do. The prayer healers/prophets are considered to be a link between God and the people on earth. One respondent stated that not anyone who could pray could assist a person. Only those appointed by God in "a very secret and special way" could do so. They are persons "who are able to pray for the water which they give to you so that you can be healed". A traditional mixture of herbs, called "Zulu mixture" also features on the *muti* list of some prophets. They also prepare *isiwasho* ("holy" water) consisting of fresh, salted or sea water, mixed in some cases with ash, and in others with white wash or with lime. That is used to provoke vomiting. It is also used for steaming and purging. Here, white is the symbol of purity. The *umthandazi* or prophet always uses *isiwasho*, which the patient/victim has to drink, in prescribed dosages. The prophets also make cords which the patient wears around the waist, wrists, ankles, neck, shoulders and head. Some make up strings with various colours such as green, white, blue, yellow and red.

A church leader who is also a prophet, prescribed the following treatment for epileptics: "The horns of a goat[1] which was slaughtered

---

[1] Such horns of goats, antelope and cattle are usually kept on the roof just above the entrance to the house. If there are a few entrances, the horns usually are kept above the one on the side where the gate to the yard is. The horns guard against evil forces. Horns are also found on the houses of some of the indigenous church leaders.

some time ago are burned, and then the person is made to vomit and his/ her whole body is washed. By burning the horns we try to protect the person from falling on the fire. The rope around the body is taken and dipped into the ashes of the burned horns. I pray to the patient's ancestors to prevent the patient from falling into the fire, and to help him/her recover completely. I put one rope around the patient's waist and one around his/her neck. Then the patient will recover".

Another prophet/leader refers to epilepsy as "a difficult disease". He said he can treat it, but "one has to work very hard. One has to pray. One cannot just do it with one's brains". He then added "One must hang a key around the neck to put the neck in place as the key ensures that the door fulfils its purpose, to keep firmly in place in the face of onslaughts, so the key round the neck keeps it in place so that it does not 'jump around'."

Much of the diagnosis of the causes of the disease falls within the context of traditional mythology, and some of the healing procedures have magical connotations.

The diseases or disabilities discussed thus far can be described as psychosomatic. They are not diseases which are peculiar to the African cosmology, but it is clear that they are brought, even by the prophets, within this context, and that the majority of them are treated with a combination of Christian and traditional methods. One finds a constant reference to traditional African healers, or to methods utilized by diviners and herbalists. The following section will deal with diseases which are specific to the traditional African world view.

C) AFRICAN CULTURAL DISEASES (*Ukufa KwaBantu*)

Reference has been made to the African cosmology in which a variety of metaphysical forces is positively active in the lives of people. Examples are the effective or protective ancestors or the negative forces which are utilized to do harm to, or destroy, other human beings. It is in this context that the "African diseases" (*Ukufa KwaBantu*) which have no western counterpart come to the fore. These are related to:
1. Spirit possession (*ufufunyane, izizwe, indiki*)
2. Sorcery (*umhayizo, uvalo, igondo*)
3. Poisoning (*idliso*)
4. Pollution (*umnyama*)
5. Environmental hazards (*umeqo, ibulawo*)
6. Ancestral displeasure (*abaphansi basifulatele*)

7. Disregard of cultural norms (*ukudlula*)[2]

As has already been indicated, colour symbolism plays a role in traditional healing methods. Black, red, white, green and blue are the major colours. Ngubane, referring to the division of culture and nature, indicates that the red and black cooked medicine, which takes out the evil, embodies the moral element; namely, that the victim/patient has lost his mystical "balance" by his own deeds or by being the target of sorcery. The mystical sickness is derived from culture (cf. Ngubane, p. 121). Only by first removing this mystical evil could healing be effected through the following process. This is the taking in of white medicine which is not cooked, ie. it is taken raw *iluhlaza*. The latter word is also used for the colours green and blue which signify 'goodness'.

The traditional background plays its role with the prophets, who often use 'cool' medicines such as water mixed with ash. Ash represents what was 'hot' but is now cool. Many prophets have special coloured uniforms which they wear when they have healing sessions . These uniforms are usually green, blue, or white, or they combine all these colours. Gall, which is green/blue, plays a significant role in traditional healing procedures. It plays a similar role in the healing procedures of some prophets. At the Durban beach, a youngish AIC prophetess was "blessed" with gall from head to toe.

The gall was from the sacrificial animal slaughtered for her induction as a diviner. In the traditional context "gall sprinkled on a nubile girl is believed to associate her very closely with the spirits" (Ngubane, p. 123). Ancestors enjoy the taste of gall and come and lick it. Parts of an animal, such as the so-called third stomach and the chyme, also attract the ancestors.

Because the traditional treatment of disease has an influence on many of the AIC healers, further aspects of this treatment should be briefly mentioned. Ngubane discerns in disease treatment an "element of morality, element of national processes, an element of mystical processes" (Ngubane, p. 131). The element of morality relates to social situations in which sorcery plays a predominant role; the element of natural processes is associated with somatic symptoms; and the element of mystical processes is associated with pollution. Referring to the traditional context in which she did her research Ngubane states that "illness arising from lack of balance related to a morality principle may show

---

[2] cf. Wessels,W.H., *Traditional and prayer healers*, unpublished paper delivered at Nermic Symposium, 1986.

themselves either by misfortunes only, with no somatic symptoms. In the case of the former only the mystical treatment is performed, to correct the lost balance (or to get away from the situation of darkness); but in the case of the latter there will be two levels of treatment—the mystical to treat the whole person and the empirical to cure the somatic symptoms" (Ngubane p. 132).

In the traditional context, the diviners are usually females. This is because women are the channels through which the ancestors of a descent group work. However, women are not channels for the ancestors of their husbands descent groups. The ancestors with whom women communicate could be male and female. Women have a special close contact with the ancestral world in spite of the fact that they are marginal. Because of the close contact, they form "a bridge between the two worlds" (Ngubane, p. 142). This explains also why women play such a great role in the established churches as well as in the AIC. Just as the diviner hears voices and receives special clairvoyant powers, so do the prayer healers (who are mostly women) and the prophets hear voices and have visions (*imibono*). Often the prayer healers and prophets are taken into the sea, and dipped into the water. The leader shouts into their ears "in order to open them up" so that they can hear more clearly the voices of 'the Spirit' and/or the ancestor spirits.

1. Spirit possession

Ufufunyane

Traditional concept: Possession by numerous alien spirits
Psychiatric diagnosis: Brief reactive psychosis (hysterical psychosis)

The possessing spirits are presumed to be foreign. They entered South Africa from Mozambique via the migrant miners, and have a great influence, especially on women. One respondent stated "It is like insanity". The patient usually continuously utters "ie .... ie .... ie ....ie." These noises are supposedly voices that come from within the patient/ victim. The spirits can speak in various languages. When the patient/ victim comes to hospital he/she is inclined to "run away". Another prophet gets a "hysterical feeling" when a person with this "disease" comes to her for help. She knows that the person has this illness because he/she cries, screams, runs away, throws his/her hands in the air, and lies down shivering and screaming. These are all signs of being possessed by foreign spirits. Some victims become unconscious, others aggressive. Most of the victims are girls. One stated "There is much of it among Mpondos" ie. members of a tribe which comes from the Transkei. Others state that they don't want to be touched on their shoulders. If touched, they scream. They start sobbing for nothing, and this continues for a long time. This is often witnessed at Durban's North Beach, where AIC often congregate early on Sunday mornings for 'baptism'. The spirits are considered to be responsible for victims' actions. The spirits take control of the victim who becomes very strong. When the victim is completely exhausted, the voices start to speak, informing the victim why they came, who sent them and what they want. According to a well-known healer, the cause of the disease is "mixtures" used by herbalists and diviners which "get the brains off". The healer said "like a drunk person, the victims' brains do not work". If pills are given by the doctor, "then the brains come back". "After the pills have been taken, I give the person water over which I have prayed. The prayer healer or prophet can kill the disease". The disease is also thought to be caused by a person spitting out *Khafula* medicine, and then calling out the name of the girl he wants to become possessed. The intention is that she becomes disturbed, or that she goes to the person who loves her, and who initiated the disturbance. Disturbed relationships and emotions like jealousy—for instance, when a young man wants to impose himself on a girl, or when a young man is jilted by a girl—are factors which contribute to a possessed condition, which is an affront to the ancestor(s) of the victim. All the respondents referred to the crying, screaming and running around of the victims when they are under the spell of these spirits, and in about two-thirds of the cases the respondents had witnessed, these reactions had been manifested. These foreign spirits can enter anyone, although it is mostly females who are affected. The condition could be ascribed to a strong feeling of insecurity arising not only from disturbed interpersonal relationships but also from social insecurities.

Sand is taken from the graveyard and, together with the herbal mixture, is thrown on the path on which the girl walks. One respondent stated that "when a man wants a woman he bewitches her, uses Zulu medicine and only touches the girl with his hands or a stick. Even a guitar, or any music can transfer it to a person". When a man is jilted "he uses a certain *muti*. He calls the girl's name while vomiting. Otherwise, he just touches the girl's shoulder with the *muti*, taking her unawares". Another alternative is that the person mixes animal fats and herbs. "He either puts this mixture in her food or he calls her name through the wind.

After this the possession begins". As medicine for this, the *inyanga* (herbalist) gives *izinyamazane* mixed with water. According to one respondent this treatment has also been taken over by the diviners. The causes of the disease are determined by prediction, ie. through visions. The respondents who were questioned referred to a variety of treatments. A prayer healer or prophet gives the possessed person water which she has blessed. This expels the *ufufunyane* as "they cannot stand things that are blessed". Another prophet mixes holy water with ash or salt, or sea water and *impepho*. This mixture is used to provoke vomiting and for purging and steaming. These processes cleanse the person from mystical defilement. Herbs, which cause the person to sneeze, are prescribed for smoking and inhaling. Prophets also lay hands on the victim and pray for him/her. This procedure is often witnessed at the beach. After the prayer, the victim turns around with speed. This symbolizes that "the Spirit", the Holy Spirit, has entered the person again.

The prophet is considered to be the best healer because he/she can "see" the disease, and "through praying" he/she gets *ufufunyane* to say "how it came into the victim and how it will get out". The victim is also given *izinyamazane*, which, after being burned, is inhaled and used to steam the body. Then "the *ufufunyane* speaks", telling the victim why it came and what it wants from him/her.

The *ufufunyane*, which usually affects females, has a tremendous impact on its victims. The power of the impact is reflected in the fact that in some areas, girls' schools had to be closed for some time. In the traditional context, "black and white medication" is used because the *ufufunyane* is "thoroughly bad", while *indiki*, which is merely "not so good", is treated with red and white medicines" (cf. Ngubane, p. 148).

Izizwe

Traditional concept: Alien spirit possession
Psychiatric diagnosis: Brief reactive psychosis (hysterical psychosis)

The evil spirits which cause *izizwe* are also considered to be foreign influences. A person who has this difficulty has the habit of belching (*bhodla*); the victim screams (especially when his/her shoulders are touched), and runs to places where he/she has never been before. Such a person avoids human contact, stays away from home, and often wanders in the bushes or mountains. *Izizwe* has the same symptoms as *ufufunyane*. When touched on the shoulder the victim screams and after yawning makes "disturbing noises". Through sorcery the victim of *izizwe* has acquired a bad spirit which negatively disturbs his/her brain. A person with this problem always feels guilty, and cries loudly, and runs to the place where the *izizwe* come from. Such a person also talks to him/herself as if insane.

What causes the affliction?

The affliction is caused by *muti* which is mixed so as to attract bad spirits (*imimoya emibi*). Once a person's name is called over the *muti* and he/she steps over it, he/she gets the sickness. In order to cause the affliction, soil from graves and ant heaps is added. The soil is chosen from the heaps of black ants called *iziBonkole*. A handful of grass collected from near the path that leads to the target's (ie. the girl's) place is added. All this is mixed, the girl's name is called over it, and the "medicine" is buried in the foot-path for seven days. The affliction is also referred to as a "man-made disease brought about by witchcraft". "Witchcraft" is here, as is so often the case, a misnomer, and should read "sorcery". After seven days, some of the mixture is added to the victim's food. The victim eats it unawares.

According to another respondent, when a girl does not react to a man's advances, he goes to a diviner. He brews the recommended medicine and "the girl will see the picture of the boy through drinking a glass of water. This could take place even at midnight, if the young man started to brew the medicine at that time. She will then desperately want to go to him, even at midnight, and she will hit everyone she meets on the way".

Who should treat it?

Seventy percent of the prophets interviewed maintained that *izizwe* should be treated by prayer healers or prophets. Only ten percent referred to the diviner, and ten percent to the herbalist. The remaining ten percent thought treatment should be affected by the herbalist, the prayer healer or prophet, and the western doctor.

Those who referred to the diviners maintained that the latter have especially strong herbs to neutralise those which have been used on the victim. *Izinyamazane* for inhalation and smoking is particularly important, but the diviners also give the victim *muti* mixed with *izinyamazane* to provoke vomiting. Those who gave preference to the herbalist as a healer maintained that herbalists provide the *muti*, and because of this, they could also neutralise it. The victim stays with the herbalists during periods of recovery. One prophet added: "The victim drinks medicated water, thus cleansing her body of the bacteria which have magically filled it. The herbalist is preferred as a healer to the professional diviner, because the latter can only cure the sickness by making the patient into another diviner".

Those who favoured treatment by the prayer healers and prophets considered them to be more effective in helping the victim because "the bad spirits do not want a prayer, so when the prayer healer and prophet starts to pray the evil spirits run away". Other statements made in this regard are as follows: "Prayer healers give blessed water to the victim, and immediately *izizwe* get the blessed water, they run away". "The whole process is evil. Through God's communication with the appointed prayer healer, all the bonds with such evil spirits are broken." "The prophet first predicts the healing methods to be utilized because the messenger (ancestor) tells the prayer healer what to do and what to use". "The prayer healer is able to overcome demons. The prayer healer blesses the water which the person uses, and the *izizwe* do not like things that are blessed".

The prophets use blessed water which the victim has to drink. After this the *izizwe* remove themselves. The prophets also pray for the victim and prepare the same mixture as is used by the negative forces. They pray over it and make it powerless. They purge the victim through provoking him/her through steaming him/her and through the use of emetics. The "holy water from God" breaks all the bonds, and the victim becomes normal again. One respondent stated "one takes a sick person to have a shower, and while this person showers, one prays for that person, so that the *izizwe* may remove themselves. The *izizwe* then run away because they hate prayer". Another prophet "pricks with a needle in the affected part, so that blood can come out, and then *izinyamazane* is given so that the blood can be licked by the bad spirits. This procedure and the use of holy water make the *izizwe* run away".

Indiki

Traditional concept: Possession by an African wandering spirit
Psychiatric diagnosis: Brief creative psychosis (hysterical psychosis)

According to the general consensus, this type of foreign possession entered South Africa at the end of the last century from Malawi and

Mozambique. It is associated with *indiki* (male spirits) and *amandawe* (female spirits) of the miners who died and were buried in South Africa. Because no sacrifices were made to integrate them into their own metaphysical society, these wandering spirits enter people of this country, which disturbs the patrilineage issue. They take the place of the real spirits of the lineages of such persons. *Indiki* is picked up and does not enter a person as a result of sorcery. The phenomenon, so it is believed, comes from Malawi. The victim becomes blind and stiff in the neck, and feels a burden on the shoulders. According to some of the respondents, the victims experience stomach pains due to a big clot of blood in the stomach; they also look as if they have chest pains and as if they have been stabbed in the chest. They suffer from headaches and they yawn continuously. The phenomenon, said some of the respondents, manifests the same symptoms as *ukuthwasa*. One respondent said it is caused by "witchcraft" which makes the victim feel that he/she has lumps in the stomach. Smoking could cause it, but some people are born with rounded stomachs as a result of *amandiki* and *amandawe*, or foreign evil spirits.

Sixty percent of the respondents stated that the diviners should treat these victims, while thirty percent maintained that they could be treated only by the prayer healers, and the remaining ten percent opted to combine the diviner and prayer healer in the healing task. The diviners are preferred because they work with the ancestors; they see the disease after studying the position of the bones they throw, and they receive also the procedure to be followed. The *amandiki* and *amandawe* are seen by the diviners through the assistance of their ancestors, and this is important, because only then can these foreign spirits be confronted effectively.

Treatment is effected through "putting *muti* on the head of the victim, and then hitting the victim with the holy stick made in the form of a two-pronged fork (*pehla ekhandla*). The *mutis* used are called *mlahla nKosi* (a kind of herb), and *bububu, mahlozana, mpendulo wedlozi* (roots). The victim should be made to vomit and then bathed. After this the stiff neck and the blindness of the eyes will disappear. The victim is also given *amagobongo* which he/she has to drink. Different types of herbs may be mixed with the *amagobongo*, which is used to provoke vomiting, and medicines are also used for *ukugcaba*, ie. putting medicines into incisions which have been made on the body. The victim can also drink, syringe, or lick different kinds of herbs, or he/she can smear his/her face with them".

The above-mentioned spirits of affliction are associated with possession cults, which Hammond-Tooke states entered the Transvaal, Natal
and Mozambique about eighty years ago. Their origin is traced back to
Zimbabwe's shave cult. The cult made an appearance among the Zulu
around 1910 (cf. Lee, S.G., "Spirit possession among Zulu" in Beattie
J. and Middleton, J. (eds), *Spirit Mediumship and Society in Africa*,
London, Routledge, 1969, p. 130; see also Hammond-Tooke, W.D.,
"The aetiology of spirit in Southern Africa", *African Studies*, 1988). The
cults are prevalent among the Tsonga, Venda, Ndau, Pedi, Lobedu,
Kgaga, Zulu and recently also among the Xhosa.

These alien spirits, which are not ancestral spirits, possess their
victims. Hammond-Tooke refers to the origin of these spirits, which
have nothing to do with spirit mediumship as is the case with ancestral
spirits, but which have to do with "spirit possession" which is recent, and
"tends to be peripheral". These spirits are traced to Tsonga spirits.
Among the Zulu, the *amandiki* or *amandawe* (Ndau) express themselves
in the "Indian" or "Tsonga" languages (cf. Sundkler, B.G.M., *Bantu
Prophets in South Africa*, OUP, 1961, p. 23). Possession leads to illness,
and various methods are used to remove these alien spirits. Through
exorcism and contra-sorcery reaction, these spirits are removed. Some
of the healers enjoin these spirits to identify themselves, and to remove
themselves from the victim. These spirits are never destroyed, and often
reurn to a victim who is prone to spirit possession. Women are affected
mostly, and the reason for this is attitudinal change. Hammond-Tooke
explains this change as "female revolt against the 'system'" which
"cannot easily be rationalized through the use of traditional cosmological
ideas—ancestors uphold patrilineal and male interests, and witchcraft is
unacceptably immoral—so new spirit entities are created to symbolize
and facilitate new attitudes and behaviour patterns. What more appropriate a metaphor for this than the image of the alien spirit?"

2. Sorcery

Sorcery is related to the deliberate placing of substances in order to
influence specific persons. The intention is of prime importance. It could
be to harm people, or to influence people for positive purposes, such as
obtaining the attention of a girl. There are various types of sorcery in the
traditional context, such as night and day sorcery. Some types are more
dangerous than others. Traditional and western medicines are mixed,
and added to the victims' food. The lineage sorcerer is responsible for

the lineage segment quarrel, and various rituals could be used to restore harmony among lineage segments. Where ancestors have been persuaded to favour certain persons in a lineage, a specific ritual has to be followed in which special black medicines are used to ward off the misfortunes which result from the loss of the protection of the ancestors.

Acts of sorcerers are also experienced by members of the AIC, and special attention is given to the various types of sorcery. Some of these are referred to below.

Umhayizo

Traditional concept: Sorcery by love potion
Psychiatric diagnosis: Hysteria

Persons with this problem are considered to be very hysterical. It is said to be just like *ufufunyane* and *izizwe*, ie. when a person is touched on the shoulder he/she starts to scream. The phenomenon appears when "you talk about a person whom a girl loves" and then "she screams and fights with you as if you are her enemy". Assumption is that "these people scream and cry when there is lightning". Furthermore, "*hayizo* screaming also takes place when a person has ancestors on her, which means she is called to be a diviner".

The condition is brought on by giving the victim *muti* with food so that the girl may develop love for someone she does not love, or for someone she has jilted. Usually, "medicated" water or food, over which the name of the girl has been called, is used with the intention of making the girl develop love for the man who obtained the *muti* from the herbalist.

Seventy percent of the prophets interviewed were of the opinion that only the prayer healer/prophet is in a position to help such a victim, while thirty percent considered the herbalist to be most effective. The prayer healers use pure water and "this sickness does not want water". Also, they have the power to pray, and "by just using prayer and water the victim recovers". One prophet stated "they pray and bath you in water while praying. Then these things run away, and they even tell you where they come from and why they are doing this". The prophets give *ubulawu* which they mix with cold water, and which they use to provoke vomiting. *Isiwasho*, is also used for this purpose. Prophets also burn herbs, the smoke of which the victim has to inhale. They may give her cords to wear around the neck and waist. She is also given holy water. The victim has to drink several cups of this a few times daily. A prophet said "the victim is taken to a bathroom, and is put underneath a shower, and while the water comes down on her I pray. These things then talk to me, telling me where they come from, and why they were sent, and for what reason." Another medicine (*inhabia*, which is not cooked, but only put into warm water) is given to the victim in order to make him vomit. It is interesting to note that although certain rituals are performed in this connection, for most of the prophets prayer is an important healing factor when it comes to hysteria.

The herbalist, on the other hand, does not pray, but uses different kinds of herbs, and other *muti* such as different types of *izinyamazane*, which the victim smokes and licks. *Tshopa* (pricks) may be administered to all the joints in the person's body. The herbalist also uses "medicated" water (but not water which has been prayed over, as is the case with the prayer healers). With this water the victim is steamed, syringed, and through swallowing it she vomits.

One observes here the influence of the herbalist on the prophet, in that apart from prayer this type of pollution cannot be cured without specific ritual acts.

Uvalo

Traditional concept: Being frightened
Psychiatric diagnosis: Anxiety disorder

The victims are "frightened" as in the case of *izizwe*; the victims become anxious and remain in a state of shock all the time; they are always scared without any reason; they sleep badly and lose body weight; they are scared that someone will harm them; they remain incomprehensibly anxious; they have abnormal feelings; and they imagine that all kinds of evil forces are against them. The condition is created by a feeling of guilt, or fear. The victims become weak and are always afraid of being bewitched. A girl in such a situation could easily agree to a love proposition, being afraid that the man will bewitch her.

The causes

According to the respondents, a male who fails to obtain the attention of a girl goes to the herbalist where he receives "oils for smearing on the eye lashes of the girl, and luck stones with doctored animal skins, which make the girl afraid of saying 'no'. He even smears his clothing with the oils, which bring extraordinary dignity to the proposing man".

Another respondent stated: "It is sometimes caused by witchcraft. Some men consider themselves to have extraordinary power over girls, and girls become unreasonably terrified, which may result in the bursting of heart valves. A *muti* called *ndabula uvalo* is used which causes shock. It is deposited at the gate of the house where the girl lives, so that when she steps over it she gets the disease".

The general opinion among the prophets is that the cause is something in the person's blood. The victim vomits, as a result of certain *muti* which is stirred before use, and over which the name of the person is called out at sunrise. A girl also uses *muti* and when she washes her face she calls the name of a man, so that when he thinks of her he will get a shock. Others use bad medicine (*ndabulo uvalo*) over which a girl's name has been called, or they get hair oil from the chemist and mix it with *ndabula uvalo*, and touch a girl's arm. Her reaction is that she cannot eat or sleep, and wishes the person to come to her immediately. She easily gets into a state in which she screams incessantly (*umhayizo*).

Who can best treat it?

In this case most of the prophets consider the diviner to be more effective in treating the victim. Forty percent referred to the diviner; thirty percent to the prayer healer; twenty percent to the herbalist; and ten percent to the herbalist and prayer healer. Here the western trained doctors do not really feature, except where there is "a bad blood blockage" because they have the technical know-how. Only one respondent referred to western methods as an alternative. One of the leading prophet healers maintained that both the diviner and the herbalist can help the victim. The prophet could also help, but not the western trained doctor. According to this person, the prophet as prayer healer is important because he/she can see and pray, while the 'ordinary' prayer healer can only work through dreams and prayer.

Those who propose that the diviner should treat the affliction maintain that he/she uses especially strong herbs to treat "witchcraft", and some of the prophets maintain that the victims usually end up as diviners themselves. Those who opted for treatment by the herbalists stated they are the "only ones who cause it, and stop it, and none other". The consensus among the prophets is that the prayer healers are effective because they use "holy water", ie. water over which God's name has been pronounced. The prophets are empowered by God to treat it.

How should the condition be treated?

Ndabula uvalo is cooked and the resultant liquid is used to provoke vomiting so severe that foam comes from the person's mouth. The herbalist has the option either to terminate the procedure, or to reverse it. In the latter case the man fears the girl in question when seeing or thinking of her, as a result of the "medicine" applied to him. The girl, too, sniffs or licks a mixture of burnt herbs and burnt antelope skin (*izinyamazane*), which will reverse the procedure instituted by the insistent man. The girl then purifies herself with other herbs. The herbalist derives methods in order to purify his victim. *Ndabula uvalo* is cooked to stop the anxiety or disturbance. The anxiety can also be "killed" by *hlungu hlungu*, a special herbal preparation. One of the prophets boils water in which *impepho* has been put, and uses it for steaming. She also gives *isiwasho*, ie. water mixed with ash, to provoke vomiting and takes the person to the river to bathe. The diviner makes the person vomit, steams the victim, and also uses emetics, and make incisions on the chest between the breasts.

This cultural illness is thus related to male/female relationships and especially to courting, where the man finds no response, or very little response, from the girl he wishes to be associated with.

Iqondo

Traditional concept: Harm to a wife's lover through sorcery
Psychiatric diagnosis: Uro-genital disease

The symptoms described by the prophets are those associated with what is commonly known as veneral diseases—the stomach expands, diarrhoea, swollen penis, the scrotum sac also becomes swollen, the person could also experience mental imbalance.

Iqondo is the result of promiscuity. When a husband hears his wife is sleeping with another man, he goes to a herbalist or diviner, or collects herbs "so as to set a trap for his wife. When the other man comes and makes love with this trap-set woman, he contracts *iqondo*". *Muti* is used to affect the person whose name is called over that medicine. The *muti* is sent with a baboon to make the person mad". The disease is caused by morally weak people; and it may also be caused by 'medicine' over which a person has walked. It was said that "the deceived husband sees to it that *muti* is smeared on the other man, so that when he has intercourse, the *muti* is transferred to him, and he contracts the disease. Sometimes the husband drinks *muti* in which needles have been put, so that if a woman is in love with another man, the moment this man makes love to her he becomes sick". A prophet/leader stated "when a man has sex with another man's wife, this man makes incisions under the navel, and alongside the vagina of his wife, and puts medicine into the incision. This protects the woman against other men". This prophet stated that many come to him for this disease, and added: One way of treating it is to take the neck of a tortoise, and pulverise and mix it with other medicines. This medicine is actually put into the above-mentioned incisions. The penis of the wayward person then becomes small, and withdraws itself, and he cannot have intercourse".

Who should treat the affliction?

Thirty percent of the respondents stated that western trained doctors are the best to treat the disease. Twenty percent referred to the herbalist and the western doctor, ten percent only to the herbalist, ten percent only to the diviner, twenty percent only to the prayer healers/prophets and ten percent to the herbalist, prophet and western doctor. It is interesting to note that the respondents, who were all prophets, were not so sure about their abilities to treat this disease. The prophets/prayer healers consider themselves more effective in the treatment of the disease than either the herbalist or the diviner. They do, however, have more confidence in the western doctor. A number stated that the western trained doctors have the ability to treat the disease, as they use injections which "touch the blood" immediately.

A few respondents emphasized that the disease could cause brain damage, and that the western doctors have been trained to handle this. As in the case of other diseases, a few were of the opinion that only the herbalist, and not the diviner, could treat the disease because he initiated it, and could thus reverse the process.

Burnt animal skins (*izinyamazane*) are well mixed with herbs, and the mixture is "sniffed, licked and jumped over" by the victim. Other herbs are cooked, and the juice is taken by the victim. Ingredients to provoke vomiting are also given. Syringing is also considered to be good for cleansing out the poison. Animal oils are smeared on the genitals "to counteract the bacteria". According to one prophet this is considered to be the fastest method used by the diviner. The diviners usually give *muti* which has to be smoked. Some of the prophets use boiled water together with *izinyamazane* which has to be inhaled. They also use *isiwasho* and prick the affected parts with needles so that blood is let.

The confidence the prophets expressed in the efforts of the western trained doctor is important, as is the greater confidence they expressed in themselves as treaters of the disease, when compared to the diviners and the herbalists.

3. Poisoning

Idliso

Traditional concept: Ingestion of sorcerer's poison
Psychiatric diagnosis: Psychosomatic GI trait disorder

In the traditional context, *idliso* implies that poisonous substances, which have been eaten, are embedded in the chest of the victim. The substance is removed through the use of emetics, and the victim takes a steam bath if he has a feverish condition. The treatment is both ritual and empirical. The patient in this case is not placed in a mystical imbalance, but always has somatic symptoms, so that the condition "is open to any prophylactic treatment" (Ngubane, p. 132).

The consensus is that the victim becomes thin, loses appetite, coughs continuously as if he/she has tuberculosis, vomits (blood in some cases), and becomes dark in complexion. The affliction disturbs the heart beat.

The condition is caused by "medicines" which the herbalist prepares, and which are put into the food of a person, either to destroy health or to kill. One respondent stated that the *muti* used is made of the hearts of a frog and an alligator. He said "the heart of the alligator is poisonous. If you eat it you either die, or become very sick". The animals have acquired mythical significance in the traditional context. The frog, for example, is a source of snake poison, and the alligator has features which give rise to fear. They pollute their surroundings, and are considered to be inherently negative creatures. Another respondent stated that food is mixed with the fat of animals, and this poison "fixes your chest together like a nest, a complaint which western doctors call tuberculosis". Yet another respondent said "it is the result of Zulu medicines, and when it spreads in your body you get asthma (really 'short breath'). It is caused by witchcraft".

The main motive for poisoning food in this way is jealousy. A respondent said "a person wants you to die. Your forefathers protect you, but even this protection cannot prevent the sickness. You become sick in any case and lose weight and cough". The word *idliso* means "to be made to eat". Another respondent stated that a person eats herbs obtained from a herbalist, which develop into something like a nest or egg in the victim's chest, causing damage to the lungs. "Because I am a prophet, I predict the cause through visions".

Who should treat the disease?

Half of the respondents wanted the prayer healer/prophet to treat the disease, while thirty percent wanted the assistance of the herbalist. Ten percent opted for treatment by the diviner, and ten percent stated that the healer categories should assist in the treatment.

The prophet has to diagnose the disease, and "see" which type of doctor should treat it, ie. the herbalist, or western trained doctor. If an operation is needed, then the western doctor should be chosen. The prophet is best able to diagnose the disease because he/she can "see" through contact with God, and the ancestors because they work under the direction of the Holy Spirit. The Holy Spirit comes first, and then the ancestors, who are mediators. The diviner only "sees" why a person is sick, but if he/she has learned about the medicines used by herbalists, then he/she is also able to assist in the healing procedure. Diviners are not usually in the position to do this because it is the herbalist who brings the pollution on the victim, as a consequence of which it is he who also knows the cure. The herbalists can reverse the process because the *muti* used is obtained from them. The prayer healer gives *isiwasho* which enables the victim to vomit, and this removes the poison from the stomach. The prophet gets advice from the messenger, and could, through God's spiritual power, "chase away everything".

How should the disease be treated?

The prophet/leader suggests certain herbs, for example, the *inhliziyo nkulu*—a type of medicine. If it is a stomach problem, *gobo* has to be cooked for one hour and be given to the person. The person should also be given cod liver oil.

One prophet said "if you cannot 'see' clearly what to do, take the patient to the western doctor".

The herbalist orientated prophet stated "I burn the body of the alligator, and mix it with the blood of the black chicken. Thereafter, the victim has to drink the mixture three times a day in order to vomit". The burned part of the alligator has been neutralised. It is poison if not burned. The black chicken's blood represents the evil intentions of the sorcerer, and if this mixture is taken, the evil will be vomited out. The mixture is considered to be a strong medicine.

The prophets have different approaches to this problem:

 i) One said "'holy water' is used first so that the victim vomits, and when medicine (*muti*) has touched the poisoned substance or food in the person, it will come out undigested, and the person will recover".

 ii) Another prophet maintained that the victim should use medicines which soften the poisoned stuff, before the patient is prepared to have it removed from his stomach, because the victim could die if emission is the immediate aim.

iii) Yet another said *isiwasho* (water mixed with ash) should be used for a whole month, as it strengthens the victim after he/she has been weakened by the poison.

iv) There are some prayer healers/prophets who recommend a mixture of sea water, Five Roses tea, milk and alum, of which the victim has to drink "cups full". Thereafter, the patient is given two litres of ordinary water which has been prayed over, to drink. The victim then vomits. The bits of poison are seen. In most cases the victim stays with the prayer healer while undergoing treatment, and the main ingredient given is sea water or salted water mixed with ashes. This is blessed by the prayer healer.

Those prayer healers who propose the herbalist as the best healer refer to his/her medicated herbs, which enable a person to vomit out the infectious medicine. Others state that the burned flesh of an alligator is used, and mixed with the blood of a chicken. Half a cup is taken, either once or three times a day. This "kills" the poison.

The disease is not confronted without certain ingredients being used. This is why the herbalist's assistance is considered important. Once again, the scientific approach is not considered, as the forces behind the scenes are not bound by the scientific laws of cause and effect.

4. Pollution

Pollution is a "mystical force" which shows no somatic symptoms, but which could have negative consequences. At birth, but more especially at death, pollution leads to a dangerous situation against which fortification is necessary. Pollution diminishes resistance to disease. It is responsible for bad luck, and a number of conditions of negative reaction which affect a person. Women who have just given birth are polluted severely, and stay away from services until gradually integrated again into the church. A corpse is severely polluted, and everything in the household and in the area is contaminated. Menstruating women are also polluted and in some churches are not allowed to attend services while in this condition. Women are channels, and their purity is of vital importance. This is especially so if their office is that of diviner in the traditional society, or of prayer healer/prophet in the AIC.

Umnyama

Traditional concept: Pollution causing bad luck
Psychiatric diagnosis: Depression (minor or major)

Persons who are victims of this phenomenon experience bad luck. For example, a girl cannot keep a steady boy friend. The victim has no luck in doing anything right. People tend to hate the victim without reason, and his/her aims are never fulfilled. The victim remains unemployed. A few of the respondents maintained that this problem is the same as *abaphansi basifulatele*.

The main causes advanced by the prophets for this condition are the following:
a) jealousy or hatred;
b) not keeping traditional customs;
c) a change in a person's ancestors who become bad ancestors and "who create a lot of bad luck" for him/her (the ancestors turn their backs on him/her);
d) making love to a person who is mourning a member of her family who has passed away;
e) "a witch sending a baboon to a person with *muti*, which is scattered in the person's house to bring bad luck";
f) witches burying a herb (referred to as *inyama wempunzi*) on a person's path. When the victim steps over it, he/she experiences a lot of bad luck;
g) secret sins or actions.

Who should treat the affliction?

The largest proportion of the respondents stated that the prayer healers/ prophets should treat such victims. Ten percent said the diviners should treat victims, and ten percent were in favour of the herbalists. The rest of the respondents suggested all three types of healer. All the respondents excluded the western trained doctor.

The prayer healers/prophets are considered to be most effective with regard to this condition because they "communicate with the ancestors in a certain way"; use "ropes", and *isiwasho* mixed with *inyama wempunzi*; and make an altar, using candles "and *impepho*", in order to bring their ancestors in contact with those of the victim. Although prayer is an important part of the healing process, the rituals used are just as important, and those used by the prophets are varied as is seen below.

The prayer healer uses *isiwasho*, which is used to provoke vomiting, and for steaming and syringing. One prophet stated that in addition to using *isiwasho*, they take a black chicken's blood, mix it with water, and wash the body of the victim with it. Again *isiwasho* is used. *Impepho* is put in water, which is then boiled, and with this water the body of the victim is washed once more. Then a prayer is said, and a white chicken is slaughtered. When this has taken place "these things run away to where they came from after having stated why they did it", ie. they state who they are, and are asked to leave the victim. The black chicken is to confront the "bad spirit(s)", ie. the ancestor(s) of the victim who has turned against him/her; the white chicken is the assurance that the "bad ancestor(s)" has been reconciled to the victim. Sea water is considered to be the best type of water. One prophet stated "I give such people holy water to provoke vomiting and for bathing in, and a black and red chicken are slaughtered. The blood is taken and is mixed with holy water and pure water. Then outside the yard in the forest, the mixture is used to provoke vomiting and for bathing in, so that all bad luck can be left in the forest".

The candles play a role in rituals connected with this phenomenon. A prophet outlined his procedure as follows: "You make an altar with seven candles which are lit; an animal is slaughtered in order to apologise to the ancestors, and you pray right through the night, asking the ancestors to give the person luck". Another prophet explained how this condition is effected by a sorcerer. He takes a goat which has a black spot between the eyes, mixes parts of its skin with *amanzimnyama* (black water), and then takes *inyama wempunzi* (meat of a goat) which he deposits at the door of the victim, calling out his name. The victim gets tired and his luck is negatively affected. He then contracts *umnyama*. According to one of the prophets, a Christian should go to the prophet who knows who the most effective herbalist is.

According to one prophet, water plays a central role with the diviner: "The victim should steam and syringe himself with medicated water and clean himself by drinking herbalist-medicated water and which he forces out through the mouth".

The treatment of this culture-specific disease is also considered to be most effective within the traditional context. Nearly all the prophets made specific reference to the indigenous healers as helpful in releasing a victim of this type of spirit possession.

The strict adherence to culture-specific diseases was evident in the discussions with prayer healers and prophets. Even those who maintained that they do not operate via the ancestors continue their healing activities on these diseases. Agnes Zulu, a prayer healer of the *Brethren Mission Church of Zion*, who works only through Jesus and not through the ancestors, stated that when people are sick they come to the church. She has a big bath at home. When a patient is very sick she "gets the word from God" and puts him/her in the water. She has dreams and visions which come to her when she is praying. "We do not pray to the ancestors—we pray to Jesus Christ. I believe in Jesus, but many prayer healers and prophets believe in their ancestors. I cannot say they are right or wrong. I know Jesus is alive. He died for me on the cross. I do the healing in His Name. I do not say I heal the person. We are only messengers of God. The cord I have around my neck is to keep the evil spirits (*imimoya emibi*) away. I received it from the prophet. If the devil is around he will not come near me."

She added, "We can help people who suffer from *uhlanya* and *isithutwane*. They come from the devil. Because you ask me about *umnyama* specifically, I would like to emphasize that it is a bad thing. Nothing comes right to an afflicted person. The more he tries to succeed, the more he fails. To help the person, a small black chicken is used, as well as sand from the graveyard, and red and black candles. The chicken is then killed and *isiwasho* is made with river water and sand from the river or the sea, and I pray over it. The blood of the chicken is mixed and put into the water. A hole is then dug far away at a secret place, and the dead chicken is put into the hole, and needles are stuck into the candles, and these are also put into the hole. The person who has *umnyama* undresses, and is put into the hole, either standing or sitting. The next day a white chicken has to be provided by the patient. The chicken is killed, and fresh *isiwasho* is made with water, salt, camphor and blood from the white chicken. The person has to drink this. It brings out the evil which the devil has brought on the person. The person vomits into a hole at a secret place, and relieves himself. All this is covered up. All those evil forces have now left the person. If after a time the person still has only bad luck, then the *isiwasho* has to be stronger".

Of importance here are the symbolic colours of the chickens and the candles; red and black are the colours of "hot" medicines which symbolize danger, which cure disease. The needles through the candles represent the obstacles put in the way of the evil forces. The black chicken, as well as the black and red candles, stand in opposition to white. In the treatment of mystical diseases, colour is always symbolic. Black and red represent what is bad, but they could represent positive 'power'. Red represents a transitional phase from poor health to good health, while white is unequivocally good. It represents purity, light, power and good health. In the traditional context, as well as with the prayer healers and prophets, there is a rigid sequence in the use of colours. Black is used first, then red (the colour of the transitional phase), and then white (the symbol of health). White medicine can be used alone, but if black and red medicine or symbols are used, they have to be followed by white. Black and red medicines are believed to expel the illness or pollution from the system, as well as to strengthen the patient against future attacks. White medicines reintroduce good health (cf. Sibisi, H., *Colour symbolism in the treatment of disease among the Zulu*, unpublished, pp. 1–18).

Agnes Zulu has brought a traditional procedure with all its symbolism and ritual significance within the context of Christianity. It is a type of Christianity into which has been integrated the traditional, in order to give a mystical treatment to a patient. The treatment correct the balance in the patient's life, which has been disturbed by evil forces. Treatment is with black, red and white substances with all their symbolic significance. In traditional society, where mystically caused diseases are manifested in somatic symptoms, two levels of treatment take place. The natural treatment corrects the somatic symptoms, and the mystical treatment corrects the balance. But if disease manifests itself only in mystical symptoms such as *umnyama*, then only the mystical treatment with black, red, and white medicines will be given (cf. Sibisi, p. 2). Is such treatment possible without ancestral intervention? In most cases, according to the prophets.

5. Environmental hazards

Umeqo

Traditional concept: Stepping over harmful concoction
Psychiatric diagnosis: Oedema and paralysis of legs

The prophets reiterated that the victim suffers from "a very unusual sickness which the western doctor cannot cure". The victim develops incurable sores and sometimes becomes mentally disturbed. This condition is ascribed to *muti* spread on the ground, placed on a foot path or buried in the ground over which the victim walks. When the victim tramples the *muti* or walks over it, he/she will become infected.

Western trained doctors fail to diagnose the disease. They fail even to see that a person is sick, with the result that the victim goes to the diviners to find out the cause. The remedy is given by the herbalist. There are different opinions among the prophets about who is capable of handling the problem of such a victim. The herbalist makes an incision of 3 mm with a razor or sharp object. Into the incision he puts powder obtained from burned parts of animals such as horn and skin, and he also adds material made from herbs. This process is referred to as *ukugcaba*. He also pricks the patient with a sharp object containing *muti*.

The main symptom of the disease is very painful, swollen legs. The herbalist is able to heal this. *Muti* is given to inhale and to drink (a tablespoon at a time), three times a day. One prophet stated that she also gives *muti* to drink three times a day. This *muti* is called *ingunduza*. It is mixed and cooked, and the liquid (*manzi omuthi*) is used as an enema. *Amakhubalo* (medicinal roots), which is mixed with *imidlebe*, ie. leaves from a specific tree species, is also given.

With reference to the herbalist, another prophet stated that western doctors cannot assist in healing the "watery unhealing wounds, or those people who simply become mentally disturbed as a result of walking over medicated ground". Only a herbalist is seen as having the knowledge to assist in this connection. The herbalist uses *umbiza* (a type of herb), which is cooked to take water out of the body. The victim licks the medicine, together with *hlakoti zomeqo* (a specific herb used for *umeqo*), so that the water may be drained out of the body. *Mbiza* is used daily, so that the victim can purge himself by urinating excessively.

Again, the traditional approach has not been discarded. Prayer "plus" is important, and the "plus" often becomes of vital significance, even if it has no scientific basis.

Ibulawo (bodily weakness as a result of sorcery)

The victim displays different types of symptoms—intense headaches, lice in the hair and on the body, and weight loss; he/she gives the impression of having psychic problems, indulges in criminal acts, and is unable to work because of swollen legs. Such a person tries to do what is right but does not succeed. Stealing, even from his own family and against his will, is an example of such aberrant behaviour. When a well-off person becomes impoverished, or "when a person does not come to you as a prophet any more, the medicines used against him are responsible for this. Witchcraft causes this 'bad-habit-sickness' which will stay with the person until treated". There are various types of *ibulawo* such as psychic and physical, and there are thus a variety of symptoms, such as mental disturbance, strokes, heart attacks etc.

The causes

The herbalist causes the disease through "black water". The witches pour medicine on the ground and call out the victim's name. When the person steps over the medicine or eats the herb he/she contracts the disease. However, it is stated that there are many things which could cause the disease because "different types of witchcraft" are applied. Neglect of the ancestors could also be the cause of this physical condition.

The sand of the grave of someone who had the disease could be used. The sand is mixed with *muti*, over which the victim's name has been called. The main motive behind this unfriendly act of bewitchment is jealousy. Either the name of the person is called over *muti* or the *muti* is sent to a person in a "sort of a dream. Once a person dreams, it gets you and causes sickness".

Who should treat the disease?

Sixty percent of the prophets considered themselves able to treat the disease. Thirty percent would also refer it to a diviner, and ten percent to a herbalist.

The prophet/leader, who referred both to the diviner and the prayer healer as effective in treating an *ibulawo* victim, maintained that they steam the person with boiled medicine and that when steamed they give the person white water, *amanzimhlophe*, ie. water mixed with sugar. He added "Then your luck starts to move". According to him, it is easy to mix such medicine. Brown sugar mixed with water (*manzinyama*) is also used, and the person is "steamed". Another prophet also uses *izinyamazana*, which the victim inhales, and which is used in incisions (*gcaba*) at the joints of the body. Then a *muti* called *ubulawa* mixed with cold water is used to provoke vomiting. Not only the prophet, but also the diviner, is seen as one who is using medicines for vomiting, steaming and "syringing", against adverse evil forces.

The prayer healers use different methods which depend on the sickness. Holy water mixed with salt, sea water, *impepho* and whitewash is prominent. The prayer healer prays, and treats the person with 'holy water'. He/she is considered to be best able to assist the victim, because he/she has the power of God to "chase away" evil spirits and he/she uses *isiwasho* to help wash away all the dirt which is causing *ibulawo* in the chest of the patient. This method "cures the patient permanently". *Isiwasho* is given to provoke and is used for steaming and emission. The victim is also given a cord ("rope") which is put around his/her waist to stop the negative things and "to ask the ancestors what they really want so that this can be done quickly."

Umkhondo

Traditional concept: Bringing bad or good luck

Both biological and environmental factors are at work in causing illness. There has always been a close relationship between the peoples of Africa and their environment. Plants are used for healing or harming and specific animals are used for sacrifices. The natural environment has special influences on the human being. Moving animals leave foreign elements behind which can contaminate human beings. Tracks of animals are loaded with adverse power, and could be dangerous. One could become contaminated with negative forces if one stepped over the "loaded" tracks. The joints then become affected, as it is here that the evil forces usually enter. In the traditional context, incisions are made on the joints and medicine (*muti*) is applied.

The balance of forces, which so many factors disturb especially in the urban setting, needs continuous attention. In the urban areas, the unknown factors are many, and any disturbance, set-back, insecurity is ascribed to misdeeds, such as the burying of poisonous and ritually dangerous stuff underneath one's foot path. Identity of cause led some prophets to state that *umkhondo* leads to *umeqo*.

This condition is also described as one whereby the victim has a bad spirit on his body. It is thus best treated by herbalists, as they use traditional herbs to 'throw' such spirits on a victim. They use *impuputho yemimoya*, for syringing and also for inhaling. However, when a person is lost because of "medicines" which make him/her wander away from home and get lost, the diviner is thought to be the best person to handle the case, because through special visionary gifts, he/she can establish where the lost person is, and bring that person back home. The victim's name is pronounced over *muti* called *isikhafula*. The diviner is a specialist in the application of certain "medicine" which gets back lost things and people.

Some of the prophets knew nothing about *umkhondo*. Those who did know about it, referred to either the herbalists or diviners as appropriate healers. One prophet maintained that when one person is stabbed, everyone in the family will die in the same manner. Stabbing is a real problem in the townships. The result is a view that it should be ritually counteracted. *Muti* with a knife stuck in it is used to bring bad luck to people.

Some of the prayer healers/prophets stated that this type of sorcery is counteracted by digging a hole in the yard at the corner of the house. Into this hole are put cords (*amatambo*) and the hole is filled in. A hole is also made at the gate, and a cord ("rope") put into it, and then the hole is filled in. Each member of the family is given a cord to wear around the waist. The cord wards off the evil and protects the person.

6. Ancestral displeasure

Abaphansi basifulatele
(Literally: "The ancestors are facing away from us")

Traditional concept: Ancestral displeasure
Psychiatric diagnosis: Depression (minor or major)

A distinction is made between ancestors who have authority and who are able to control their progeny and those who are not in this position because they have already receded into the background. In Zulu society, the parents of a man, his father's father and his father's mother are most important ancestors, followed by his father's brothers (Ngubane, p. 51). These are the effective ancestors who can punish or reward. The non-effective ancestors have no such jurisdiction. In the traditional context, the ancestor influence is tremendous. At birth a special sacrifice to the ancestors is made for each child through the slaughtering of a goat. The child receives its name and is put under the protection of its ancestors. The breaking of this relationship with the ancestors leads to tremendous tragedy. This relationship is still firmly accepted by many in the AIC.

Bad luck is the lot of those who are disobedient to their ancestors. This is also the case in the AIC. Those who are disobedient feel hot for no reason, and cannot get a job. The victim or the family experiences a lot of misfortune. Inability to get a marriage partner, eruption of family quarrels and incomprehensible loss of property are some of the negative experiences. One prophet stated: "You can slaughter many goats, but when the ancestors have turned their backs on you, nothing will come right".

The cause of this condition could be summed up as follows:

a) dreaming about people who have died. If this happens, bad luck such as accidents will follow;

b) calling of a hated person's name over *amanzi amanyama* (black water) mixed with *muti*. This is done to the whole family of that person so that he experiences bad luck;

c) failure to uphold all the traditional customs;

d) the negative intentions of a "late relative", ie. ancestor, who has become a bad ancestor to the victim, set upon ruining his life;

e) neglect of the ancestors (*abaphansi*). Their anger is provoked as a result of the victim's neglect to perform certain rituals;

f) jealousy of a person leading to bewitchment. "Someone is making bad medicine to make our ancestors run away from us". One respondent explained: "If some of your relatives are jealous about your prosperity or good luck, they go to the cemetery and take sand from the family grave, and use it as *muti* to create bad luck. They vomit on the sand while they call your name, so that you are continuously confronted with bad luck".

It is significant that in the case of this affliction, not less than sixty percent of the prophets interviewed were convinced that the victim is best served by the prophet or prayer healer. Only ten percent referred to the diviner, the same percentage to the herbalist, and the rest to all three types of healers. All excluded treatment by the western trained doctor. In spite of the fact that the prophets/prayer healers are associated with a western orientated religion, they have much more confidence in their own ability to assist the victims than they have in the ability of western trained doctors.

One prophet recommended the prayer healer because he is able "to make a simple altar " to treat this problem. Another said "They are able to speak to ancestors by just praying". A third stated "With their prayers and holy water they are able to heal people". The prophets who recommended the diviner stated that they used herbs "to talk to the ancestors". The following statements were made. "The diviner is the nearest person to the ancestors"; "They use *isiwasho* to call on the ancestors to bring luck"; "They make the communication easy between you and your ancestors"; "They pray for their patients". The herbalist's forte—he uses medicine which induces the problem so that he can also reverse the process—was again highlighted.

Various remedies were proposed by the prophets. One prophet stated that "if the person is young the prophet should take *mtale* and *madlozana* (roots), get *babhubu* and mix it, get *hlanhla mhlophe* (white luck) and mix this, and make the person vomit and also steam him with it. Your enemy who does not like you, or is jealous of you, takes grave sand, especially the sand of your father's or mother's grave. This is how the herbalists treat it. The herbalists bring the ancestors into contact with the needs of the affected persons". The prophets who emphasized the efficiency of the diviner in this connection stated that the diviner is the nearest person to the ancestors, and that the family should slaughter a goat or a cow for forgiveness. The rituals are considered to be important. One prophet added "They slaughter the animal for the ancestors, and burn *impepho* and talk to the ancestors while they wash the victim with the slaughtered animal's bile. And then all the people have a meal together".

One of those who recommended only the prophet as a healer stated "You make an altar with seven candles which are lit, and slaughter an animal, and talk to your ancestors while the prayer healers are helping you in your prayers. The prayers continue for a whole night, and the church members have their meals only after the service, so fasting also takes place".This prophet added that he "slaughters two chickens and prays over the water and the ash. Water and ash is mixed in order to prepare *isiwasho*. All the persons of that family are taken out of the house, and bathe themselves in the forest. They take the same holy water and use it to make themselves vomit." Another prophet "boils water together with black water (*amanzi emnyama*). The mixture is used for steaming and drinking, and also to provoke vomiting." Prophets are able "to speak to the ancestors by praying first". They also "slaughter an animal, and call upon our ancestors to be with us, and bring good luck.

We burn the *impepho* while talking to the ancestors, and we also pray over water and ash, and take the whole family outside the house to wash with that mixture".

The prophet who recommended treatment by the diviner, the herbalist and the prayer healer stated: "One can scold the ancestors if they do not respond, just as when they do nothing for those who have *uhlanya* and *izizwe*".

Here again, the indigenous practices for treating specific indigenous diseases are utilized, and prophets, diviners, and herbalists are not rigidly separated in the minds of these respondents, but cooperate with one another.

7. Disregard of cultural norms

Ukudlula

Traditional concept: Disregard of ritual practices
Psychiatric diagnosis: Obsessive compulsive disorder: Kleptomania

The victim of this disease cannot resist stealing, and is a kleptomaniac. The victim is repeatedly involved in offensive things, things which he/she despises. It is said that "The victim is forced by his/her brain to do it".

This condition is caused by:
a) disobedience to authority and parents;
b) bewitchment. For example, if a person steals a diviner's medicated object, that person will forever be subjected to stealing if he/she is not cured;
c) non-observance of the customs when a relative has passed away, or failure to mourn, or the committing of an evil deed during the time of mourning.

Half of the respondents referred only to the prayer healers or prophets as being able to help an afflicted person. Twenty percent referred only to the herbalist, while a further twenty percent referred to the diviner, herbalist and prayer healer. Ten percent referred to the diviner only. The largest majority referred an afflicted person only to the prayer healer or prophet because the rituals in this connection are not as effective. In fact, only prayer is effective because "it is difficult to treat the disease". The disregard of ritual practices is in a sense an offence against these practices. The result is that they will not have the desired effect.

Furthermore, the prayer healers use water which has been blessed. It is "by using the word of God that a person recovers". Prayer healers are also able to pray to and talk to the ancestors asking them to forgive (*xolela*) a person. "The prayer healer/prophet can put hands on, and pray often for the person". For treating this disease the herbalists are preferred to the diviners because of the effective herbs they use. The problem is, after all, cured by using Zulu medicine.

Various treatments are proposed by the prophets for this problem. Herbs are ground and deposited at the place where the person steals. The herbalist can treat the problem "through enema up in the mountains". "The victim must syringe and drain the effect through the mouth (vomit)".

The prayer healers and prophets give the victims cords to wear around the waist, and also they pray for the person, who is given *isiwasho* to drink everyday "with a spoon". The prayer healers "take such a person to a river with running water, and they wash the person's body in the river while they keep on praying for the victim, so that he can get rid of the problem. Then he is taken back home, where he is given *isiwasho* to provoke vomiting and for steaming. Then the healers light the *impepho* and talk to the victim's ancestors, asking them to assist him to get rid of this habit. The healers take water, and mix it with salt and sea water on the body, and "an animal is slaughtered to apologise to the ancestors". A prophet stated "I make an altar, and light seven candles with yellow and blue colours and pray. I slaughter two white chickens, and remove their blood and fat. I burn the fat and blood with *impepho*, and talk to the ancestors over the smoke, asking them to stop this habit of the person".

One prophet, who recommends diviners, herbalists and prayer healers as being able to assist an afflicted person, outlined his own procedure: "I speak to his ancestors, and tell them they have failed to warn him properly. A goat is slaughtered to persuade the forefathers to change the mind of the person. The bile of the goat is taken, and poured over the body of the person, and I again speak to his ancestors to persuade him to discontinue his devious actions, and to change his ways".

The prophet who maintained that diviners could help an afflicted person best stated "I mix the heart and fat of a black sheep, and dust from the road (*izibi zendlela*), and also *muti* called *bulimazi*. A cord is taken and smeared with this mixture, and put under the person's pillow. It will stop him doing the things he has done before, for ever.

None of the respondents, who were all prophets, relied only on prayer as a healing influence. Certain rituals are necessary and the herbalist's, and to a lesser extent the diviner's, assistance are called upon.

D) Various other diseases mentioned by the respondents

ibumbo (spell):

Veneral diseases are difficult to handle, and here western trained medical practitioners are considered to be specifically helpful. This disease is contracted when a person is surreptitiously trapped into getting *muti* on his sexual organs while sleeping with someone else's wife. The prophets use certain medicines for this disease, which cannot be healed through prayer alone. Specific medicines are mixed with those which are used to bring about the disease, and this mixture heals the person.

Hlangothi (lala ngohlangothi—lie on one's side): The victim sweats, and feels tired all the time.

Izintwala: Lice in the person's hair (on the head, eyebrows, and body). People dislike such a person. The condition is ascribed to *muti* poured on the gate of the house of a person, or a footpath where he/she is likely to walk. Jealousy is the motive and the actions bring bad luck. One of the prophets suggested the following: "Cook *impepho* together with dust from the pathway. Give it to the victim for vomiting, steaming and purging. Also, take blue butter with this *muti* for smearing on the affected hair on the body".

Umfutho wegazi (high blood pressure): The condition is considered to be caused mainly by the food a person eats. One prophet stated: "I mix epsom salt, sina leaves, and other things. I cook this mixture for fifteen minutes. Then I give the person a cup of this, and he has to take it three times daily".

iBuba: This refers to the discharge from a woman's vagina "which sticks like glue. Where it has passed, it leaves dark itchy patches. When these patches start to get better, lice will then appear on those patches. They will stick to the woman's vagina, even inside, and affect her womb, and if this continues, she will not be able to bear a child". It is caused by "Zulu medicine" which is put on the floor and the woman walks over it. The prescribed treatment for this is *ukuphalaza* (vomiting), and *ukuchatha* (enemas).

Ukushaya (stroke): The person suffering from this condition feels tired in all the joints, gets very painful headaches, loses balance, falls down, and feels something hitting him/her very severely. This is because people send to him/her *impundulu*[3] or *utikoloshe* (a hairy human being with short legs—feared especially by women) or a baboon which he/she cannot see. It is invisible because it is smeared with *muti*. By way of treatment "the victim is given *muti* to inhale through his/her nose, and *isiwasho*".

Isichitho

Traditional concept: Charm to cause estrangement between lovers

This refers to a situation where a woman's husband does not like her any more. When he sees her he wants to give her a thrashing, and send her away. This woman should take *isiwasho* in order to vomit. She should steam her body, use emetics, have incisions made in her skin (*gcaba*), and put a cord around her waist. This serves as fortification against the onslaughts of the husband.

The situation is mainly due to the fact that the husband has a girl friend who wants him to divorce his wife. The medicine she uses is called *sichitho* which she pours on her face. She calls the woman's name saying loudly that the husband should chase his wife away.

Isibhabo: a person experiences pain on his chest as if something stabs him there with a sharp instrument. A prophet stated that "ropes with different colours, especially red, are put around the waist of the victim and *isiwasho* is also given to provoke vomiting. Incisions are made on the person's chest".

There are numerous treatments proposed for the various diseases. The prophets are considered to be the most effective by some because they have all the metaphysical forces at their disposal—those of the African, and those of the Biblical worlds. They are in contact with the messengers from these worlds.

---

[3] A bird believed to be used by women in witchcraft.

CHAPTER FIVE

THE TASK OF THE PROPHET CONCERNING DEMONS, DEMON POSSESSION AND EVIL SPIRITS

Two samples of fifteen prophets each from Soweto and the environs of Durban were approached concerning demons, demon possession and evil spirits. This brings the number of prophets interviewed in the Rand/ Soweto and Metropolitan Durban and surrounding areas to more than seventy. Other regular interviews have continuously taken place at the Durban beach, where many come for "baptism", which includes exorcism, for receiving more of 'the Spirit' to increase spiritual power, for purification and for wholeness. Not only do the prophets put their patients in the sea water, but they themselves have to undergo this ritual to remove from themselves the evil forces which have left their patients, or simply because they get contaminated and unclean after having been in touch with the demons. They also enter the water to fortify themselves against demons whose power for evil is unlimited.

The task of the prophet (*umprofeti*) and/or prayer healer (*umthandazi*) is that of guardian over their assembled house church or over the congregation in the house church. They have to detect the presence of demons or evil spirits at the door and remove them from persons entering, as well as any evil that might have been brought into the building, before the healing service may commence. Only then may Bible reading start and the prophet or prayer healer say a prayer and be sure that the situation is congenial for healing procedures.

The belief in these destructive forces increases in a socio-economically deprived and unstable situation and the roles of the diviner, herbalist, prayer healer and prophet gain in significance. The socio-economic and political situation is responsible for the insecurity that prevails in the African context—a situation which is projected on demons, as a concretisation of the adverse situation with its numberless adversaries. Such insecurity creates further insecurity, which accounts for the increase of those offices which are symbols of guidance and assistance. Sorcery and evil spirits, regularly referred to as demons, are reflections of an extremely insecure situation where blacks have had to move within what many consider to be the minefields of *apartheid* laws, alienating conditions of work and all the dividing and unjust factors of a large-scale impersonal society. In this situation not only have the diviners increased, but also the prayer healers and prophets, mainly because they can exorcise and heal, create a future as it were, in an unfriendly, often gruelling situation. *Prima facie* they abstain from politics, but deep down in their existential situation they use other methods than political parties and trade unions. This is one of the main reasons why the Ethiopian movement, which initially had a hand in the formation of the South African Native National Congress in 1912 (ANC since 1925) did not maintain close association with it when its political emphases became stronger. Reconciliation in order to obtain peace is the main aim of their ministry.

The enduring belief in witchcraft, sorcery and evil spirits has been greatly neglected in the established churches and their seminaries and theological faculties. This belief still has a prominent place in the daily lives of many Africans as it is often related to disharmony between individuals and between groups, to socio-economic and political circumstances, to misfortune, illness and death. Evil forces and not natural causes are seen as being active behind the scenes, and as responsible for these calamities.Witches and sorcerers are considered to be negative forces. The sorcerer is a poisoner and uses magic, while the witch uses her/his personality (witches are usually women), which is considered to be so powerful as to accomplish goals without the use of magic.

In traditional society the herbalist or medicine man has a vital role in detecting who is responsible for the witchcraft or sorcery used against a victim. He assists in restoring relationships, as conflict or jealousy is usually the main cause for the application of negative instruments against persons disliked or considered to be enemies.

In a survey executed in the Greater Durban and Natal area (cf. Zulu, P. and Oosthuizen, G.C., "Religion and World Outlook", in *Afro-Christian Religion at the grassroots in Southern Africa*, Lewiston/Queenstown/Lampeter, 1991, pp. 334-363) it is stated that:
i) "there is a dialectic between the belief system of any people and the material conditions in which such people find themselves"; and
ii) "religious expression is also man's attempt to explain space-time events, especially where he finds himself powerless in dealing with temporal forces...." (*ibid.*).

Religion can be used either as an instrument to maintain the *status quo* and retard change, as was the case with the Afrikaner churches (which supported the *apartheid* system during the most important era in which South Africa could have changed to a more just and open society), or to effect change.

The AIC were socio-politically as well as religiously inspired, an attempt to delegitimise the existing socio-political order which made itself felt in the mainline missions and churches. The AIC movement involves commitment to a modernization process in that it encourages changing leadership stereotypes, helps to overcome ethnic and communal limitations, grants to women responsible roles (through changing from a passive to a creative orientation, assisting one another in need, in ill health, in a situation of socio-economic and political deprivation), overcomes the static concept of the church and takes the African world view and what it implies seriously. Here is a movement which has taken African advance seriously, and which confronts the forces against this advancement with a realistic approach to the situation in which Africans find themselves. This movement opens up the future; as the diviner confined those adverse forces on the way to the future, so the healers in the AIC also confront them, but within the orbit of the indigenised church, which understands much better than a mainline church of colonial origin what the forces are which the African sees as being in his way.

Spirit possession, too, is a different way of explaining adverse situations. These are seen as pollution, as not natural, and as such fall within the context of African cosmology. Evil spirits are considered to be responsible for the type of illnesses which western-trained medical practitioners fail to detect. Illness here refers not merely to physical but also to mental and psychical discomfort, though it is seldom related to insanity. Spirit possession can increase with increased tension, as a result of the movement away from the traditional way of life and its world view to a more "modern" way of life and its world view—that is, from a situation where a person is attached to a group (for example family peers) to one in which he/she becomes more individualized. During the initial stages of such a situation, spirit possession becomes even more prominent; so does personal purification through cleansing.

No wonder that baptism has become such a widely practised purification rite for many in the indigenous churches, and that exorcism has become closely associated with it. Baptism has developed various connotations, for example, a means of driving out evil spirits, of receiving "more of the Spirit", of receiving strength (fortification), a healing procedure, a means towards discernment of well-disposed and ill-disposed forces. Through baptism the ears of the prophets especially are opened to hear more clearly the voice of the Holy Spirit and/or ancestor spirits. It provides "luck" against the bad luck brought on a person by evil forces.

The orthodox churches have taken a negative attitude to the indigenous healers as if they are *per se* evil. The indigenous churches in general, on the other hand, have taken the adverse forces seriously within the context of the African cosmology and confronts them as real problems, as the consequences of witchcraft, sorcery, demons and evil spirits. Much of society's injustices are categorized in African cosmological terms. Where the major concern is the transition from the old to the new, and where a person becomes marginalised in moving from an established traditional situation to the periphery of a new situation, much suffering is experienced and this is reflected in spirit possession. Evil spirits are considered to be the main obstacles with regard to development and progress. They symbolize reaction to change as well as the vicissitudes of the new situation. Those undergoing the transition fear not only disobeying the ancestors who sanction traditional customs but also the reaction of elders and parents. On the other hand, the new situation forces them to question the traditional way of life and beliefs, and this leads to deep psychological tensions. These changes not only affect the youth and those who work within the changed context, but also the women whose contact with modernization forces has been delayed, and who experience the contact as a cultural shock. This accounts for the large percentage of women who consider themselves to be the targets of evil powers. In this context also, women are bridges between the metaphysical world and the existential situation, with the result that they are the pin-cushions of the adverse forces and are in continuous need of purification.

Witchcraft and sorcery have been largely ignored by the missionaries in Africa because of their deep-seated westernised disposition on these matters. Their highly intellectualised disposition on witchcraft, sorcery, magic, spirit possessions and the reality of demons (with the exception of Satan) has made them turn a blind eye to these forces, which are considered to be out of bounds to anyone associated with Christianity and thus to be totally ignored, whatever their influences might be. The ideological approach of the missionaries regarding these issues has kept the missionary churches largely away from the specific problems of Africa. Of course, no one is happy to see anyone a victim—either in imagination or in reality—of evil forces, but these forces should not be ignored as a result of stereotyped, preconditioned traditions in western-influenced churches when, at the same time, people existentially experience them. They are forces to be reckoned with as they reflect the *Sitz im Leben* (the life situation) of people.

Christian and western-orientated hospitals have adopted negative attitudes rather than trying to understand these phenomena, with the result that no dynamic therapy has developed to treat people when it comes to illnesses which are located in the African cosmology. Recently, psychologists and psychiatrists, whose work has taken them in this direction, have given these issues more attention. The adverse influences can only be addressed through knowledge and not merely by ignoring them as if they are non-existent.

The indigenous churches have taken these issues so seriously that they offer continuous assistance and pastoral care to their flock in a context which they understand.

The antisocial effects of sorcery and witchcraft in a society where harmony in social relationships is vital, affect the very health and well-being of people. This aspect has always been taken into account by the AIC. Reconciliation is thus an important factor within the context of the church. Reconciliation not only implies prayer and putting things right with God but also has to do with man's sin against his fellow human being. It implies that prayer, however important it may be, will not solve the issue on its own. Relationships have been destroyed and disharmony created, and this has to be rectified. Restoring relationships remains a vital issue in Africa (a basic role of the traditional healer).

Reconciliation with the person's community in the traditional context is important. This aspect is taken seriously within the AIC revival services. Such reconciliation in traditional society has to do not only with the living but also with the ancestors, and this aspect is of great significance for many in the AIC. Transition from the microcosmic traditional worldview to the marcocosmic worldview causes many of the set customs, rituals, commands and taboos to be affected, and thus disturbs the relationship with the ancestors. It also leads to sickness, misfortunes, bad luck, attacks by various types of evil forces, and could even culminate in death.

There is a fixed relationship between personal sin and personal affliction (*John* 9:1-3) and although this seems to work in the same way as the Hindu *karma*, it is different from the latter because in this case there is the possibility of reconciliation with those affected, and thus the avoidance of the negative consequences of one's acts. In *Karma* one has to undergo retribution for one's misdeeds. Here sin is not seen lightly, but its consequences can be alleviated through genuine reconciliation in one's concrete situation. Sin involves alienation from one's community and one's family, which for many is as disastrous as being alienated from

God. For some, alienation from their communities is even more disastrous than alienation from God. Each person is seen as responsible for
his/her own sin. The emphasis on individual guilt is important, and this
is recognized in the AIC.

The impression is often given that too much emphasis is put on
witchcraft, sorcery, magic and spirit possession within the AIC. The
deep-seated psychic element involved in all sorcery should be recognized. The real antagonist in Zionism is the sorcerer—it is as if Satan is
pushed into the background because of the strong stress which is placed
on the looming presence of this evil force. Satan is not seen to work
through certain rituals but to tempt people directly to what is morally
wrong, such as violent acts which disturb the peace of the group. Satan
attacks the group, the sorcerer attacks the individual; Satan is spiritual,
the sorcerer is human (cf. Kiernan, J.P., *The role of the adversary in Zulu
Zionist Churches*, unpublished, 1985). However, a more realistic functional approach to sorcery is called for than to ignore it or wish it away.
Witchcraft is less problematic to the prophets in the AIC than the
sorcerer. Sorcery, however, is regularly referred to by them as witchcraft.

Public confession during the service plays a significant role in most
of the AIC. Here the emphasis is placed on the person who has been
wronged—only this person is in a position to give absolution, and not
any intermediary. When mutual trust has been restored the offending
person can be reintegrated into the group. The prophet through dreams
and visions receives information on who is responsible for acts which
disturb harmonious relationships between individuals. Antisocial behaviour is a serious moral offence in the AIC. The attitude with some is
that a witch cannot be converted, because he/she is the symbol of evil.
Most witches are women. In Zionism the adversary is always confronted
but never really overcome. The scapegoat mentality, whereby the destructive instincts are projected onto an individual, is now projected onto
the adversary who continuously confronts the group.

This projection of their reactions against an adversary, unifies the
group. Among themselves public confession takes place and restoration
is effected. Their small AIC communities take the place of the extended
family and here the church acts as an intensely sensitive community in
which the spiritual nerves are deeply interrelated. Here, one can speak
of a corporate personality. Here, members are protected and fortified
against their adversaries through the ritual acts they observe and the
sacred objects they use and wear, such as cold water which is prayed

over, uniforms, cords, medals, photos of leaders, and holy sticks. These acts and objects fortify them against their enemies. Traditional fetishes and amulets, which continue to have a hold on the subconscious, cannot be erased with the stroke of a pen or with Bible texts. In this context, the church has adopted its own protecting objects—even the pious reference to Bible texts could have the same function as fetishes and amulets.

It is still to be established how the Zionists have been influenced with regard to their uniforms, candles, ash and water, etc. The colours of the uniforms are interpreted in the traditional way, with blue signifying love, green faithfulness and white purity. The use of candles probably derives from the mainline churches but here the Holy Spirit or 'the Spirit' is represented by white candles, and the ancestors by those with green, red and yellow[1] colours. Ash in water, or *muti*, which is used to strengthen the Zulu king at the First Fruit Ceremonies, conveys strength in the AIC context. Illness means loss of strength, of numinous power, the power which is behind and in everything in various degrees according to African cosmology, and this power (*umoya, amandla*) has to be restored.

Staves go back to the Old Testament, recalling especially that of Moses, through which he effected miracles. The staff also recalls the stick which in traditional society an African male carried, signifying authority. It not only serves as a fortification against the enemy, but also attacks the evil spirits and demons at healing sessions when rubbed against the body of a victim. These evil forces are "thrown out", exorcised at the sea, river or dam, or during regular services, and in this way diseases are driven away. The illness is not returned to the sorcerer or evil doer, as is effected through the practices of the herbalists. It is clear from the above that the African cosmology cannot be erased overnight in the minds of those nurtured in it. When aspects vital for them are not ministered to in the churches, ie. if their deepest needs are not meaningfully addressed, they revert to the traditional securities. The historic churches, the missionary societies and their missionary outreach have to a large extent alienated the indigenous ministers—who emulated their masters during the colonial era—from many of their flock. The situation has gradually been changing since just before and after independence, but alienation from the ministry of the Church in Africa has

---

[1] When healing procedures take place the ancestors of the officiant and those of the patient have to meet (often described as having to be reconciled). Usually the white and yellow candles are used each representing the ancestor or a group. The white candles often also represent the Holy Spirit as well as the ancestors of the officiant.

helped to give the indigenous churches and the development of the indigenous church movement a decisive impetus.

The metaphysical forces of adversity are not fictions of the mind for large sections in the African communities, from the uneducated to the educated. Mr X, with a university degree, a member of the *Christian Catholic Apostolic Holy Spirit Church in Zion*, came to the beach, where he planted eight candles in the sand, lit them and put ten- and twenty-cent pieces alongside the candles. Another man stood beside the candles with staves. Mr X related that he was being attacked by evil spirits which were "thrown up on him" (*phosa* = to throw, bewitch, cause lightning to strike a person) by the evil acts of jealous colleagues in the office where he worked. They were practising sorcery against him. This was effective, but not as effective as they hoped. He stated: "What they did not realise is that the armies of Pharoah perished in the Red Sea, as mighty as they were, when they persecuted women and children in the desert. It was only one man with a big staff who prayed to God who caused their destruction.

The people who believe may go anywhere ... my days are numbered by Jesus Christ, not by witchdoctors ... the greatest secret is not known by these people. He has principles which will never change ... I failed one of my major subjects three times, not because I am a fool but because they bewitched me with *muti* ... but I had a vision on Saturday 16 August 1986. I felt like singing songs which had to do with the new world ... I also wrote to Michael Cassidy of Africa Enterprise ... they prayed for me.... I could feel the difference ... a very great difference.... and in spite of witchcraft.... I could feel the power of prayer and that I was free".

One of the major tasks of prayer healers in the AIC is to assist victims of witchcraft and sorcery, which is often described as spirit possession. With the rapid social change experienced in industrial sectors of the community, and especially in fast-developing urbanized areas, traditionally-orientated people experience great difficulties in adapting and fall back on old securities to guard them against what for them are the activities of evil forces in the new situation. The Zionist adversary has therapeutic value in the sense that it is an external danger which has to be confronted, not a danger which is internalized and so leads to the formation of severe individual neurosis. As is obvious in the earlier section on the handling of bewitchment, sorcery and spirit possession, the prophets concentrate on these phenomena as the major external dangers which have to be confronted in order to protect interpersonal relationships. Bewitchment and sorcery evoke mistrust in the environment, and in the AIC this mistrust assists in keeping the group together.

The dangerous situation in which the AIC find themselves derives from their independent existence among many forces. The forces can take hold of a person and direct his/her life without the person being responsible for his/her acts. In the AIC, public confession emphasizes personal guilt, but in sharing his/her predicament with the group, the person confessing finds deep inner satisfaction. Furthermore, these people are able to express their inner feelings within the context of their world view and this in itself has therapeutic value. To a large extent, the AIC has retained sensitivity towards the indigenous culture. Since the colonial era, indigenous culture has received more attention in many established churches than it did during that era of foreign domination. The leadership of these mainline, so-called "mission", churches was often not only de-Africanised but also colonialised, thus becoming estranged form its own people and irrelevant to the future of the African people.

The established churches in general have hardly any rituals counter-acting the effects of witchcraft and sorcery, while the AIC give attention to these aspects. They may be judged as bordering on non-christian practices, but the utilizing of such practices has therapeutic value. Many members of the mainline churches would appreciate pastoral attention given to those who feel plagued by sorcery, witchcraft and spirit possession. Unfortunately, many indigenous ministers are so condi-tioned that they ignore these issues as being below the dignity of advanced people. Life, health and wholeness are vital issues within the African context and the forces that wish to harm a person through trying to destroy them have to be taken seriously and counteracted. Here, symbolic acts and signs are of great significance, for example, the various rituals that are performed, the water and ash therapy, the objects used, such as holy staves, oil, cords, emetics, even the slaughtering of chickens and animals. Theological problems arise from the often-created impression that these rituals take place in the traditional rather than the Christian context.

Exorcism is a major activity in the AIC; shouting in the ear of a person (which is also done to open his/her ears to the injunctions of the ancestors and the Holy Spirit), hitting the spirit-possessed person with staves, or with the hands, especially on the shoulders and arms, are acts which drive out the evil forces. This takes place at practically every healing ceremony. The continuous attention to these forces is a major feature in an overwhelming section of the AIC. At the beach, confessions are made to the prophet, prayer healer and the "woman guardian" (*umkhokheli*) by those who wish to be blessed in the water. Young boys confess also to the *umkhokheli*. The adult men go to the prophet, minister or bishop. The prophet of the *The Christian Tabernacle Church of God* stated at the beach "if you want to get rid of the evil spirits, fast for seven days, and then they will rapidly remove themselves when you touch the sea water". The established churches discourage these activities, which has given the AIC prayer healers/prophets and others the advantage of becoming known as effective healers who understand these matters. In spite of the fact that the established African Church members often formally reject phenomena such as demon possession as outmoded superstition, many of their members receive assistance from the AIC healers or remain with these problems unsolved in their spiritual lives. But even in the established churches interesting changes have taken place in the African context during the last two decades.

Scripture takes these issues seriously, as is seen in the attitude of Jesus Christ to demon possession. Spirit-possessed people ask for serious attention, and a church in the African context which ignores this does so to its own disadvantage, as it is culturally irrelevant in this respect. Revival services of the AIC, in which spirit possession is treated, usually have members of the established churches present, seeking help. The approach of the AIC to the demon-possessed is appreciated, in spite of the fact that they have had no formal training in handling such phenomena, which often arise from psychological and social problems. Insanity and epilepsy are often ascribed to spirit possession. Social circumstances lead to psychological experiences of tension which are described as spirit possession.

Different types of spirits could take hold of a person or influence his/her life. A specific ancestor may have turned against a descendent, troubling him/her through dreams, illness or misfortune. Ancestor misfortune is never as serious as that sent by witches (cf. Hammond-Tooke, W.D., "The aetiology of Spirit in Southern Africa", *African Studies*, 1988). Such ancestors usually allow rather than send evil, ie. they withdraw their protection from members of their progeny (cf. Kiernan, J.P., "The 'problem of evil' in the context of ancestral intervention in the affairs of the living in Africa", *Man* 17, 287-301). To be deprived of such protection in a situation where vertical and horizontal relationships are of primary concern is for many Africans more serious than death.

It has been indicated that witch beliefs and accusations are ways of explaining suffering and misfortune in personal and social life. Certain persons are in a position to bring about evil, of which there are two types. The first type consists of those with an inherent, mystical quality. They go about invisibly causing misfortune and even death, as in the case of witches and their familiars, such as animals, snakes or birds, which are sent at night to do their evil work. The second type consists of sorcerers, who use special medicine (*muti*) to disturb people, cause illness and even kill. Evil in Southern Africa is considered either as evil incarnate (the witch), or evil inherent in matters on which the injunctions of the sorcerer have been expressed (cf. Hammond-Tooke, and Berglund, A.I., *Zulu thought—the patterns and symbolism*, Cape Town, David Philip, 1976, pp. 236-266). Evil is associated with antisocial attitudes and actions such as envy, hatred, jealousy, angry attitudes, which threaten the basis of social life. These negative forces are bound to increase in situations where individualism prevails at the expense of social cohesion, as is evident in situations of rapid social change.

Apart from ancestral spirits (some effective, others not because they are only in the distant background, such as three generations away), there are also witches and sorcerers, the "spirits of affliction", which are believed actually to possess the individual and which are associated with possession cults in which such spirits actually enter a person's body. These spirits have appeared in South Africa and Mozambique during the last eighty years. The evidence at the disposal of those who study these phenomena points to Zimbabwe as the locus of origin. The Nguni in South Africa had "spirit mediumship" rather than "spirit possession" (cf. Hammond-Tooke). While spirit mediumship is an integral part of the Nguni traditional religion, spirit possession entered from across the South African borders. Today, however, spirit possession has become a major issue in South Africa, with exorcism a regular feature in AIC services. Possession thus takes place by alien spirits, not (or only very rarely) by ancestral spirits. Illness precedes such possession by alien spirits. Therapy involves exorcism, where the spirit is called upon to react to questions put to it, manifest itself and leave the victim. Women are possessed more often than men by these alien spirits. This type of affliction is seen as a response to social change, and indirectly as a reaction against the traditional system dominated by the ancestors who uphold patrilineal and male interests. Hammond-Tooke states "so new spirit entities are created to symbolize and facilitate new attitudes and behaviour patterns".

Masamba ma Mpolo indicates that even in the case of bewitchment, such beliefs are functional in various respects. For example, from the psychological angle, they assist a person to deal with the personality crisis which he/she encounters as a result of social pressures. The victim is "allowed", as someone of worth within the context in which she finds herself, to mistrust her environment—bewitchment is thus related to a process of identity formation, to a network of psychological dynamics. It has another function, namely, the symbolic acting out of inner guilt feelings. The influence of evil spirits or "ancestor presence" on a person is so strong that he/she could hardly be responsible for specific actions and hardly feel guilty about them. And yet, a deep sense of guilt can develop. Masambo ma Mpolo refers to a patient who was married, had one child, was divorced and developed acute anxiety and neurosis. She experienced a repetitive dream in which her grandfather told her to slaughter a goat at the village for her uncles, who were against the untraditional way in which her marriage was performed. She eventually adhered to her grandfather's injunctions which came through the dreams she experienced, and in that village "she experienced a total catharsis and returned to Kinshasha a new person" (cf. Masamba ma Mpolo, "Kindoki as diagnosis and therapy" in *African Theological Journal* 13, 1984, 3, p. 152).

The established churches reacted against such phenomena as "pagan" while the AIC gave attention to them more than a century ago in Southern Africa. The AIC in general refused to reject these acts as merely "pagan" because, although they may not be "Christian", they are realities which need close attention. Syncretism is not *per se* superstitious but, even if it raises problems, through it the Christian message can touch the depth dimension of African existence. Africa's first and second century Christianity has not completely alienated itself from traditional spirituality. Healing is still basically a religious and holistic activity, and exorcism is not a circus act but of vital significance for the very existence of a group. The demonic powers, the forces of evil, are considered to be real—in this context this is not merely superstition. Popular African religiosity accepts these forces as real. Although the AIC do not reflect theologically in a scholarly manner on these issues, they give attention to them. They have helped through the years to retain the equilibrium of the African community in this country in spite of its adverse socio-economic, political and racial dispositions and its rapid social change. The prophets' approach to demons and evil spirits could be deduced from responses received from AIC prophets in Soweto and in and around Metropolitan Durban. The prophets in Soweto are highly urbanized;

those in Metropolitan Durban and its outskirts are in more regular contact with the rural areas. Of the more than seventy prophets approached in these areas, the large majority's activities are related to the negative forces which confront their church groups. Many still attach great value to the African indigenous healers who understand the beliefs concerning spirit possession and demons and the consequences of the acts of these adverse forces. All the replies to a rather exhaustive questionnaire came from the prophets who act as healers and advisors, thus restoring the role of the medicine man/diviner in the AIC context. The replies were as follows:

A) DEMONS AND POSSESSION

Question 1

What do you understand by demons?

1. Demons are evil forces which work for Satan, and Satan assists them in fulfilling his aims.
2. Demons are Satan's agents, or fallen angels who rebelled against God and they are now loyal to Satan. They are all out to do any type of evil against God's laws.
3. Demons are those forces which inhabit some people. These people claim to have ability to foretell. Some claim to be faith healers. Their medicines are made by people from certain roots and herbs. They are forces which work within *inyangas* (herbalists) or *isangomas* (diviners).
4. Demons are evil spirits which are removed from people and transferred to pigs. This is why the consumption of pork is avoided.
5. Demons are evil spirits produced by ghosts.
6. Demons are bad spirits which possess people through horrifying dreams.

A few did not know/were not sure.

Question 2

What do you understand by demon possession?

1. Demon possession occurs when the Devil enters a person in order to influence him/her to such an extent that this person performs unfamiliar, undesired, ridiculous and even unnecessary things.
2. It takes place when someone's life is not under God's control; demons

find it easier to possess such a person. It also occurs when a person has a negative attitude towards God's laws; the demons take advantage of such a person.

3. People who are possessed are viewed as having super-spiritual or magical powers which enable them to perform unusual feats.
4. It happens when *inyangas* use herbs and roots to make other people sick or even kill them. *Inyangas* and *isangomas* are regarded as possessed people.
5. A possessed person may cry, jump about, speak aloud or feel dizzy.
6. A possessed person is characterized by the experience of horrifying dreams and is susceptible to illnesses.
7. A possessed person is usually mentally deranged and suffers form hallucinations.
8. A possessed person fails to make any progress.
9. Demon possession means that a person is controlled and abused by an evil force to such an extent that his own will is completely overruled, while the Holy Spirit gives scope to the free will of a person, ie. the Holy Spirit co-operates with a person.

Question 3

What do you understand by evil spirits?
1. Evil spirits are the same as demons.
2. Evil spirits are the forces which work together with Satan to promote anything evil on earth. They are forces which work against righteousness and order on earth.
3. Evil spirits are agents of the demons and they are even worse than demons.
4. They are those forces which perform evil deeds through "witchdoctors", and they continuously encourage them to do evil deeds.

Question 4

How does a person get possessed?
1. Demon possession occurs when Satan and demons take control of a person's life to such an extent that the person performs unusual deeds or acts. A possessed person may believe that he/she has to act in an unusual manner.
2. A person gets possessed when he/she is not in God. Demons take advantage of such a person and they live in him/her. This is common

among non-Christians.
3. "Witchdoctors" use herbs to cause a person to be possessed. People who are seen as having some super-spiritual or magical power are the ones who are partially possessed by evil spirits.
4. The victim gets sick and ends up being possessed. This is caused by witchcraft.
5. Ancestors, not only evil spirits, may possess a person when they want to use a person to convey messages.

Question 5

Is spirit possession the same as what is described as illness by a western doctor?
1. Spirit possession is what western doctors may describe as illness. This is because western doctors call everything illness even where evil spirits are involved.
2. It is more than illness and is related to *Ukufa kwaBantu*, ie. it is a specific African illness or disease; it is stronger than ordinary illness and it is much more complex to cure.
3. A western doctor is not acquainted with spirit possession unless he/she is a Christian, because the Bible speaks about this.
Some did not know.

Question 6

Has spirit possession increased during the last ten years in your area?
1. Yes, because there are many people who seem to have the spirit of prophecy and there are many faith healers who have to cope with spirit-possessed people.
2. Many people visit the respondents with the sole purpose of seeking aid concerning spirit possession. This problem has increased greatly in the urban areas.
3. While the majority of respondents emphasized the above-mentioned increase of spirit-possessed cases, a few stated that spirit possession has decreased due to western civilization and progress.
4. For a few it remained constant.

B) WITCHCRAFT AND SORCERY

Question 7

What is witchcraft?
1. Witchcraft is the result of jealousy and evil desires, which compel a person to achieve his/her undesirable plans by using *muti* (medicine) to kill other people.
2. It is part of Satan's work in utilizing the human mentality to harm other human beings. This destructive power may take any form but it ends up in killing other human beings.
3. The evil deeds of *inyangas* (herbalists) cause them to end up being witchdoctors. They use herbs and roots (*muti*) to bewitch those whom they resent.
4. Witchcraft is effected when someone's food has been poisoned with the aim of killing that person.
5. Witchcraft involves the use of African medicine in order to harm people physically, mentally and spiritually.

Question 8

How does witchcraft operate?
1. It is Satan's force within some people, working to harm or destroy other people, either by effecting unkind acts against them to hurt them physically or mentally, or by killing them.
2. It emanates from the heart of a person who, for example, is jealous of someone's prosperity and, as a consequence, utilizes ways and means to harm or to kill that person. It involves the mixing of herbs or medicines and the transference of such a mixture to the victim concerned, by devious means getting it into the victim's food, drink, or certain parts of the body, or onto the path on which he/she walks, or into the house, and so on.
3. Witchdoctors use herbs and roots as well as evil spirits to persecute or kill others; the combination of evil spirits and *muti* over which the person's name has been called is considered to be the most effective. Some did not know.

Question 9

What is sorcery? (Cf. reference to it in the Bible: *Deut.* 18:10; 2 *Kings* 17:17.)

1. Sorcery is African magic through which incredible acts are performed which people see as the result of magic. Though some people do not initially believe in these acts, they end up believing in them because of what they experience. It is a man's power over nature which allows him to do unusual things.
2. Sorcery is the same as witchcraft, except that it is more subtle and dangerous than direct witchcraft. Objects and ingredients are used in sorcery; in witchcraft the psychic forces of the so-called witch are utilized.
3. Sorcery occurs when a person has unconsciously been made to eat something which is poisonous or has been killed by lightning.
4. Sorcery occurs when a person has been put under the spell of spirits such as *amandiki, izizwe*, through the use of objects and ingredients.

Question 10

How does sorcery take place?

1. A witchdoctor may use herbs and over those herbs call the name of the person to be victimized. As a result such a person may eventually suffer from *amandiki* or *izizwe*.
2. A person who actually performs sorcery is really aiming at hurting, harming and even killing other people.
3. The demons use a person as a medium for the performance of supernatural acts which amaze people or terrify them. These acts could be the result of the influence of Satan.
4. African magicians use some animals or objects to perform peculiar acts. (This is actually witchcraft.)

A few did not know/were not sure.

C) Witchcraft in the present situation

Question 11

Have rural migrants to urban areas more difficulty with spirit possession than those who have been there long? If so, why?

1. Yes, because they are attached to their traditional way of life; they are still attached to superstitious perspectives. They use *muti* (medicinal/

herbal mixtures) to cause illnesses such as *ufufunyane, izizwe, amandiki* and the like. They have the ability to call up evil spirits which can attack many people.

2. Yes, because their life style is such that they are living in fear of invisible forces. But as soon as they begin to adapt to urban life, they begin, on the whole, to experience relief from such fears.
3. Yes, because rural people are not highly enlightened; they are uneducated, so that they fail to make realistic judgements on intangible matters.
4. Yes, this is the case because religion has never been successful in assisting rural people to abandon their traditional practices. They do not get real religious education and they "lack western experience".
5. Yes, this stems from the fact that they do not have enough contact with other cultures and their customs.
6. A few stated that experience of rural or urban life is irrelevant, since urban prophets are approached by urban as well as rural people and they come with identical problems. Rural people have their own prophets to counteract such evil spirits.

Question 12

How do people get rid of witchcraft and sorcery?
1. Through prayer and faith in God.
2. They approach faith healers, prophets, *inyangas* and *isangomas*. A few approach western doctors.
3. Through prayer and the utilization of holy water for vomiting, steaming and as an emetic.

Question 13

What role does the *inyanga* play in removing witchcraft?
1. An *inyanga* is qualified in using herbs/roots. As a result he may know how to deal with anything pertaining to herbs—even those which are used by witchdoctors in trying to kill others. The *inyanga*, as an African doctor, knows how to help people by providing the appropriate herbs.
2. The *inyanga* provides protective medicines against witchcraft. He diagnoses illness and provides remedies. The *inyanga* uses bones to identify and diagnose illness and knows how to remove the effects of witchcraft.

3. A few maintained that the *inyanga* is capable of removing the effects of witchcraft.

Question 14

What role does the *isangoma* play?
1. The *isangoma* is important since he/she "points out our enemies, especially those who bewitch us".
2. An *isangoma* has a major role in removing witchcraft/illness. He/she can be helped by his/her ancestors in healing people. He/she diagnoses and predicts, and provides traditional *muti* for healing purposes.
3. The *isangoma* is not as well advanced in the knowledge of herbs as is the *inyanga* (herbalist).
4. For a few the *isangoma* is the same as the *inyanga*.
5. The *isangoma* has the ability "to prophesy and foretell the future".
A few did not know/were not sure.

Question 15

Do the established churches understand the problems of bewitching?
1. Some do, while others do not.
2. No, they do not understand these problems.
3. They deny the existence of these problems and they simply ignore them.
4. They do understand, but in many cases they pretend that they do not recognize these problems.
A few did not know/were not sure.

Question 16

Do the Zionist churches understand the problems of bewitching?
1. Yes, because even Zionists are possessed and they like to talk about such problems as bewitching.
2. Yes, they have faith healers and prophets, and they organize prayer meetings and healing services for the sick. It is, however, believed too that they also become involved in bewitching, especially when they fight for leadership among themselves.
3. There is "the Spirit" which works among Zionist prophets, and these prophets know how witchcraft works.

Question 17

Does belief in evil spirits affect the thinking of people in the modern situation?

1. Yes, this is because anything whose existence you acknowledge, whether good or bad, will always control your actions as well as your responses to certain stimuli. This also means that a person in such a situation cannot live freely, but will always feel more motivated by fear of offending evil forces than fear of God. People are in great need of enlightenment, which implies understanding all the forces. In this case, knowledge becomes the major factor in conquering the evil forces, and this involves a fundamental process of transition from an emphasis on washing and emetics to one on the strength of an "enlightened mind".

   This theme came through with a minority of the respondents, and is basically related to the struggle between traditional customs and the Gospel. These respondents wish to emphasize that the penetration of the Gospel inoculates people against the evil forces with the result that the traditional practices become obsolete, or are even taken as a sign of disbelief in the efficacy of the Gospel. Others, on the contrary, say that it is precisely because the traditions are forgotten or neglected that people experience the many adverse circumstances. All this reflects the problem of the struggle between the old and the new, between the traditional and the "modern", between—according to many of those in the original pentecostal churches and the classic Ethiopian, Zionist and Apostolic churches—spiritual enlightenment and traditional retardation.

2. Yes, it creates problems in that people cannot think positively, for example, about what should be done and how to progress. They are more concerned about bewitching than about progressive responses. This indicates how progress has been hampered by a situation which forces people to think in terms of sorcery and bewitchment, with all its negative consequences.

3. It is a hindrance where bewitching and sorcery bring certain diseases upon people, such as mental disturbances, fear, distrust, malrelationships, etc.

4. A few stated that it does not affect the thinking of people in the modern situation—at least not much in the urban areas.

D) Women and their role concerning African-orientated diseases

Question 18

Are more women possessed than men? If so, why?

1. Yes, this is the fulfilment of prophecy that in the last days many things will take place. Secondly this happens because evil spirits try by all means to win everyone to follow them and to listen to their demands and many women are affected.
2. No, according to a minority of the respondents, there are not more possessed women than men. Spirit possession is due to the fact that many read the Bible, which speaks about spirit possession, and they even hear Christians talking about it.
3. Many churches and many faith healers/prophets aid the possessed and are active among both men and women.
4. No, there is no great difference between men and women in this connection since people have always been possessed. (NB: One could agree with Lewis that the high incidence of possession in women in this case also "cannot very possibly be ascribed to any inherent biological prediposition on their part. On the contrary, the facts here point to a common denominator of deprivation, frustration and discontent" (cf. Lewis, I.M., "A Structural approach to witchcraft and spirit possession" in Douglas, M., *Witchcraft, Confessions and Accusations*, London, Tavistock, 1970, p. 214). Another factor is the definite middle position women have between the metaphysical forces and those around them. This accounts for their predominance in traditional society as diviners.)

Question 19

Are there more women faith healers/prophets than men?
The majority of the respondents were convinced there are, as women traditionally played a mediator role between the ancestors and their progeny. Some stated that the sexes are almost equally represented, there being slightly more female than male faith healers/prophets. A few stated that they are not sure. Others maintained that women are more easily converted into Christianity than men. The fact is that there are more women prayer healers than men, and more prophetesses in specific areas and denominations.

E) Protection from sorcery

Question 20

Can objects such as staves, stars, photos of leaders, uniforms and candles ward off evil spirits?
1. Yes, candles ward off evil spirits because evil forces retreat from light. But faith in God is more effective, stated some of the respondents.
2. Many of the respondents agreed that these objects are effective while some added that this depends upon their use in accordance with the guidance of the Holy Spirit, on what has been suggested by the Holy Spirit. All these objects have a repelling function.
3. A few stated they have not any special power, that they are not specially effective.

Question 21

How does this compare with the medals, crucifixes, rosaries in the established churches?
1. Yes, rosaries and crucifixes are useful in protecting a person just as are the staves, candles, cords, stars, uniforms and other objects used by the indigenous churches.
2. It is the Holy Spirit which tells a person in the indigenous churches what to use.
3. The attitudes to these objects differ according to people's churches, and these attitudes are influenced by the depth of a person's belief in the effectiveness of these objects.
4. Through dreams and visions those in the indigenous churches are informed what to use, while in the established churches the objects used are available to everyone who is a member of the church.
Some did not know/were not sure.

Question 22

What do you do round your house to ward off evil?
1. Put candles at the corners of the house. Pray over ash which is mixed with water, then sprinkle this mixture inside the house. Hang ropes/ cords inside the house and a flag.
2. Hang ropes and a crucifix inside the house, and sprinkle holy water, ie. water mixed with ash and prayed over.

3. Put a candle at every corner of the house and at the gate of the yard.
4. River stones and candles are put at the corners of the house.
5. Yellow flags and protective plants are put around the house.
6. Holy water with salt is sprinkled inside and outside the house to ward off evil spirits.
7. Rosaries are worn by some as protection against evil forces.
8. The *inyanga* is called in to apply protective measures around the house, which then fortify the house and the residents against witchcraft.
9. A few stated that they only put their trust in God and believe that He will protect them.

F) REASONS FOR BEING PLAGUED BY FORCES OF EVIL

Question 23

Are there many people who are plagued by evil forces? Why?
1. Yes, this is because there is a lack of enlightenment. Witchcraft is still widely practised. By witchcraft, sorcery is meant; some respondents do not make a distinction between these two activities.
2. People are plagued by these forces because they do not observe their traditional customs, ie. they are not enlightened so as to see these customs in their true perspective.
3. There are not many people plagued by evil forces because the Gospel has penetrated the lives of people, and it has managed to demonstrate God's power in protecting people and this is conspicuous in urban areas. Here there is a firm belief in the power of the Gospel message vis-à-vis these forces.
4. Yes, because people do not attend services where the congregation can pray for their protection against evil forces.
5. Because people do not visit African doctors or faith healers/prophets.
6. Yes, there are many people plagued by evil forces because these forces see that the world is coming to an end, therefore they try by all means to fulfil their objectives as soon as possible.
7. Because of the population explosion there are many people, which leads to an increase in the activities of these forces.

Question 24

Should a bewitched person be taken to hospital? If not, why not?

1. No, western doctors will fail to cure such a person since they have no experience how to treat *Ukufa KwaBantu*, ie. they do not understand African illnesses. Western doctors fail in their treatment of such illnesses. Only such persons who have eaten poisoned food (*idliso*) should be taken to hospital.
2. Such a person should be taken to a faith healer who has proved himself/herself in the handling of these types of diseases.
3. Some stated that such a person should be taken to African doctors such as *inyangas* and *isangomas*.
4. A few maintained the victim should be taken to a hospital.

Question 25

Should certain traditional beliefs be taken into consideration in healing procedures?

1. Traditional beliefs should always be considered whenever a person is practising healing. Any healing practice should largely be effected in the context of traditional beliefs.
2. A few of the prophets emphasized that the Holy Spirit always gives guidance on what should be done during the healing process.

Some did not know.

Question 26

Are dreams important or should they be ignored?

1. They are very important and God uses them for communication purposes. Through dreams certain information is relayed or the meaning of something explained.
2. Dreams are important, since faith healers rely on them for the diagnosis of illnesses and for suggestions from the ancestors and from the Holy Spirit for healing methods and procedures.
3. A few prophets maintained that they are sometimes useful and sometimes useless, depending on the source from which they come. Messages can be sent through dreams by the Holy Spirit, by the ancestors and even by bad spirits.

Question 27

Do the AIC take witchcraft seriously? Why and how?
1. Yes, this is because they have their own faith healers as well as prophets to provide healing for the victims.
2. Yes, this stems from the fact that they arrange prayer meetings and healing sessions during which they pray specially for the sick and perform various healing procedures.
3. Yes, they provide protective devices such as holy water, ropes/cords and uniforms to restore a person's health and to retain it. Protection against evil forces is a major concern.

Question 28

What do sorcery and witchcraft do with regard to interrelationships?
1. They destroy people's relationships because of the hatred and jealousy behind those acts. Such acts also affect the mental, physical and spiritual health of people.
2. They destroy relationships even between relatives.
3. They cause enmity or hostility between rivals, as the acts of sorcery and witchcraft are utilized to destroy or disturb the aims, success or prestige of rivals. They are even used in sport.

Question 29

Does confession play a role in solving the bad relationships brought about by witchcraft?
1. Confession to whom the wrong has been done is important, not only because it may solve the witchcraft problem, but because it may resolve any problem. A wrong is done to someone and it is no use just to settle this to God in prayer—the person(s) against whom the wrong was done should be approached in the correct manner. Public confessions are also important.
2. Sometimes, it does help if "the Spirit" tells a person to do it.
3. Only a few maintained that confession does not play a role, and that only prayer can lead to positive results.

Question 30

Can the ancestors be responsible for witchcraft? Why?
1. Yes, if they are angry about something; they may even punish deviants.
2. Others stated that they perform protection functions and they provide for the needs of their relatives.
3. A few prophets maintained that only herbs and medicines are responsible for witchcraft, and not ancestors, "because they are holy and they are close to God".
4. A few stated that those ancestors who had evil hearts when they were still alive can be responsible for witchcraft. As a result, they continue with their evil actions after death.
5. Others considered witchdoctors capable of using ancestors to bewitch.

Question 31

Why should an animal be slaughtered?
1. To thank the ancestors.
2. "It is our traditional practice to slaughter animals when we want to communicate with or commemorate our ancestors".
3. To thank God.
4. A few respondents stated: "to have a party", ie. such slaughtering no longer has religious connotations, it has been demythologised. The ancestors are not invoked. Thus, here also, the road of "enlightenment", according to those with this point of view, is being followed. The few who hold this view are largely in the mainline AIC. This approach could be similar, in the view of some, to that of Hindus who maintain that yoga is merely related to fitness exercises, in spite of the existence of different types of yoga which are not merely physical exercises but which are embedded in Hindu religion. Basically, however, those who take this stand reject sacrifices to ancestors.

Question 32

Is prayer enough to counteract witchcraft?
1. Prayer is enough to counteract any kind of a problem, not only witchcraft. Even holy water used in such cases is converted from ordinary water to holy water through prayer.
2. The majority of the respondents, however, stated that prayer is not

enough by itself, but should be coupled with other means, ie. ritual acts and *muti*.

Question 33

Should one leave these problems to God or do something oneself?
1. Yes, everything should be left to God and if God wants to do anything, He will communicate it through His prophets. This is because God is capable of solving all kinds of problems.
2. A number of the prophets stated that God has given one a mind to think with, therefore it is essential to do something about one's situation.
3. "He/she must approach prophets or *inyangas* or *isangomas* to get some form of assistance", was the reply of eighty percent of the respondents.

Question 34

Can witchcraft be responsible for bad relationships? How can these be restored?
1. Yes, it has to do with bad relationships, but these can be restored by having faith in God as well as through prayer.
2. Bad relationships are caused by evil forces which want to destroy good human relations, and this cannot be restored only through prayer. In the African context retribution is necessary—the one to whom a wrong has been done should be approached in order to rectify the matter.
3. They can be restored by consulting African doctors as well as faith healers.
4. Witchcraft leads to bad relationships, which can only be restored by prayer and confession. Witchcraft disturbs relationships so that they are difficult to restore.

Question 35

Is it enough just to preach against witchcraft?
1. Preaching can be strong and effective to combat any evil practice.
2. Preaching is not enough, but should be coupled with prayer.
3. Preaching, praying and holy water are useful in combating witchcraft.
4. No, preaching is not sufficient; the *inyangas* and *isangomas,* as faith healers, should be consulted to provide remedial aid.

Question 36

Is confession in public—before the congregation—important?
1. It should be made before the congregation, but it should be genuine and meaningful.
2. If it is for the benefit of either the public or the congregation, it should be made in public but if it is not, it is not important, ie. it depends on whether the person has to restore his/her relationship with the public or the congregation.
3. No, it is not compulsory, but depends on the type of confession which is made and the reason for confessing.
4. For a few respondents it is not important at all.

G) THE ROLE OF TRADITIONAL HEALERS AND WESTERN-TRAINED DOCTORS

Question 37

Should diviners be consulted to diagnose one's sickness?
1. One should consult the *isangoma* for any problem; the *isangoma* should name the sickness, which implies that he/she utters a word of rebuke over the evil forces responsible for the illness.
2. No, but one should trust God only and pray.
3. A few stated that one should consult western doctors for the diagnosis of one's illness.

Question 38

Should one consult the *inyanga* to diagnose one's sickness?
1. Yes, to diagnose sickness and to name it, ie. to expel the evil forces responsible for it.
2. No, it is better to trust God than traditional doctors.
3. A few stated that Christians are not allowed to consult the *inyanga*. Here the *isangoma* is not mentioned. Surveys have indicated that the *isangoma* is much more highly respected than the *inyanga*. Many of the respondents emphasized that the *inyanga* gives *muti* to kill.
Some did not know.

Question 39

Who is the more effective: the *inyanga* or the *isangoma*?
1. Some considered the *isangoma* to be more effective in restoring health than the *inyanga*.
2. Others considered the *inyanga* more effective in restoring peoples' health.
3. Most of the respondents considered both effective. Traditional healers have thus not been obliterated in a modernizing milieu but still have considerable influence.
4. A few stated that neither of them are effective, but only God.
Some did not know.

Question 40

Is the western doctor helpful with regard to the *Ukufa kwaBantu*?
1. Western doctors are unfamiliar with African diseases and are not helpful.
2. A few stated that they are helpful only to a limited extent; only those who have the ability to pray and heal can be helpful.
A few did not know.

H) INDIVIDUAL RESPONSIBILITY FOR MISDEEDS

Question 41

Must wrong done be confessed to the person wronged?
Nearly all said "Yes" without any further explanation. A wrong done against someone cannot merely be rectified by mentioning it to God in prayer, in the "isolation" of one's vertical relationships. Rather, because the wrong has disturbed interrelationships it should be rectified in this context.

Question 42

Blame on evil spirits for one's wrong deeds; how far does this affect one's self-criticism, ie. how far need one look into oneself for one's own guilt and sin?
1. Many agreed that evil spirits influence people's behaviour, but that does not mean that one is not responsible for one's misdeeds. In the

traditional context, the evil spirits received the blame for negative acts, which lessened personal responsibility.

2. Only one respondent denied that demons or evil spirits are active among human beings.

I) THE EFFECTS OF WITCHCRAFT AND ATTENTION GIVEN TO THE VICTIM

Question 43

Does bewitchment, sorcery and evil spirits lead to mental disturbance? All believed that a person who is bewitched has become mentally disturbed as a result of this and may be dangerous to the community.

Question 44

Does the bewitched person receive much attention? From whom?
1. Yes, his/her family approaches remedial sources such as faith healers, traditional and western doctors. The relatives feel responsible for such a person.
2. Yes, almost all people, in particular the relatives, are forced to take care of such a person.
3. A few referred only to doctors, nurses and hospitals.

Question 45

Should a pastor or priest react against witchcraft?
All the respondents agreed by saying "Yes", because witchcraft defiles human beings.

Question 46

Is the sea more effective in removing evil spirits? What happens to the evil spirits when removed by the sea, or wherever they are driven out? Do they drown in the sea or do they enter other people again?
This question was put only to the prophets of the greater Durban area and the outlying squatter areas.
1. The sea water and prayer are effective in removing *ufufunyane* and *izizwe*.
2. The African disease can be treated by praying, steaming, vomiting and drinking of holy water. Sea water is very effective in provoking vomiting in order to get the evil spirits out, and in washing them off

from the body. Sea water is effective in regard to all African diseases.
3. The evil spirits are thrown into the sea, where they get confused but do not drown. They will enter other people again.

Question 47

Can a witch be converted?
All agreed by saying "Yes", but with the provision that he/she repents from evil deeds and has faith in God.

The above responses give sufficient evidence of a people in transition from one set of beliefs and traditions to a new set, with only a small percentage discarding overtly the old and in a dynamic manner accepting the new. However, taking into consideration the present situation in the West with regard to belief in metaphysical forces and the way to approach them as well as the proliferation of western cults, makes it difficult to establish simple contrasts between the African and Western approaches, because many similarities prevail.

Reference has been made to phenomena such as sorcerers, demons and witches in the Christian church up to the sixth century and to the seemingly chaotic situation which prevailed as a result of the rapid growth of Christianity, especially during the fourth century. The first and second century of Afro-Christianity reveals the same trends, and the emphasis on demonic forces and exorcism, with special concentration on the removal of demonic forces, is thus part of the development of church history, and should be seen in this context. Possession by malevolent, capricious spirits, which explain illness and affliction in much the same way as witchcraft and sorcery are explained, are equally comprehensible within the African world view and within the history of the early Christian church. Witchcraft accusations reflect social tensions, while spirit possession in general and those foreign spirits such as *indiki, amandawe* and *ufufunyane* relate to situations of stress and conflict mainly in the domestic sphere. Lewis refers to such phenomena as peripheral possession cults which are contrasted with central possession cults. These peripheral possession spirits play no part in upholding the moral code of the societies in which they operate; they are foreign to these societies and they usually relate to the peripheral strata of those societies where deprivation, frustration and discontent prevail. They relate to social tensions especially between subordinate and superior (cf. Lewis, I.M., *Estatic Religion: An anthropological study of spirit posses-*

sion and shamanism, Pelican Anthropology Library, Penguin Books, 1971, p. 32). Where a victim of witchcraft puts the responsibility on a rival or enemy, affliction is attributed to malevolent spirits, ie. forces not within the fellowship, in this case the church community, but external mysterious forces. Witchcraft and sorcery are the darkest side of the evil activities which the prophet has to confront, a role in which some prophets have built up respected reputations.

CHAPTER SIX

"BAPTISM" AS A PURIFICATION RITUAL IN THE AIC

A) A SYMBOL OF TRANSCENDENCE

Whatever the reasons for the tremendous development of the AIC may be—there are many and it is not possible to discuss them all here—one of the main reasons lies with the interpretation of baptism as a sacrament and a means of obtaining grace and numinous power. This symbol assists those who take part in it to receive the benefits for which it stands, namely, to be in the transcendent world which manifests itself through various benefits bestowed generously on them, if they fulfil the necessary requirements such as fasting, attending the preceding nocturnal revival service, and confessing their sins.

Each symbol has a manifold of meanings; it unites heterogeneous realities in itself. It "constructs" a bridge between the micro- and macrocosmos. In this manner it becomes the expression of the totality. As it gives expression to the manifestation of the transcendent, the symbol implies the continuing association of the people with the holy. It is related to the reality of a situation with which the human being is existentially involved.

This accounts for the many aspects relevant to the individual's life that are associated with baptism in the AIC. Baptism is called the mission's sacrament because of the decisive existential implications this had and still has in the life and work of the church in the African context.

The symbol is related to reality of the situation; it is not acknowledged with the mind in the first instance but in a psychical experience. It represents a complex reality which reaches out far beyond every expression in words. This is precisely the attitude to "baptism" in all its connotations at the sea, where many AIC from various parts of South Africa come for healing. It is the symbol in the AIC which gives orientation and meaning; it changes chaos into cosmos. In their environment, work situation, living conditions and the foreignness of a secularised impersonal world, much of the initiants' inner equilibrium is disturbed and they receive through baptism the necessary orientation to continue. "Baptism" is thus a normalisation act; an act through which balance is established; it has not only great psychiatric value but also great physical value because of the influence of the psyche on the body.

The symbolic religious geographical centre, such as a cosmic mountain, a holy city, a fountain, or the sea, establishes a central meeting place between heaven and earth, between transcendence and the here and now. In some religions the temple becomes the micro-cosmic image of the Universe, in others it is the cosmic mountain, and it seems that the sea has taken over this role in many AIC. The sea has become for many the symbol of the presence of numinous powers.

Not only is the symbol's geographical association of vital importance but so is its association with the time in which the events first happened. Holy time is reversible and it repeats and represents the original time. With the new year there is the repetition of cosmogony; with the great *Umkhosi* (the first-fruit ceremonies) among the Zulus, the new time cycle is introduced. The original time, when the event occurred to which the symbol refers, is holy and strong and its reappearance leads to participation in its powers. What happened at the River Jordan and the Sea of Galilee during the time of Jesus is repeated today at the river and the sea, and Jesus spent more time at the Sea of Galilee than at the river Jordan. John the Baptist baptised Jesus in the River Jordan; Jesus did much of His work at the Sea of Galilee. As a result of the symbolic repetition of the original, those taking part in the ritual at the Durban beach become part of early New Testament history.

Because baptism is the AIC symbol of transcendence, not primarily of being initiated into the church, initiants are assured of the victorious outcome of the struggle of the divine powers against the demonic powers of darkness. They receive life through the removal of sins effected by baptism; they receive "the Spirit" because they have been cleansed and "the Spirit" is a source of strength.

B) BAPTISM IN THE ZIONIST CONTEXT

The symbol of baptism among Zionists is strongly influenced by the Christian tradition but they have given it an emphasis which it did not have in most of the established churches. In the mission context it is prominent because of its association with adult baptism and it is much closer to the early church's baptisms. Traditional African purification practices could also explain the emphasis put on this sacrament in the Afro-Christian context. It has, of course, also a Christian background as the sacrament of baptism was much more in the centre of the life of the early church than is the case today.

This symbol which has such a powerful position within most of the AIC should be evaluated against Carl Jung's concept of the symbol in contrast to the sign and allegory. For him, the human being may aspire to higher levels or could also retrogress to a lower level, where the symbol becomes a dead form. There are two ways, according to Jung, of symbol formation depending on the increasing and decreasing of spiritual activity. The same outward form could be for the one a sign of spiritual expansion and for the other a shell from which the living content has long since evaporated.

Much of the latter is true with regard to baptism in the western world, where for the late Karl Barth, the eminent Swiss theologian, a "baptised heathendom" exists. Over against this baptism has always been a dynamic sacrament within the churches in the mission context. The history of baptism within the church, before the modern scientific mind overruled everything, reveals the very central place it had in the church. It would be an interesting exercise to compare the approach to this sacrament of the primitive and early church, when adult baptism predominated, with what developed in the indigenous African churches, where more adults received the sacrament than infants.

C) Symbols in the African context

The question is: Are there certain symbols that speak very strongly to Africans and are these reflected within the churches? In spite of denials by some, there is enough evidence of a specific traditional African approach. The indigenous/independent African churches have a specific African character. That contrasts with the western techno-scientific approach.

Certain symbols and images occur fairly regularly among African authors on this continent, in spite of differences among them. Such symbols and thought patterns are unity, harmony, peace (many a child in Africa and especially South Africa bears the indigenous name for 'peace'), the emphasis on life which comes through death and which is symbolically expressed in many of their rituals, the removal of the forces of darkness, the emphasis on humanity and personhood within the context of community, the role of water as a life-giving force.

These emphases, according to Jung's approach, are evidences of man's collective consciousness. They belong to the whole of humanity but could be and are so often suppressed by other symbols and thought patterns. But even post-modern man—man of the split atom, of quantum

physics, of biomedical advance, the one-dimensional man—instinc-
tively harks back to origins. There is an undercurrent within human
existence, like an undercurrent underneath the surface of the ocean,
which gives him a spontaneous sensitivity for a primal approach, which
finds expression in art, music and dance: the emphasis falls on the
emotional rather than on the individual.

In spite of the strong emphasis in our time on the rational and the
development of scientific and technological language, there are signs of
reaction against this, as is evident in the influence of not only Eastern but
also Western mysticism, especially on the youth. They look for identity,
for new means of communication, for a sense of community, for a
situation in which experience instead of belief is central, where a person
attains a new spiritual level through his experiences and himself becomes active to obtain what his religion professes. In communication the
emphasis is on hymns, dreams, tongues; here liturgy is flexible, the
service is 'made', ie. with no fixed liturgical order, with the emphasis on
spontaneity. The self-propelled machines, computers, robots; the whole
modern technology with its emphasis on a programmed existence in a
society ruled by production and consumption, aroused a reaction from
the youth, many of whom found a haven in Eastern mysticism and
Pentecostalism or 'born again' movements. This development has been
active for decades in the AIC, which have their own type of reaction
based on their own background.

Symbolism used by the AIC to penetrate deeper into their existential
situation is not always understood by others outside their circle but it
speaks directly and strongly to many African people. For western youth
it is their communes; for the AIC it is their face-to-face congregations,
of which there are over one hundred and fifty thousand in South Africa,
their baptisms and special ceremonies at pools, rivers, mountains,
elevated places and the sea.

The symbol must be understood in the context of the individual and
the group. In the AIC the uniform is not merely a piece of clothing that
covers the body but a garb that elevates a person to the heavenly spheres;
the staves are not merely sticks but vehicles of power, the "flag" is not
merely a piece of cloth attached to a stick but an object which keeps the
evil forces away; the "crosses" are not crosses in the traditional Christian
sense but are resemblances of pieces of wood which symbolise the
cancelling out of evil. One piece of cloth on the uniform represents
disharmony, another put on his cancels this out and establishes harmony.
The X symbol signifies the cancelling out of evil. These pieces are in the

form of the spokes of a wheel—after the equilibrium has been restored life can advance again. Life, symbolised by the circle, can continue. The sick usually appear at the place of baptism—the pool, river or sea—with crossless uniforms signifying that disharmony prevails, and penitence.

Usually the archbishop, bishop or baptiser walks into the sea with outstretched arms lifted upwards and a big cross displayed on the back of his/her uniform. He (or she) challenges the demons, monsters and evil spirits of the sea. The fact that the group moves rhythmically in a circle before the baptism, that they plant candles in a circle, and that the person baptised in the sea is turned around and around, shows how important the symbol of the circle is, ie. the symbol of harmony, of life and perfection, of togetherness. It is basic to the African sense of community; it plays a greater role in the average Zionist Church than even the symbol of the cross which is carved out or fitted onto the "holy sticks". The circle is associated with rhythm and rhythm is a means of making contact with the transcendent power(s); healing is effected within a circle; the circle is the most obvious place for the restoration of harmony. In the circle they dance before getting into the water; they get into the mood for the great event, namely the washing off of their sins in the sea, the driving out of evil spirits, the restoring of health, the receiving of the power of the Holy Spirit; here, transcendent power is relayed among themselves thanks to the activities of the transcendent forces which are either the Holy Spirit or the ancestor(s), or both; here, in the circle, they act jointly before entering the water individually.

D) THE IDEA OF REBIRTH AND THE FULLNESS OF LIFE

The idea of rebirth is uppermost in the traditional African cultures. The *rites de passage* are associated with this cycle of death and life. The *rites de passage* are closely related to the ancestors; the ancestors mould the child in the mother's womb; they bring to life the dead person. The newborn baby is not accepted as being a person and as being associated with the life cycle until it is shown to the ancestors and until it receives a name; the young person has to die from the ways of the youth during initiation in order to get protection and real life within the community; death leads to after-life. This accounts for the central position held by the rites associated with funerals, for they are rebirth rituals. With most African peoples the corpse is put into the grave in the form of a foetus. Death is a new birth.

Baptism symbolises a transition from death to life which is effected through purification by fasting, washing, vomiting and confessing of sins. Life is given through the water at the pool, river or sea. The more one has of the fullness of life, the stronger one is and the greater one's contact with transcendent powers. A situation of chaos is restored to cosmos; it could fade again but the restoration possibilities are always there—fading and restoration itself is a cycle. Mass restoration gatherings during Easter are a familiar sight in South Africa and elsewhere. Such gatherings took place in the traditional societies with their first-fruit ceremonies, such as the *Umkhosi Omkhulu* among the Zulu, when they were "eating" with their ancestors and the royal ancestors (*amakhosi*). Here much dancing, singing and handclapping took place.

Baptism as a symbol of transition from death to life is so strong that it has received a number of connotations within the AIC, connotations such as rebirth, healing, power and good luck, as well as of being invited into the church, being purified from sin, being freed of evil spirits, and receiving 'the Spirit' or Holy Ghost and becoming thereby enlightened (capable of visions) and able to prophesy. It has a strong rebirth emphasis among Zionists, for whom the main focus is new life, renewal of life over the forces of darkness and destruction (which overtly refers to negative spiritual forces and covertly to the physical forces which govern their circumstances). Baptisms by the sea are preceded by watch-night revival services, at which the emphasis is put on the outpouring of the Holy Spirit or closer contact with the ancestors, when new life is conferred on the participants. Purification is central, whether it takes place on the holy mountain, at the holy fountain or at the sea. Whether they claim a river, a pool, the sea, or a mountain—it is not the place as such that receives precedence but its symbolic value. Fasting before and during the watch-night revival service, which culminates at the sea, prepares for the gifts of baptism. Water mythology is not strange to the African. In African mythology running water and the sea played a definite role in man's origin. The reeds and the water of the river are closely associated in their cosmogony. Some of the staves are made of reeds and are used by spiritual leaders, which is reminiscent of John the Baptist at the River Jordan.

E) The development of baptism in ecclesiastical-historical perspective

Brief reference to the historical development of baptism will put various issues with regard to the Zionist practices in a clearer light.

The consensus is that adult baptism predominated up to the second half of the 2nd century. Justin maintained that infants were born, without willing it, but they should themselves be reborn, willing it. To this most of the Zionist churches will agree. Children are "baptised" but baptism is related to the receiving of the blessings which Christianity can give, such as healing, protection from evil forces, inner strength, a good relationship with God—the baptism is done in an *ex opere operato* manner. Only later can the child confess its faith and become a full member of the church after having received the baptism of faith.Tertullian saw baptism as *obsignatio fidei*, ie. sealing of personal, accepted faith. For Zionists this takes place usually at the age of 12 but mostly after the age of 15. It was only around 125 AD that children of these ages were baptised after instruction and if they had truly confessed Jesus Christ to be their Lord and Saviour. After Augustine's doctrine of original sin and the consolidation of the State Church, the practice of infant baptism was fully accepted in the western church. From the third century onwards, baptism was increasingly understood as effective in removing original sin, ie. in an *opus operatum* context. Infant baptism strengthened this approach, with the result that it contributed to the *corpus christianum* fallacy.

The early church fathers emphasized that with baptism a change of lordship takes place within the adult baptised. Not the demons, but God takes possession of him (Justin, Irenaeus, and others). Baptism is a seal (*sphragis*) which is assured through the holy names of the baptismal formula, anointment, crossing, and/or the baptismal water. In this way the person is sealed as the possession of God or Christ; he is sealed off from demonic attacks, and angels and demons acknowledge him as God's child. This is a transition from death to life, an emphasis put on baptism by the early church fathers. Baptism was a contract with God. For the AIC the contract stands if it has been entered into by those who are able to understand what it implies, and for them the contract includes many issues other than death and resurrection in Christ. 'Baptism' has become a purification rite which is repeated many times on the same person—every quarter, every month, or even more.

Around 200 AD, the emphasis was on catechetical instruction which eventually concluded with baptism. Origen understood the symbol (*sumbolon*) as complete and thorough cleansing through the Logos but as also giving power to the person baptised as a result of the pronouncement over him of the names of the Triune God. With this most of the Zionist churches will be in full agreement. For Origen, the degree of cleaning depended on the attitude of the receiver. Many Zionist leaders go through even a week of fasting before they baptise people. They expect such fasting from those to be baptised, but not the same number of days.

For Tertullian, baptism effected forgiveness with absolute certainty, even if an unrepentant person administered the sacrament. For him, the baptismal water had wonderful power; it is a "holy stream", an eternal fountain, divine water; it is saving water of salvation, healing water (cf. *John* 5: 2 ff ; 9: 7) or the fountain of life. Some of the Zionists attach such great significance to the purifying effects of water that it is used in the church after confession of sin and they drink it from small cups. Tertullian's emphasis on "holy baptismal water" could typify him as one of the earliest forerunners of the Zionist churches, indeed. Also, according to the well-known church father, Irenaeus, baptismal water gives life, immortality. For Ignatius, water in which the demons settled (also a Zionist belief) had to be cleansed and sanctified through Christ's baptism, through Christ's blood (Augustine), through the mediation of an angel (Tertullian) or the Holy Spirit (Ambrose), who moves over the water and who is responsible for the rebirth of the baptised. With this the Zionist churches are in full agreement. In the undisturbed water—some baptise from 4 am on Sundays at the sea before it has been disturbed by bathers—which is blessed and sanctified by the baptiser, the flock are baptised and cleansed ie. from demons, the perpetrators of sin. For the Zionists, water at the pool, river or sea, that has been prayed over, is consecrated while the flag that they usually plant alongside them on the beach also keeps the evil forces away.

F) Baptism outside the established churches

Whether baptism outside the established church is valid and thus acceptable was a really contentious issue in the church. For Cyprian, the "unbroken belief" of baptiser and receiver, which is only possible in the church, was necessary. It was valid only if done in the name of the Trinity or Jesus. Those against baptism outside the church were united in their belief that the receiving of the Spirit was possible only in the church.

The same question with regard to AIC baptism arises at times in the various churches today. The ecclesiological norms invariably apply and not necessarily the objective understanding of this sacrament in the context of the AIC. The question asked is whether the church is a church. Are the 4000 AIC denominations, with their 8 million members and adherents and their variety of practices, churches in the scriptural sense? From a phenomenological point of view their baptisms fulfil the requirements attached by any church to this act, in spite of the emphasis on exorcism and purification.

G) THE *OPUS OPERATUM* APPROACH

The gnostics had various types of baptism such as the water baptisms of the mystery cults, fire baptism, and spirit baptism. (Some AIC administer a waterless baptism by laying on of hands, which is termed Spirit baptism, as does, the 4-million-strong *Kimbangu Church* in Zaire.) From the second century, under the influence of the mystery cults, baptism was perceived as an initiation rite and had received some mystery aspects: fire exorcism in preparation for baptism; prayers and fasting during the days before baptism (there are prayers and fasting before baptism in the AIC); watch-night service during the last night (very familiar with AIC—*umvusilelo*, ie. revival service); anointing the whole body as protection against the devil (also found in some of the AIC); and a baptismal act that included confession of faith, putting on white baptismal clothes, crossing, processing of garlanded initiants with candles in the church, under the leadership of the bishop (just as some of the AIC at the sea, their baptismal "font", wear baptismal clothes and go in procession to the sea with the bishop or baptiser leading and "opening up" the water with prayer).

Augustine maintained it is actually Christ who baptises, who as "visible word" (*visibile verbum*) acts in the outward baptismal act (*sacramentum*) and as "invisible grace" (*invisibilis gratia*) completes the work of salvation (*effectus sacramenti*) in those baptised. The outward act (immersion in water and anointing) is only the symbol of the work of salvation.

The AIC in general differ from Augustine—the symbol is not merely a *signum* in the sense of a mere sign. Baptism has in itself dynamic value and it has specific effects which cannot be ascribed to a mere sign. They are closer to those who interpreted the act of baptism as freeing a person from guilt and punishment. For Zionists, water that has been prayed over, and especially sea water, conveys spiritual benefits. They will agree with Thomas Aquinas that God is the principal cause and the baptismal water the instrumental cause of the spiritual work of grace. For the AIC, although it is widely practised, baptism is not a mere convention—it has deep-seated significance. All the Afro-Christian religions emphasize the importance of this sacrament and its deep inner relationship with the work of the Holy Spirit, as if it were associated with rituals that make use of magic. There is also a repetition of the sacrament in the AIC, although some emphasize that the first ceremony is only an "initiatory" baptism in a river, which is thereafter repeated at the sea. The repetition does have associations with magical power. Nevertheless, in spite of the many theological questions that arise from this, the established churches should look at their own attitudes to the sacrament which has lost its centrality in the church. It is indeed a dynamic sacrament in the AIC—something which should not be overlooked. It has become, to a large extent, a purification rite.

H) Liturgical aspects

As in the primitive church, so in many AIC a person to be baptised has to fast for a few days—the baptiser and members of the congregation have to share in such fasting. Furthermore, baptism has usually to be preceded by a revival service (*umvusilelo*) which could start on a Friday evening and continue to the Sunday morning, before the participants leave for the place where baptism is administered.

In the early church baptism took place preferably where there was running water. Immersion three times was prescribed and the trinitarian formula was pronounced "over" the person baptised. In the AIC such baptism could also take place at the sea, as in the case of *The New Holy Church in Zion of South Africa*, the leader of which stated that they do it at the sea because it is not easy to get an adequate spot at the river. On one occasion, six new members baptised at the sea after the *umvusilelo* (revival service) were immersed three times and the trinitarian formula was used, namely "In the Name of the God, the Son, and the Spirit". Immersion is the only procedure accepted by the Zionist churches.

I) Consecrated water and baptism

The major precondition of AIC baptisms is that the water has to be consecrated—even the powerful water of the sea. The baptiser enters the sea first—some do this with outstretched arms—and blesses the water before baptism. This water, to which ash is often added, is also used for healing purposes. The AIC regurlarly dance around water to be used for healing purposes; the dancing is accompanied by singing and drumming. From the 8th or the 9th century, consecrated water was included in sacramental acts and was considered to have an enlightening and a remedial and sanctifying influence. This is precisely what the AIC emphasize—the consecrated water gives them "the Spirit", of which the burning candles, planted in a circle or otherwise, are a symbol; it is used for healing and it symbolises spiritual devotion. Exorcism played an important part in the baptismal ritual of the early church, as it does within the AIC context. The Reformation reduced the emphasis on baptismal water and moved away from the elaborate liturgy regarding baptism. The Zionists reinstituted not only an elaborate liturgy but gave a dynamic significance to baptismal water.

Zionists baptise their holy staves and crosses (with which they *inter alia* touch a sick person in order to relay power); their flags (which, even if they are sometimes not opened, are planted alongside the circle where they gather at the beach) are also baptised; and they themselves are baptised in their uniforms. Such acts remove the evil forces that pollute these objects.

J) FLAGS

The flag also plays a role in the baptism ceremonies of some AIC. Some bring the flag to be baptised in the sea—it is folded and tightened with strings. Others plant it alongside them on the beach or at the place where they baptise.

It is not certain where the flag originated from—most probably from John Alexander Dowie, who started the Zionist movement in 1896 in Chicago and whose church is the initiator of the movement in South Africa. He introduced the flag in his church but its use has undergone a transformation.

The flags have various functions:
(a) they open the way for the believer to the place of public worship;
(b) evil spirits are removed from a place of worship or baptism through the flag;
(c) flags are planted near the place of worship or baptism as a sign that the place is safe and that the various liturgical and ritual activities cannot be obstructed by evil forces;
(d) those who wish to receive catechetical instruction gather at the flag;
(e) The flag serves as a protection against witchcraft;
(f) it could also be a sign of the power of the prophet or leader to cure disease, or to confer "the Spirit". It may be in various colours, mainly blue, green, yellow and white—seldom in black or red;
(g) the colours serve different purposes in driving away evil spirits, and

often depend on the dreams or revelations of an exorcist. They are the softer colours which are associated with trust, love, and purity, as in the case of the uniforms.

Flags are put on top, or in front of, houses, where they serve to ward off evil. In some cases, the flags are detached from the flag pole or staff to ward off the intense dangers that arise, for example, at the moment of internment at a burial service. Flags are prominent on many huts and houses where lightning is experienced as a real danger.

Thus, because exorcism plays such a significant role, the flag has a place at the baptismal ceremonies of many of the AIC. It is often the only "watch dog" over their possessions on the beach, while they are singing and handclapping and drumming in or near the water with the baptismal ceremony in progress.

K) Baptism at the Durban Beach and its various connotations

Baptism is used in the wider connotation here because this is how the AIC evaluate this sacrament—it is dynamic, it can be repeated, and it is associated with holy water. Fasting precedes baptism as well as revival services.

There are various reasons for baptising and the best is to let the AIC speak for themselves:

1. When a person is initiated into the church he/she is baptised—either at the sea or at a dam, a pool, or a river. For some, such baptisms take place preferably where there is running water, implying that the "initiatory" baptism should take place at a river and later "baptisms" at the the sea. Others consider baptisms at the sea as also taking place in running water.

   They usually baptise in the name of the Father, the Son, and Holy Spirit.
2. "If somebody backslides the person is brought here to be baptised in order to wash away the sins... which are very hard to... take out of a person"—according to the "prophet" of the *Apostolic Full Gospel Church of Zion*. This "prophet" is a plasterer.
3. They are baptised to get new life, according to Archbishop Phewa: "When they put you down you are dead; when you come up you are new... *impilo entsha*. We pray for a person that he gets new life."
4. You must give them power. "I have already baptised them once—after that I give them power." According to a minister of the *Bantu Christian Church in Zion*.

In the AIC great emphasis is put on the acquisition of power (*amandla*) through baptism at the sea. Power is obtained not only through immersion, "thrashing out" the evil spirits and laying on of hands, but also through the initiants swimming in the water with uniforms on or just lying on the sand so that the waves go over them— a familiar sight at baptismal ceremonies. Just being at the sea in a uniform, even without entering the water, gives power. Two elderly Zionist women, for example, visited the sea; both put their uniforms on but only one entered the water—the other maintained that merely being present there in her uniform gave her power and a good feeling.

5. Getting 'the Spirit' or Holy Spirit (*umoya oyingcwele*) is an important theme in all baptisms. The choruses also reflect this. The Holy Spirit reveals secrets to them at the sea. One said to me, "I see you are a church man; the Holy Spirit told me that." When they are baptised, candidates usually spin around, which is a sign of the Holy Spirit entering them; others shake, which is also evidence that "the Spirit" has entered them.

6. The Secretary of the *St Matthews Apostolic Church of Christ in South Africa* at Sebokeng, the black township that often erupts in violence stated: "We came specially to baptise in sea water. We believe in 'spiritual water'. Our members drink the sea water in order to *palaza* (vomit); this works the stomach, it cleanses everything... it strengthens one's manhood... We can have another baby again... baptism gives one inner well-being."

7. Infant baptism is combined with baptism of children who have just passed the puberty stage. They were baptised in the church when they were small and are now baptised in the sea. They are called aside at the sea and instructed before the sea baptism by a *khokheli* (a Mama, a female leader).

While this baptism takes place a group sing with candles in their hands:

Thina (we)... *Ewe* (Yes)... *Ewe* (Yes)... *Thina* (we) *Nkosi yami* (My Lord).

The candles in their hands are symbols of the light that the Holy Spirit gives. Often the candles are put in a circle on the sand. The candles also assist the minister or prophet to see invisible things as well as to look into the future. Often candles with various colours are used; white candles always symbolise the presence of the Holy Spirit when lit.

8. Exorcism is deeply associated with baptism—hitting a person on the shoulders, on the arms, on the legs, accompanies the baptismal act. Away from the sea or water, "holy" staves are regularly pressed against a patient in order to remove the evil spirits. Often the "baptised" (especially after this procedure) will say "I feel free". The staves are usually not pressed on a person in the water.

One respondent had a uniform made of sugar bag material. His explanation was "it will help me when we want something; or when bad spirits come, nothing will happen." In traditional society, such evil spirits are an omnipresent reality and various rituals are performed to ward them off. When entering the sea one sometimes hears the chorus:

Zonke izinto zaluhlaba (All the things of the world) *zidukisa umoya wona* (take your strength/spirit away).

9. Sick persons are brought to the pool, river or sea to be "baptised", ie. to receive the power from the water. Sin and sickness are correlated—sin weakens a person physically and psychically—and baptism removes sin so that the sick person is strengthened.

Even sick babies are brought to the sea to be dipped in its water; for example, upon my asking a parent why he and his wife brought such a sick baby of about nine months to the sea, the reply was: "The prophet said that she has to be brought to the sea and be put into the water, to get power." The diagnosis and instruction of the prophet is accepted as if from a specialist. The father said that the medical doctor using white (western) medicine "cannot get nothing" ie. he could not diagnose the sickness of the child. Such baptisms give life, *impilo entsha*, for the sicknesses are cultural diseases associated with evil spirits and sorcery.

10. There are also ecumenical gatherings of the AIC at the sea, where they are baptised together in order to get "the Spirit". They come in contact with "the Spirit", who strengthens the bond between them.

11a) There are some who come to the sea unaccompanied by a minister or leader. Two young men, Jetro Mtshali and David Nene, for instance, came from a men's hostel situated in a black township. After putting their gowns on over their usual clothes, they went from the ablution block down to the sea, where each lit a candle. Both came to receive power and good luck and to pray for their families, whom they had left up country, and to have the evil spirits removed in the sea. They conducted their own special ceremony.

11b) Established church members come to commemorate their ancestors who have passed away; for example, one group who sat in a circle with three candles in the centre and with a cross planted in the sand, were mainly Anglicans and Catholics. It was a special occasion at which a woman prophet took the lead.

12. Baptism also implies getting rid of traditional medicines and traditional medical practitioners whose office extends beyond healing to "prophecy", ie. seeing things and generally consulting. One leader stated: "We throw the *isangoma* (diviner) things into the sea and then the *umoya* of Jesus comes to us."

13. Dancing and rhythmic movements accompany most baptisms. Dance is the most universal of all acts and in dancing the dancers are protected from dangers and evil spirits. It strengthens and brings down numinous power on whatever they dance around, such as the container with water and the sick person. From the Synod of Aquiles (318) to the Council of 680, a struggle reigned in the church for three hundred years about dancing in the church. At the latter Council, the standpoint of Augustine prevailed namely *chorea est circulus, cuius centrum est diabolus*, and so dance was forbidden absolutely. The Zionist will say that in the centre of the circle there is power and the Spirit—not evil. During the whole of the Middle Ages dance was considered to be suspect, while Calvinists maintained it was sinful. Dance is rhythm in which all sense of space and time could be lost and contact made with the transcendent world. This makes dance inevitable in the AIC. Before going into the water those to be baptised sit, walk fast, or run rhythmically (a form of dance) in a circle.

14. The most important prerequisite for an effective baptism ceremony is the *umvusilelo*—revival service—at which the participants prepare themselves to receive 'the Spirit' as well as to be in a position to receive the other mentioned blessings which baptism brings.

The context in which baptism is evaluated is so intense and so extensive that this sacrament cannot be described with full justice in the language and terms of most of the historic churches. It has much more meaning than they ascribe to this sacrament, as is evident from the above exposition. The main question regarding the AIC is not whether the historic churches accept their evaluation and use of baptism but whether, for them, baptism has a positive meaning and rôle in their situation. It certainly does provide direction in the lives of many AIC members in South Africa. It relieves their tensions, frees them psychically from the forces of evil, heals them, strengthens relationships, gives them an insight into their destiny and strength for the road ahead. It offers them the guidance of the Spirit and an acceptable framework to work in in contrast to that experienced in daily life, which often means confrontation, alienation, subjection and frustration. Here, they learn the power of positive thinking without ever having read Norman Vincent Peale or other people who offer their spiritual remedies for coping with the pressures of the modern world. They have found their own remedy, in what the church terms a sacrament and what for them has a medical, psychical, spiritual, social and even economic connotation. Here, the secular is not dissected from the spiritual. In this method of exorcism and spiritual renewal, the prophet plays a vital role.

CHAPTER SEVEN

DIVINER/PROPHET PARALLEL

This empirical study has indicated that the prophet has a vital role in the indigenous churches—even more than was the case during the first three centuries of the existence of the Christian Church. While this office was then related mainly to the proclamation of the Christian message, it has become associated in Southern Africa mainly with healing in a holistic sense, but also with the daily needs and personal issues of members of those churches which have such an office. It is to be found in most of the AIC. This in itself is proclamation and accounts for the dynamic growth of the AIC in *apartheid* South Africa. A small percentage of prophets who are mainly other-world orientated, emphasized personal salvation.

The AIC prophet fills the vacuum left in the missionary established and directed churches, where none of the church offices compensated realistically for the loss of the diviner, the traditional 'prophet', healer, welfare consultant, seer and adviser. The African type of prophet (the traditional 'prophet' is referred to as diviner) is more than a healer, irrespective of whether he/she is a Christian or not. The diviner is also deeply involved in social relations and is responsible for social cohesion in the society. This is achieved through specific ceremonies, rituals and the observation of taboos. The roles of the diviner are set out aptly as follows:

  i)   as healer, either through divination or provision of *muti*;
  ii) as the centre of social integration and cohesion;
  iii) as seer or diviner;
  iv) as the protector of the people, their possessions and their environment, particularly against lightning; and, most important,
  v)   as the religious head of the society and mediator between the ancestors (*amadlozi*) and their descendants, either for love and protection or in propitiation for omission of required rites in contravention of the social code." (Cf. Griffiths, J.A. and R.W.S. Cheetham, "Priests before healers—An appraisal of the *iSangoma* or *iSanusi* in Nguni society", *S A Medical Journal*, 62, 11 December 1982, p. 959).

The prophet is also a consultant, although the healing function predominates in many ways in the AIC prophet's case. The priestly role which the diviner has in the traditional society has largely been transferred to the minister in the Christian context. The diviners' functions and roles are thus much more extensive than are the roles of those who act as prophets in the AIC, and yet these prophets give an invaluable dimension to the AIC activities, which accounts largely for their growth. In all matters in which the diviner is consulted, she is informed by the ancestors, and her activities take place in some state of altered consciousness which may be effected by trance, self-hypnosis or some ingredient such as snuff etc.

A) How does the work of the prophet differ from that of the diviner?

The prophets in the metropolitan Durban area emphasized, in the words of a female prophet, "that the prophet goes to church, uses *isiwasho* and prays. He/she works under the power of the Holy Spirit but the ancestors may be consulted. The diviner does not go to Church, believes in and works only under the power of ancestors." A number stated that the diviner uses bones to 'protect'. Although the Bible is seldom used in healing procedures, one prophet stated that he uses the Bible and added "when we predict the patient says 'Amen', ie. if the diagnosis is correct", which reminds one of the responses from clients when the diviner tries to establish the cause of an illness or misfortune, or the whereabouts of something lost. A few stated that they get visions from the Holy Spirit and do not go to the cemeteries to consult ancestors, as is the case with a number of prophets.

The woman prophet from *The Bantu Independent Ethiopian Apostolic Church of South Africa* was emphatic that she works with the Holy Spirit only "and when I do consult the ancestors, I always do it under the Holy Spirit". She added that "the prophets are able to pray for people. They use *muti* and *isiwasho* or sometimes only *isiwasho*. Diviners use *muti*, work under ancestors and do not pray".

The prophets in the Rand/Soweto area stated that the diviners use traditional herbs and medicines which could also be utilized for killing people. A few of the prophets on the Rand referred to the fact that diviners are consulted for killing and this they found abhorrent. One of these prophets remarked that the diviners "do not pray or believe in the Son of God—I do."

The prophet from the *Apostolic Church of Christ in South Africa* (who had Std I education and lived in a rural area) emphasized that his work is "not very different" from that of a diviner "because I would always start working as the prophet and if nothing happens then I would apply everything which a diviner would use because I am using both. Actually, I have a double engine at my disposal, namely, one engine from the Holy Spirit and one from the ancestors". Another prophet who also acts as a diviner stated, "I feel that I am very powerful for I am using two callings and as a result a disease or sickness has no chance to escape". The mixing of traditional and 'modern' ingredients is also considered to be very powerful. There are a few who do not have this double-barrel approach, but none reject the diviners, or oppose them, although they maintain: "the diviners do not read the Bible and abide by its commandments"; "we don't peep at bones but pray instead"; "a diviner uses pure medicines (or raw herbs), but I use *isiwasho*"; "the diviner depends on the ancestors to guide and give him/her the message—I depend on God to give me messages or answers regarding peoples' problems".

A prophet of the *Corinthian Church*, who came to sea for power— with his staff, as he must have something in his hand to get this power— added that he came on the injunctions of the Holy Spirit; that his Bishop, Johannes Hlabehlangane Richmond, one of the most senior and re-spected prophets in the Greater Durban area, who "sees" when he is praying, told him to put the chains around his shoulders. He can see through the staff where the sea is dangerous; even if the ancestors are not there, "feelings tell me where the dangerous sections of the sea are; I use *impepho* to dream and then the ancestors visit me; the cords on me fight illness and keep the demons away. Then the Holy Spirit comes, by whom I am controlled and not by demons. Previously, when I was plagued by the demons I went to the witchdoctors but they could not help me. At last I found help from Hlabehlangane. I now pray with candles....the candles work with the Holy Spirit. This candle I have in my hand is different from the one I bought in the shop. I cannot give it to a sinful person. A person must first be cleansed before he touches it. I listen to whatever the Holy Spirit tells me. All of us have the Holy Spirit....we want power". The white candle symbolizes the presence of the Holy Spirit, as the burning of *impepho* symbolizes the presence of the ancestors. But a prophet of the *New African Voice of South Africa*, relating the mythology concern-ing the big snake in the sea (and also in the rivers) stated, "we use candles....if the big snake comes from the sea and a person is taken into the sea, such a person will return....we burn the candles before we enter the sea to ask the king of the sea to let us in safely".

Among the prophets in metropolitan Durban and on the Rand, there is either a full acceptance of the diviners' approach, a partial acceptance or a complete rejection. Those who reject the diviner see him/her as one who does not pray, who does not use the Bible, who has no contact with God but only with the ancestors, who uses bad medicines which could also be utilized to kill and get people out of the way by those who hate them or are jealous of them.

Nothing is said about how effective they are. Nevertheless, it has become obvious from the discussions so far that both the diviner and the herbalist have a role to play for most of the prophets. The prophets in Greater Durban evaluate the work of the prophet as good and would encourage people to become prophets, "if they follow God". They enjoy their work as prophets and are excited to see their patients or victims healed. A prophet in the metropolitan Durban area maintained that when she "tried to get away from being a prophet" she became "seriously ill" and remained ill until she returned to her prophetic task. One stated that although his healing is somehow different from that of other Zionists, he is nevertheless a "full Zionist". In the established churches many follow the "Zionist way" when it comes to healing procedures.

B) CO-OPERATION WITH DIVINERS

Information on co-operation with diviners is difficult to obtain. Only one of the metropolitan Durban prophets, a male, stated that he co-operates with them, while a female prophet stated that she visits their sessions occasionally. The few who have been trained both as prophet and diviner practise their profession openly. They are avoided by the stauncher Bible orientated groups, but some individuals do approach them for assistance. Margaret Ncamane, who trained as a diviner on a farm in the Ndwedwe district, Natal, became a member of *The United Zulu Apostolic Church in South Africa* six months ago. Although she no longer wears the reddish coloured outfit of an *isangoma*, she still has the diviner's beads around her shoulders. She acts as a healer in this church, prays to *Nkulunkulu* (God), to Jesus and to her ancestors. She accepts the existence of 'the Spirit'. Her minister stated that "we want 'the Spirit' to increase so that she will be a prophet and not an *isangoma*". The minister stated that the church would not expect her to discard the use of *muti* when she becomes a prophet.

Sixty percent of the Rand prophets do not co-operate with diviners, but most of them utilize diviners' and herbalists' rituals, and some of their medicines in their healing procedures. Those prophets who do have contact with diviners state the latter also do good work for the community in using traditional ways of healing, and they do not see why they should not co-operate with diviners. The main problem with the diviners is the fact that they could also kill people with herbs; this applies also to the herbalists. Nevertheless, there are prophets who co-operate with diviners in spite of their rejection of the "killing aspect" in their functions. One prophet's own father is a diviner and the prophet, who hails from a rural area, co-operates with him.

C) ARE THERE CHRISTIAN DIVINERS?

The question arises as to whether a diviner could be a Christian. The prophets consulted in the Durban metropolitan area stated that diviners could become Christian diviners if they were prayed for, and instances of such conversions mentioned. They then change their diviner's outfit for a church uniform when accepted into the church, after having been immersed in the river or sea (preferably moving water). After prayers have been said for them, they become prophets and cease to be diviners, although they need not discard all their divination practices as is obvious from the above.

A leader-cum-prophet, of a very active church in metropolitan Durban, had the vision that he should "baptize" five diviners in the sea for seven successive Sundays, which he faithfully did along with others who joined his church. He then considered them to be purified. The seven successive Sunday baptisms, at 4h15 in the Indian Ocean, were accompanied by singing and rhythmic movements. Seven here is the symbol of completeness; of transition from seeing things only in part to seeing everything in its full perspective. The diviners had to leave their skins, ropes, beads, etc., on the beach before entering the sea. At the last Sunday immersion they were told that they could put these objects on again but that their healing procedures should be basically under the guidance of Jesus which, however, did not exclude calling upon the assistance of their ancestors. The prophet himself, apart from prayer, also utilizes herbs, *isiwasho* and other ingredients. This prophet/leader regularly takes diviners to the sea to be "baptized" or purified, and, according to him, they now call upon Jesus during their healing procedures instead of only on the ancestors. After "baptism" in the sea they are allowed to put their diviner's clothes, amulets and beads on again, but they then do their work "primarily in the name of Jesus".

Some make a distinction between Christian and non-christian diviners on the basis of the medicine they use. Christian diviners use God's advice to make their medicines. These do not include the "carcasses of animals", as was stated by a spokesman of *The Holy Church of Zion of South Africa*.

There are established church members who have left their churches and become diviners, such as Elizabeth Lokuthula Dimba (72 years of age), born a Methodist, who became a diviner twenty years ago. The spirits of her uncles called her. It was impossible to resist them—she was bleeding, vomiting blood and had a terrible headache. She had to go to hospital, stayed there only two days, and left. "I went to a senior diviner who gave me nothing except she was burning *impepho* and talked to her ancestors whom she called by their surnames. She then proceeded with the first stage of my initiation as a diviner and continued until I qualified. I never visited the church again but I cannot do anything without the help of Jesus Christ. When a person comes I pray first. God must help me. My power comes from God and through me it goes to the patient". In her house, where she has a diviner's initiation school, hangs her church membership certificate of years ago, and her Temperance Society Certificate. This highly respected diviner also receives Christians from the established churches; they come to her for healing and with other problems. One of the most respected diviners round Durban is the wife of an AIC bishop. Christianity and traditional religious practices have become integrated and acceptable. Although she is the image of a diviner in outfit and bearing, and also has a special diviner's hut alongside her housing township near Durban, she emphasized that she is a Christian and a member of her husband's church.

Some emphatically reject working through ancestors, as in the case of the lady minister of *The Apostolic Holy Zulu Church in Zion in South Africa*, Rev E. Sibeko, who makes a distinction between the prayer healer and prophet—as a junior who only "put hands" and a senior who works through visions. She related how she was called—an old lady came to her during the night in a dream and wanted her to become a diviner but her parents took her to a "Zion lady" who prayed for her, and then "I had the Holy Spirit. I work with the Holy Spirit and not with an ancestral spirit."

For the Rand prophets, Christian diviners, ie. diviners who repent and join the church, do exist. A person could be both a Christian and a diviner; he/she could become a Christian by "accepting God in faith" and by coming to the church to be baptized. A Zulu prophet who lives in Soweto, and originally came from a rural area, stated that he is "a Christian and a diviner", a member of the *Apostolic Church of Christ in*

South Africa. Another prophet "doubts if ever a Christian could be a diviner". One of the prophets maintained that "there are Christian diviners and there are diviners who are Christians", explaining the difference. The "Christian diviners" are those who were Christians and subsequently took the diviners course, while the others are traditional diviners who subsequently accepted Christianity.

A variety of views concerning diviners were expressed:

a) a diviner could not be a Christian without repentance;

b) there are Christian diviners;

c) Christian diviners do not exist as diviners cannot possibly be Christian;

d) there are some who are trained either first as a prophet and then as a diviner or first as a diviner and then as a prophet; only through faith in God and baptism can a diviner become a Christian. As healers, diviners are more stringently trained than prophets. There is no term as yet in the indigenous languages for the office of diviner-cum-prophet.

D) ORIGINALLY CALLED TO BE A DIVINER

Only one of the metropolitan Durban prophets had the experience of being called first as a diviner. She was a Zulu woman, with Std IV, who stated "I was called to be a diviner but I prepared to be a prophet. I slaughtered a goat in order to bring my ancestors close to each other and to the Holy Spirit. Then they accepted my calling as a prophet which I experienced in my dreams. My ancestors then told me what to do and I became a Christian diviner".

Forty percent of the Rand prophets were called as diviners. Those who were diviners "repented their sins first and then went to the church where the prophets prayed for them and gave them faith. The qualified prophets instruct such a person in the healing procedures and the various activities of a prophet. The diviner who wishes to become a prophet has to be trained by a qualified prophet. Usually he/she would be taken to a river or sea for immersion; he/she would be bathed, hit on the shoulders and body, made to vomit and given an enema. An animal would be slaughtered and he/she would be taught how to diagnose illnesses, how to assist in cases of misfortune and how to heal.

One of the Rand prophets related that he was approached by his ancestors who informed him that because he was "sick" (the same "sickness" as in the case of the calling of a diviner), he needed to become a prophet, to 'predict' and to heal. He then acknowledged their intervention through sacrificing a goat to them. Another was called by his ancestors to be a diviner but refused. He sacrificed a goat to his ancestors, who then acceded to his request to become a prophet. A respondent who had first been called to be a prophet, and later was also called to be a diviner, stated "Actually my ancestors are the ones who gave me my second calling, after which I sacrificed a goat to them". Another prophet first had "the idea" of becoming a prophet: "it was a clear one. I informed my ancestors who seemingly did not object".

The reconciliation of traditions can be a traumatic experience—it depends on the speed with which it takes place. When traditions are in transition, it is not simply a matter of discarding the old but of reconciliation taking place and much depends on how smoothly such reconciliation is effected. Some are consciously involved in this process while for others it is subconscious—depending on the importance of the cultural or religious aspect in the lives of those who have to take the reconciliatory step. In the case of the call to divinership, a person may attempt to ignore the call of the ancestors but yield eventually. Others become prophets but check it out with their ancestors in order to make sure that mal-relationships with them do not develop. Usually a special sacrifice is made in order to "apologise" to the ancestors.

The ancestors allow them to become prophets after the sacrifice, which is usually a goat, never a sheep. A prophet of the *Sardis Church of the Holy Ghost in Zion* stated that he was initially called to be a prophet "and nothing else". Later he had a dream in which he was admonished to become a diviner "but I prayed about it and it never came back again". Here no sacrifice was made, only a prayer was launched. Whether a person can become a prophet instead of a diviner actually depends on the ancestors. The person needs to be immersed and an animal, usually a goat, has to be slaughtered in order to appease his/her ancestors. He/she would get cords, be given enemas, be made to vomit (usually at the riverside or sea), and given some cleaners (*isiwasho*). The same procedure of mixing white ash with water (*isiwasho*, a cleanser/internal purifier) is also utilized with regard to the initiation of diviners.

There are some who see the change from diviner to prophet as forsaking the works of darkness, and as the commencement of a new life believing in God and working for Him as a prophet. There are a few among the prophets who do not even talk to diviners. One prophet prays to God asking Him for protection from acting or practising as a diviner, "but to remain a prophet forever". There is thus a temptation for some to hanker back to traditional activities. Some went through the training of both a prophet and a diviner including all the rituals and ceremonies which prospective diviners have to undergo.

In contrast to those who were trained either as diviners first and prophets later, or vice versa, there is also a prophet who had no training but who was called and given the message to proclaim. The Holy Spirit acts through her, which makes training a superfluous affair. This type of prophet is found especially in the mainline AIC.

E) RITUALS UNDERGONE BY A PROPHET IN ORDER TO BECOME A DIVINER

Those who maintained that they knew prophets who became diviners referred to the dreams through which the ancestors sent messages to these prophets requesting them to be diviners. After this, they were allowed by the ancestors to become prophets, but "they then continued using medicines (*muti*) and bones". It is not unusual to find a string of coloured wool round the neck of an *umthandazi* (prayer healer) or prophet, with small bones, usually that of chicken, attached to it or sometimes even strings around the head with yellow, red, green and white colours.

A number of the Rand prophets described those who became diviners, after having been initiated as prophets, as "not having enough faith. Their ancestors succeeded in pulling them out of the church and they then qualified as diviners". Some doubt whether such persons were real prophets. A prophet who becomes a diviner has to sacrifice a goat after completing a training period with other diviners. They are taught which herbs to use for specific diseases and how to use them. All the Rand prophets knew of prophets who became diviners. The strongest statement against diviners came from a Swazi prophet with Std V education, who originated from the Wakkerstroom area, where Zionism originally started. He maintained that "only those who are prophets in disguise end up being diviners. I regard the two—prophet and diviner—as in constant conflict". This is not an ideological conflict but an institutional conflict as he does not object to traditional medicines. He sees a competitive relationship, in which power is involved, between the prophet and the diviner, for acceptance as a healer. The competition has become more severe recently as the diviner has been more readily accepted as a respectable healer during the last decade by many members of churches. The diviners are seen as being able to remove pollution, and as advisers. In some indigenous churches such competition is obviated when the same person acts as diviner and prophet.

None of the prophets from the Durban metropolitan area were treated first by a diviner before the "Christian power" could function. Although most of the Rand prophets stated the same, thirty percent of these respondents were treated first by a prophet and later by a diviner. One prophet was persuaded by his family to consult a diviner when he was sick as ancestors are called in by the diviner to assist in healing procedures, especially with regard to cultural diseases.

F) THE ACCEPTABILITY OF MEDICINES USED BY DIVINERS

Of the metropolitan Durban prophets, thirty percent said medicines are unacceptable, but a third of these added "but we do use it because some sicknesses are easily healed when we use traditional medicines of diviners". A prophet from the *'Correntian' Church in Zion* described how she was called by the ancestors. She became very ill and had visions at night when she was half asleep. The prophet prayed for her and *amagobongo*, the diviners' *muti*, was used during training. In her dreams she was shown different types of medicines which she had to use for healing purposes. She became a prophet after they prayed for her "until I had the Holy Spirit".

Some of the Rand prophets stated *inter alia* that they use all the herbs "which are not for killing". Some of the acceptable medicines mentioned were incense (*impepho*), red soil, red ochre, blue stone and emetic products, snuff, ash, vaseline, epsom salt, salt and vinegar, for vomiting, steaming and emetics. A prophet who was initiated in Empangeni emphasized that "there is nothing wrong with diviners". Here is both an ideological and institutional acceptance of traditional healers.

Thirty percent of the Rand prophets stated emphatically that traditional medicines are not acceptable, and one added "diviners do not work for God". This is both an institutional and ideological rejection. The medicines are also rejected in the struggle to acquire what they consider to be the newly discovered truth, and to influence and control people within the context of their understanding of the Christian message. The rest, however, had no problems in utilizing the diviner's medicines for their healing procedures. The reaction in these cases is against the office of the diviner as an institution, but not against it in the ideological sense for there is an appreciation of its healing procedures.

The prophets in the metropolitan Durban surroundings emphasized that the prophet's activities included diagnosing the illness of patients and methods to heal them, the prediction of future events and analyzing the causes of misfortune. These were also highlighted by the Rand prophets. One stated, "I preach about the things of the other world as I am also a bishop of the church". Another concentrated on the vertical dimension. He stated, "I repent and lead people to repentance and admonish them to follow God in truth and honesty".

The combination of the office of leader and prophet, ie. of minister and prophet, does not imply that such churches have no other prophets. Most of these leaders want prophets in their churches because their ministerial duties are usually very demanding, especially when it comes to keeping the group intact. As a charismatic person the prophet is solely a medium of the power of metaphysical forces, in particular of 'the Spirit' (umoya), which in most cases refers not only to the Holy Spirit, but also to the ancestors. Prophets divine the sources of evil, detect hidden moral weaknesses. They see through people, especially where they have to establish the source of an illness, as physical afflictions could be the result of moral transgressions.

Just as diviners are feared because of their ability to 'see' into a person's past, prophets are also sometimes feared. Their office could lead them to subjectivity for they receive their office directly from the metaphysical world without the intervention of an institution. Thus it is important that they work under the control of a minister whose authority is based on the rite of ordination as exercised by the church. The social relationship between leader, whether bishop or minister, and prophet is thus of great importance for a group. As the minister has to exercise his institutional authority carefully, his prophet task—when these are combined—could suffer or his church could suffer if he is forthright in this. The mystical power of the ancestral forces which is autocratic, absolute and unpredictable, could contribute to subjectivity when prophets operate through them and 'the Spirit', whose injunctions are not always consistent with Scripture.

The prophets protect the people of their churches by predicting their future, warning them about problems they face, helping them to avoid misfortune, helping them to get healed when sick, and by praying for them. One stated, "I light candles and pray and tie ropes around their bodies". Others stated "if I see any coming danger and illness I give them ropes and *isiwasho* to protect them against it"; "my predictions and prophecies warn and guide them in their future life and this is how they will defeat the devil"; "through *isiwasho* and prayer meetings we cast out demons and evil spirits". Others emphasized that the protection that their patients or victims receive comes from "the messenger(s)", as they themselves, as prophets, do not have the power in themselves. The "messenger", in the singular or plural, is the guiding ancestor(s). Another prophet specifically referred to "only God" as "the one who protects us all". The above emphases of various prophets do not imply that they are only this world orientated, ie. that their ministry concentrates only on healing, interrelationship problems etc. They are, however, deeply concerned about the daily issues of the adherents of their churches.

In reply to the question about what they consider to be the greatest problems black people face in their areas, the prophets of metropolitan Durban stated: sickness and unemployment; that some are unable to have children; that some have children by way of caesarean operations; evil spirit possession; witchcraft and sorcery; and that some have criminal problems.

On this question, the Rand prophets stated *inter alia* that the greatest problems of black people are: headache, body pains, bewitching, kidney problems, menstrual problems, stomach pains, pregnancy pains, bad luck, blood pressure and conflicts, food poisoning, insomnia, insanity, fear of lightning, labour, marriage, fear of evil spirits, swelling of bodily organs, heart attacks, unhealed sores and wounds, sterility, dizziness, bad dreams and unusual or terrifying visions. Not one referred to political issues, and hardly any reference was made to socio-economic issues—and this from black respondents living on the Rand and particularly in Soweto. This should not leave the impression that these issues do not matter. In fact, their political views are often strongly contrary to the *status quo* but they seldom express them and preferably not in public. Adherents in the different indigenous churches assist one another and, as a result of their stoic approach to life, they manage to survive and make ends meet. Many have maintained—and some have even raised— their standard of living during the last few years of chaos and turmoil.

On the question of what they consider to be the greatest problems in the country, the prophets from metropolitan Durban referred to finance and the cost of living. A few emphasized the following: "A prophet is not allowed to get involved in politics"; "I have only one thing to do—that is to prophesy and heal people and nothing else"; "prophets are not allowed to involve themselves in politics, so I have nothing to do with the black people's problems". The last remark comes from a Zulu female prophet with Std 1 education. The word "Zion" does not feature in the name of her church—significantly it includes the designation "Ethiopian" and "Apostolic". Most of the churches which use the designation "Ethiopian" are conservative but are less apolitical than those who are "Apostolic" and "Zionist". Reference has already been made to the socio-economic and political involvement within the AIC without members being involved in outside organizations related to these dimensions of their existence.

The political attitude of the Zionists is steadily changing and reflects their approach to socio-economic issues. Those who suffer with regard to food and shelter are readily assisted by co-members in these churches.

H) THE BLENDING OF TWO WORLDS

How and why?

Theologically, the Zionist movement is a blending of two worlds—traditional African and Christian, with emphasis on healing, purification rites, food taboos and indigenised services with a dynamic undertone. In this context the prophet plays a great role. However, the question is whether or not the prophet is a replacement of the traditional diviner.

It is obvious from the above that the prophet figure is parallel to that of the traditional diviner. This is clear in the calling of a prophet, the training and the various aspects that receive attention with regard to his/ her disposition to prophethood and its implications. Not only is the prophet entered by 'the Spirit' and/or ancestor spirit, but dreams, visions, water, ash, objects as well as procedures regarding patient/ victim, all play roles in both the diviners' and prophets' activities. Both have to do with natural illnesses (*umkhuhlane*) but especially with spirit possession or 'pollution'. While Zulu diviners often act in groups, especially in their healing procedures, the same is true of the activities of the prophets where the singing and dancing of the congregation play an important role.

The findings of these surveys indicate clearly that there is a whole range of similarities between the Zulu diviners and the Zulu Zionist prophet. Pauw is right when he maintains that these similarities "do not merely consist of a number of isolated aspects, but it is a comprehensive similarity involving a complete pattern: Zionist prophet follows the diviner prophet in all important aspects" (Pauw, B.A., *Religion in a Tswana Chiefdom*, OUP, 1960, p. 205). Pauw further states "The belief in the Spirit, however, does not completely displace the belief in ancestors in Zulu Zionist Churches, and in spite of substituting it in some instances, it is nevertheless used to uphold and sanction it in others". (*Ibid.*, p. 207). To substantiate the latter, Pauw refers to Sundkler's statement that "Spirit and Angel are concepts which Zionists use rather indiscriminately....the Angel's main reproach in churches of Zionist type is that the ancestral spirits have been neglected". (Sundkler, B.G.M., *Bantu prophets in South Africa*, OUP, 1948, pp. 249ff).

As indicated above, the prophet type of office and leadership is found mainly in Zionist Churches, where the emphasis is on preachers and healers; not in the Ethiopian type of Churches, where the ministry is more of a priestly type stressing, for example, the continuation of the church tradition. The former is based more on the pentecostal approach; the latter more on the traditional, historic type of church. The prophet is sometimes the real leader, exerting the kingship type of leadership, ie. he (very seldom "she" in this case) is the most important religious, ceremonial figure and healer. There are a few large independent church movements in which the kingship type of leadership with its system of rank prevails. The Zionist type of church has a variety of office-bearers (evangelists, deacons, preachers, faith healers, prophets, ministers, bishops, archbishops, presidents) and in a few the prophet is the main leader. In most of these churches a syncretic strain can be discerned— as is evident from much that has been stated by prophets during discussions and interviews. This has also been witnessed in their healing procedures in which diviners' practices are adapted within the Christian context, with purification rites, taboos, certain healing procedures, counteraction of sorcery and witchcraft, etc. The Zionist leader has the authority of a king and, often, the healing powers ascribed to the king although the office of prophet is usually separate. In most churches the prayer healer (*umthandazi*) is of a lesser rank than a prophet (*umprofeti*). In some churches women are the prayer healers (*abathandazi*) and men mainly the prophets. However, if such a church has a woman prophet, she acts as a senior (*mama*) among the women prayer healers.

The prophets use various methods in healing. It is clear from the empirical research, which involved over seventy prophets, that to speak in general terms about the procedures of prophets does not give a true picture. The above mentioned expositions prove this point. For some, special vestments, scarves and other symbolic attire with specific colours are important. One could say that, for all, water mixed with ash (referred to in *Numm* 19:9) is vital for healing as is ash mixed in water for diviners.

As in the case of diviners, many illnesses are ascribed to spirit possession which has been "thrown" on a victim through witchcraft, a term nearly always used for sorcery. Illnesses could also be ascribed to ancestors, turned sour because of being neglected or for other reasons. Such ancestors do not "possess" someone as is the case with other evil spirits. Relating diseases to the metaphysical world immediately puts them in a serious context. The prophetic healers are considered to have a clearer insight into the psycho-therapeutic aspects of healing. They go to the source of information on these matters through their ability to understand the ancestors' messages, which come through dreams or "insanity", ie. through visions. They are thus informed of the spiritual causes of diseases and psychic disturbances. This is also considered to be the forte of the diviners. The western trained medical doctor either is unaware of all this or has little understanding of it.

Furthermore, while the diviner and the prophet patiently enter into the background history and beliefs of each patient, in most cases this aspect is completely ignored by western trained doctors. Christianity, as practised in the historic churches is also not directed to what are, for many Africans, very real issues, such as the powers of the ancestors, the tremendous potency of witches and sorcerers, and the forces they have at their disposal. The prophets have to counteract these forces and here the traditional thought patterns take over, as in the case of about eighty percent of the prophets interviewed. Illnesses are put within the context of traditional cosmology. The diagnostic and therapeutic work are existentially, but not formally, brought into context. Thus, the prophet's therapy is aimed at confrontation. The solution does not lie in traditional reconciliation but in the elimination of the adversary through counter methods used under the guidance of 'the Spirit' and/or ancestor spirit(s). The evil spirit has to be exorcised. While this was done by the diviner under the guidance of an ancestor spirit(s), the prophet calls for assistance from 'the Spirit'/Holy Spirit and/or messenger(s) ie. ancestor spirit(s), also referred by some as 'angel'. In this context, prayer alone is insufficient. A visible act or ritual should also be enacted, just as in the case of the diviner.

The prophets take spiritual causes (the evil forces) seriously and combat them in a way which appeals to the African mind. The symbolic objects as indicated above represent power—no less than the power of the magical medicinal objects of the diviner or herbalist, through which evil is driven out and fortification and security are effected. Here the support of the church group is important. It has first to be established what type of disease the patient experiences—usually this is indicated in the dreams and visions—then, what the intention of the adversary is and what these forces demand. The forces are categorized as evil spirits or demons which should be exorcised. Witchcraft and sorcery are seen as the causative factors in illness. Various objects and ritual procedures are used. It is here that one questions the superficial descriptions of romanticists who act as if the prophetic practices are based only on the Holy Spirit as source through prayer. Only about twenty percent of those interviewed in the Greater Durban and Rand/Soweto areas concentrate only on the Holy Spirit and prayer. The dreams and visions give authority to the work of the prophets, as these come from the Holy Spirit and/or ancestors. Dreams are sent by well intentioned ancestors, by bad spirits, by diviners, or by ordinary spontaneous dreams. Visions are instant and are from well intentioned ancestors. The link between dreams, especially visions, and prophecies is very close. Prophets declare that they are led by 'the Spirit' and/or the ancestors in their dreams, but a large number emphasize the instant insights they receive through visions.

In the Old Testament "vision" is the word used for nearly all revelations that come through a prophet. True and false prophets could have visions (Vriezen, Th.C., *The theology of the Old Testament*, Oxford, Blackwell, 1962, pp. 245-6). The biblical prophet's visual experience was never described with the word *chazah* (behold), but rather with the word 'see' (*ra'ah*). The false prophets were "beholders"; they gave their own visions. For the Old Testament prophets, the visionary world of revelations was a direct experience of God's presence. For the Zionist prophet, 'the Spirit' and/or ancestral spirits are very much to the fore.

In the Old Testament the dream also has a revolutionary character. Dreams play an important part in stories; for example, those associated with Joseph and Daniel in the Old Testament. But dreams are not a means of revelation with any of the major prophets, except perhaps with Zecheriah and Joel. The prophets received their revelations in a 'vision' or by the word (Vriezen, p. 243). In the Zionist Churches which accept the office of prayer healer (*umthandazi*) and prophet (*umprofeti*), a distinction is often made, as has been indicated, between those two offices. This is done on the basis that the *umthandazi* work mainly through dreams while the prophets get their information from 'the Spirit' and/or ancestor(s), mainly through visions which are immediate. In the Old Testament the dream is a means of receiving God's Word but could, like the vision, be an experience of God's presence (*Gen.* 28:11ff). The dream did not play an important role for the prophets of the Old Testament. Jeremiah was of the opinion that revelations by dreams were only given to false prophets (*Jer.* 23:25-32; 27:9; 29:8). Jeremiah did not reject them on the basis of principle, but he was radical in many respects (Vriezen, p. 244). The "possessing" aspect of the Spirit is not mentioned either. He also rejected the sacrificial ritual.

In the Old Testament the dream oracles were considered largely to have been given only to those outside Israel, the heathen (*goyim*). In the later form of prophetism in Israel the dream hardly played any role, although it was not rejected but accepted. The Old Testament revelation was thus entirely different from that of the nations around Israel, where dreams were considered to be of vital significance (Vriezen, p. 244). Communion with God was generally personal, immediate with the major prophets and not through dreams. Zionist prophets in general emphasize this immediate contact with the supernatural world through visions. Such dreams and visions also play a role with herbalists and diviners in their healing practices.

The Zionist prayer healer's dreams cover much the same aspects as the diviner's dreams, in which symbols such as different types of water, colours, cords and certain animals predominate. Dreams are an important means of communications with the Zionist prayer healers and although visions predominate with most prophets, dreams have specific communication value for them.

The Old Testament prophet and the AIC prophet

While the diviner and the AIC prophet emphasize healing, the biblical prophet's task is to bring the "Word of God". God's word was the major emphasis in Old Testament prophetism. No forces other than God direct the Old Testament prophets. The majority of the Zionist prophets, on the other hand, concentrate on healing and 'prediction', ie. informing people about which forces are affecting them adversely. They have no special task in the proclamation of the biblical message. Those who are influenced to join these churches do so because of their success at healing. The Old Testament prophets gave the proclamation of the word a dynamic dimension; the Zionist prophets give their churches a dynamic stance because of their healing activities and 'predictions'. In the Old

Testament God gives the prophet a word (*dabar* or *imrah*) (Vriezen, p. 25ff). The vision that the prophet receives in the Old Testament is often a word, a message (*Hab.* 2:1-5). The prophetic word not only preaches salvation but brings it near and makes it reality. For them the word of God is dynamic, but *dunamis* (power) is not used in the context of some kind of mysterious power.

In the Zionist context, the "messenger", particularly 'the Spirit', plays a vital role. In the Old Testament the messenger of Yahweh, also referred to as the angel of the Lord, is the visual manifestation of God. The messengers can be manifested as people or as angels. They represent God. In most Zionist Churches the messenger (sometimes, although seldom, these days referred to as *ingelosi*) is the ancestor, and "the Spirit" (*uMoya*) refers to the Holy Spirit, who is the source of power and is often interpreted in these churches as the vital force.

"The Spirit" in the Old Testament is an activity of God's power. It is a power proceeding from God, an inspiration from 'strengthening', a 'quickening', and an 'animation', which fills man with spiritual gifts. (Vriezen, pp. 249–250). "The Spirit" can "possess" a person (1 *Kings* 18:12, *Ezek.* 9:1). It can "inspire" a person to do something (1 *Sam* 11:6); it moves to ecstasy (1 *Sam* 10:6); it is a life-giving force (*Job* 27:3; 33:4); it fills man with spiritual gifts (*Ex.* 31:3), with knowledge, and with strength; it renews man inwardly, and it inspires man to preach. "The Spirit of God" is God working in the world in many ways, making His faithful experience His power. The major prophets "never connect revelation with the operation of the Spirit, except Ezekiel (once) and Deutero-Isaiah... Jeremiah, especially, is completely silent on the subject of the Spirit of God.... behind this attitude we must see an inward opposition to the spiritualism of false prophets" (Vriezen, pp. 250–252). This is also the case with Paul. Jeremiah is in such direct communication that he has no need for any intervention of the Spirit (cf. *Jeremiah* 31:33).

Nevertheless, where the Spirit does play a role, it puts the human being totally in the service of God, and prepares him to do the work of God. The Spirit is the possession of God and can never be the possession of any human being, but it establishes a union between God and man. The Spirit is an inner recreative power which prepares the human being for communion with God.

In the Zionist Churches the Spirit has the significant role of giving power, and, as indicated earlier, the traditional African emphasis on power lends particular weight to this interpretation. The power associated with the Holy Spirit is a life force so vital in the African context that

Jesus hardly plays a role in the healing procedures. Sickness means weakness, and vital force means life and health. Furthermore, the charismatic gifts of the Spirit such as *glossolalia* "to see", "to predict", are associated, for most people with the Spirit, as well as with the ancestral spirits. The Old Testament prophet is a proclaimer of the Word. The Zionist prophet is a healer, a guardian assisting those who experience misfortunes and other difficulties, and a real helper in need. The prophets' association with the Spirit and/or ancestors (as indicated, twenty percent of those interviewed rejected ancestral contact) and the sympathetic attitude with which they approach the victim/patient, gives great credibility to their office within, and even outside, the Zionist Churches.

There are some who question the theological position of the prophet. They ask whether the activities of those who maintain they are guided by ancestral spirits, and who practise various tradition-oriented rituals, can be classified as Christian. Is the prophet a mouth-piece of God? Is he/she called by the Holy Spirit? Or has the prophet accommodated diviner practices within the context of a church, which in most cases makes the office of the prophet merely parallel to that of the diviner? It has been established how closely the approach of most prophets resembles, that of the diviner, but some of these prophets are often critical of certain practices of the diviners. A few said that the diviners and the herbalists work under the injunctions of evil spirits. It has also been established that prophets try to convert diviners. Specific reference has been made to this. Sundkler had already came across this phenomenon, stating that "while on the one hand Zionists have formed their religion on the pattern of the *isangoma* system, yet on the other they are very careful to point out that of course they have nothing in common with such people". However, "The basic pattern from which Zulu Zionism is copied is that of diviner and witch finder activities rather than that of the historic Christian Church" (Sundkler, 1948, p. 242). This may be the basic pattern but the activities are not basically the same.

Is the indigenous church prophet a modernized diviner?

A question that is asked is whether the prophet is a modernized diviner. To speak of "prophet" in general terms raises many problems, because the point of departure could differ from one prophet to another.

The parallel between the calling of the diviner and of the prophet has been indicated. Furthermore, the diviner reinstates the importance of the ancestral spirits in the lives of many, as could also be said of a large number of the prophets. Also most prophets have an *ukuthwasa* experience, when "the Spirit" and/or ancestral spirit approaches them to become a prophet, and they become ill. The illness is sometimes long-term and no cure is possible by western means. Like the diviner, the prophet goes through a period of apprenticeship when, *inter alia*, sacrifices are usually made to the ancestral spirits, when purification rites are observed and when interpretation of dreams, the reception of visions, diagnosis, prediction and healing are learned. All these aspects are also to be detected in the calling and training of diviners. It has been indicated that some prophets have been trained as diviners, a phenomenon which has increased through the last decade. Not only church members, but also some prophets, call in the aid of diviners, and in some cases, of herbalists. Some potential prophets considered assistance from diviners essential, in order to be able to utilize power from the sources to which the diviners have access. They wish to use this power in their ministries as prophets.

The combination of traditional and Christian forces is thus essential to these prophets, especially in their healing tasks. In the churches established by missionaries, diviners were looked upon as nothing but agents of the devil, but in most of the African independent/indigenous churches their traditional significance in the community is taken seriously. The real strength of the church is seen in the acceptance of the power of 'the Spirit', with which the ancestral spirits can serve as mediating forces. The diviner who wishes to become a prophet has to get the approval of the ancestral spirit(s), and could go through a period of illness. His/her initiation includes purification rites.

'The Spirit' (*uMoya*) to which most of the prophets refer, is described by Sundkler as "a general state of being divinely possessed, whereas *ingelosi* and the Voice are channels by which *uMoya* reveals itself and make its will known" (Sundkler 1948, p. 249). The word *ingelosi*, angel, is also used for an ancestral spirit. Today *ingelosi* is much less used than *idlozi* or *amadlozi* (ancestral spirit(s)). The ancestral spirit assists in the diagnosis and treatment of illnesses. When epidemics break out it is a sign of ancestral wrath. The ancestor is not only a communicator but also a helper. He/she informs the prophet what disease affects the victim, how the patient should be treated and what type of medicines should be used. Water mixed with ash, over which the prophet has prayed (*isiwasho*), is a standard prescription. The ancestor also informs the prophet about the colour of the vestments to be worn, and often about the type of sacrifice to be made, particularly in real crisis situations. In spite of the attitude of some western doctors and hospitals, special welcoming ceremonies are observed when a patient returns from hospital. The sacrifice to the ancestors, the prayers and various rituals are reminiscent of the traditional approach to sickness and healing. Sacrifices open up the way to ancestors and are a means of expressing gratitude and of asking for help and protection.

The "Voice" has to be clearly heard. The result is that the prayer healers and prophets, when "baptized" for strength in the pool, the dam, the river or the sea, have to allow the leader to shout into their ears, so that they open up and are able to hear clearly what the ancestors say. Evil forces could disturb the ability to hear the "Voice".

The concepts of the Spirit, the angel, and the ancestors have been the source of much subjectivity in interpretations and approach. Differences often lead to secessions. The induction of the Holy Spirit also leads to many secessions in pentecostally-oriented churches. No wonder then that, in 1980, there were officially three thousand two hundred and seventy independent/indigenous churches in South Africa—in reality, at least a thousand denominations more. One among the many other causes for this is the role of the ancestral spirits in a large number of these churches.

Why divination by some prophets? Why syncretism?

The practices of some of the prophets are referred to as divination against certain forms of witchcraft and sorcery. The Zionist prophet uses his/her power. As a result of socio-economic, cultural and political tensions, especially in the urban areas, the assistance of the diviner and of the prayer healer/prophet becomes important. The forces are so strong that the Bible study and prayer approach are considered inadequate. Much more is needed to counteract witchcraft and sorcery too strong for the western approach, and this "much more"is the utilization of traditional methods. In any event the patient/victim who comes from a traditional background will not be satisfied with only Bible texts and prayer. Rituals are expected, but these are often streamlined. The modernization process and the uncertainty it brings intensifies the search for security against the ever threatening forces of destruction—forces which threaten to destroy that which has been a fortification against them. Referring to this, Sundkler observed four decades ago that "some Zionist prophets in this situation form, as it were, a modern movement of witch-finders, who assist and in many ways replace the heathen witch-finder or diviner. The pattern of heathen divining is closely followed, but it has been reshaped to suit modern conditions" (Sundkler, 1948, 255). Schlosser maintains that the process of diagnosis and of healing in the Zionist Churches, as executed by the prophet, is nothing less than a Christian form of traditional exorcism (cf. Schlosser, K., *Eingeborene Kirchen in Süd- und Südwest-Afrika*, Kiel, Muhlau, 1958, pp. 205-6).

Here one finds syncretism of the traditional approach and Christianity, where the traditional elements are utilized in the Christian context. The rituals and ingredients used, the procedures observed and the various symbols deployed have a miraculous effect when correctly brought into play. Prophets are considered to have supernatural power which comes from the supernatural world. One seldom hears, among the prophets, that Christ gave the various gifts to them. For most of the prophets, "the Spirit" of power takes precedence and in this context the ancestors have a significant role to play. However, the prophet has a specific position, and understands the problems of victims/patients much better, it is claimed, than any western trained doctor and better even than the diviners. Their supernatural contact with "the Spirit" and/ or ancestral spirit(s) gives them insights into the nature and causes of illnesses which is not the case with the others. Prophets are thus considered to be more convincing in their diagnosis and procedures than the western doctor.

A variety of remedies is given, a variety of techniques is utilized and the healing process is in the hands of a robed person, who has supernatural contact and thus supernatural power. The traditional and Christian forces are combined and the event impresses as a result of the ritual, prayer (word therapy), candles, cords, holy water, staves, drums, singing and rhythmic movements, etc. The prophet receives information, usually instantly, on the type of illness and how it should be cured. Few questions are put to the patient, unlike the situation with the western doctor or with the diviner's *vumisa* practices, in which leading questions are asked. A few do use this method, during which "Amens" are often heard. Some observe a sooth-saying or divining ceremony, which is referred to as prophecy. Not only is the disease diagnosed, but the witch or sorcerer is also identified. Hidden sins are 'seen' in the individual and in the church through such prophecy, ie. it is made known to them by 'the Spirit' or even by ancestral spirits. While traditional Africans scold their ancestors when severe drought or epidemics continue after sacrifices have been made to them, those in the indigenous churches do not practice such scolding as these events are seen as judgements from God on man's sin.

According to Vilakazi, the traditional Zulu religion is based on two pillars, namely "ancestor worship" and magic. Vilakazi emphasizes that in all his experience as a Zulu, "living among Zulu carriers of the culture, and in the field, I cannot remember a single instance when I heard a prayer by a traditionalist offered to *uMvelingqangi*. It is always to the ancestral spirits that prayers are made in cases of sterility in women, in cases of illness or when the cattle are dying unaccountably. In diagnosing the cause of the disease or misfortune, the diviner discovers the cause either in witchcraft and sorcery and/or in the anger of the Spirits, not of *uMvelinggangi*" ie. Go (cf. Vilakazi, A., *Zulu transformations*, Pietermaritzburg, University of Natal Press, 1962, p. 89). This deep-seated approach still has its influence in many Zionist Churches. Vital force is a normal issue in the African context—such power can be used positively or negatively. If used positively it heals, it wards off evil, it can bring rain. It works on the presupposition that the human being can influence the supernatural forces; black magic is related to sorcery which is effected because of jealousy, hatred and suspicion. In some of the indigenous churches these issues play a significant role. Ash and water, which has been prayed over, is very powerful and its effects could be miraculous. The prophets often use what are considered to be powerful ingredients and procedures in the traditional context because of the fear among the patients/victims of the powerful effects of witchcraft and sorcery, fear of the activities of potent evil forces which have to be counteracted by potent means. In this context prayer is, for some prophets, not as effective as the age-old anti-witchcraft and anti-sorcery practices. For some healers the Bible and prayer are mighty weapons against these forces but most prophets regularly use "cleaners", such as *isiwasho*.

In a situation of social, economic and political upheaval, specific traditional beliefs become stronger because of the tensions experienced. These beliefs are considered to be most effective in carving a way to the future. Through them the sorcerer, the great disturber of the future, is neutralised, his "poison" revealed and removed and harmony restored. Through transference of power by way of inner and outer cleansing, the utilization of various objects, bodily contact and the laying on of hands (illness implies bodily weakness), the person receives health. Sundkler maintained that "the actual belief in witchcraft is vital in the Zionist Church. Both Zionist prophesying and Zionist healing are based on such a belief. No healing is complete until the prophet has found and removed from the patient's hut some horn or bottle, supposed to contain "*ubuthaka-thi*-poison*" (ie. bewitched poison) (Sundkler, 1948, p. 264). This is no longer such a predominant feature. Divination is used even against those who refuse to join a specific church.

Preference for the prophet as a contextualiser

Special attention is given by leaders of indigenous churches to having prophets in their churches. Church leaders have stated, when asked about this, that when looking for a prophet(s) it is important to get the right person with special gifts. Prophets are considered to be extremely important, they have insights and power which they receive from the supernatural world. Their visions and predictions are a great asset to the church and they are consulted on most of the important matters pertaining to the church. They decide on the colours of the uniforms which members will wear, assess candidates for leadership positions in the church, indicate the sins and adversaries of the congregation, express the wishes of 'the Spirit' and/or ancestor spirits and "predict" the future development of the church. The prophet is consulted on all important issues in most indigenous churches which have instituted this office. Of the three categories of healing—through immersion in a bath, dam, river or the sea; through healing during church services; or through consultation with a prophet—the latter takes a significant position. The prophet, mainly in the Zionist and Apostolic type of churches and in a few Ethopian churches, has the gift of 'prediction', healing and divining.

There is a strong desire among many females to become prayer healers and prophets. The prayer women, referred to as "half-prophets", are given *izikali* (holy sticks) for healing purposes and authority to visit and pray for the sick and to follow healing procedures with them.* This is also the conclusion of West in his research in Soweto (cf. West, M., *Bishops and prophets in a black city*, Cape Town, David Philip, 1975, p. 98). The prayer women usually rank below the prophets; most of them have no training while most of the prophets, as indicated above, receive training and go through initiation procedures.

The life history of a prophet is, in many respects, parallel to that of a diviner, as stated above. They are called and go through a period of illness which is only successfully treated by another prophet (cf. also

---

*Some Bishops carry an iron rod based on *Rev.* 2:27 "and he shall reign with a rod of iron, as when earthen pots are broken in pieces..."

West, 1975, p. 98). When a person is called to become a prophet there is a strong resemblance, as indicated, to the calling of a diviner: illness, nervousness, ancestors tell the person to go to a certain person to be trained, the training includes purification rituals which are vital, and singing and rhythmic movements (dancing in a circle) are part of the initiation procedure, as in the case of a diviner. White ash mixed with water, used during initiation of a diviner, is also used in the case of a prophet in training.

There are also parallel characteristics between diviners and prophets as far as their behaviour and activity after initiation are concerned: they both work under the injunctions of the supernatural world—ancestors in the case of the diviners; the Spirit and/or ancestor(s) in the case of prophets. The diviners, when called in dreams play a significant role. The same with the prophets. Both receive revelations about their own purification before becoming either diviners or prophets; both have the ability to predict.

The diviner's hair remains uncut as does that of the prophet, who refers to *Judges* 13:5 and 1 *Sam* 1:11 in this connection. There is also some similarity with diviners in the prophet's special vestments— although in most cases these do not differ from those of the other members of the church—cords with symbolic colours; the way the cords are attached; as well as the parts of the body to which they are attached— around the neck, wrists, ankles, around the waist and cross-wise on the shoulders. The prophet can often be clearly distinguished in a group because of the long hair, the special objects and the vestments.

The diviner also uses holy sticks but these often consist of the tail of a beast assembled on a short stick, while the prophet uses the rod or staff based on *Ex.* 7:9-12 "And the Lord said to Moses and Aaron when Pharoah says to you, 'Prove yourselves by working a miracle' then you shall say to Aaron, 'Take your rod and cast it down before Pharoah, that it may become a serpent'.... and it became a serpent .... the wise men and the sorcerers... the magicians of Egypt, did the same by their secret arts.... every man cast down his rod, and they became serpents. But Aaron's rod swallowed up all their rods". The prophets' staff is a miracle worker—with it, evil spirits are kept away, driven out, and through it, its owner receives the power of 'the Spirit' and can heal. It is one of the main objects used in exorcism. The "gifts of healing by the one Spirit" (1 *Cor* 12:9) are seldom distributed without the holy stick/staff (*isikali*). It is regularly purified and thus ritually strengthened in running water, in water mixed with ash and in the sea. All the staves are bundled together and put into the sea—the purification rite applied to these staves also symbolizes the unity of the group.

It is evident from the above empirical studies that although approaches to the prophets vary in detail, there is "considerable uniformity", as West has also observed (West, p. 104). The reintegrative work of the prayer healer/prophet is of great significance. Their warmth, empathy and integrity are greatly appreciated. As indicated, their approach to the patient/victim evokes confidence in the prophet as healer on the part of the patient/victim. Their world views are not foreign to each other and, through diagnosis, that which is an enigma to the patient becomes clarified in such a way that his worldview becomes meaningful. Inner turmoil is replaced with understanding. The diagnosis and the discussion of it with the patient/victim lead to a relationship between patient and healer which is important for meaningful treatment. Through prediction the prophet knows what the circumstances of the patient/ victim are. The patient/victim is treated within a familiar worldview and without the traumatic break that hospitalization brings. The emphasis is on togetherness, or reintegration—not on hospitalization, ie. individualization in distress. The prophet's church takes a caring interest in the patient/victim, not only in his/her problems but in the whole life situation of such a person. Relatives remain in contact with the patient/victim and this gives him/her personal support. Here they can pray together and provide moral support.

Some prophets charge for their services, but where they do so it is much less than the diviners, some of whom are considered to be charlatans. Furthermore, the prophet is linked to a church and, in the case of an indigenous church, it is usually a closely knit community which plays a supportive role in healing and in need. In most of these communities the sense of responsibility to one another is greater than in any other association or church. This in itself has healing and therapeutic significance, especially in situations of stress, discomfort and misfortune. Here, healing is also integrated with worship, something which cannot be said of most of the established churches.

It has been pointed out that in traditional medicine the emphasis is on suggestion, confession, catharsis and group support, which implies removal of evil forces through vomiting, steaming and emetics, ie. purification. These emphases are very strong in the indigenous churches, where spirit possession is approached through confession, purification rites, dancing, singing and handclapping. The group is essential for shared experience at the church service, whether in the church building (although very few indigenous churches have church buildings), a house, the veld, open spaces in towns and cities, the river or the sea. These are holy places where people remove their shoes, on the basis of *Ex.* 3:5. This verse relates how God commanded Moses to take off his shoes "for the place on which you a standing is holy ground". It is this group therapy which assists the adherents of these churches to adapt to the urban environment. Many of their problems, especially crises, are explained in the context of physical weakness, which is described as illness. This puts it outside the sphere of the ordinary and therefore in need of extraordinary methods which only the diviner/herbalist for the traditional people or prophet for many in the indigenous churches, can provide. Here the western trained doctor is basically an *ignoramus*. As in the case of the diviner, the prophet explains in a comprehensible manner to the victim/patient what has led to his/her condition. The prophet has thus laid the foundation for a contextual procedure which sometimes seems simplistic, strange and not rationally orientated, but resorts rather to the sphere of magic. Nevertheless, here is found a holistic approach which includes body, mind and soul in the healing process. In crisis, adherents turn to their religious anchors, and in the indigenous churches healing is not practised outside the domain of religion but is fully implicated in this context. Through healing successes, prophets often attract adherents to their churches where the emphasis is no longer on the ethnic group or on kinship relations. The church group occupies an important place in the life of each person. Some prophets attain a special reputation of being able to drive out evil spirits. Couples who experience marital problems may appear before the bishop or come to the prophet to have the "bad spirit" removed. This "bad spirit" may not be an evil spirit *per se* but could be an ancestral spirit which has turned against them and is negatively influencing their lives. With others the problems of alcohol and addiction to *dagga* are treated by the leader in the church or by the prophet or prayer healer, while the congregation sing to the accompaniment of drums and rhythmic movements (as with exorcism at the sea where these issues, as works of demons and evil spirits, are treated in the same way). Other treatments include putting staves against the person (usually not in the sea since the sea water is strong enough); laying hands on the person, who is forcefully hit (often manhandled) on the body to get the evil forces out and loud praying and shouting take place, ending in *glossolalia*. The "victims" of these evil forces are often shivering when they come out of the sea, exhausted.

Such sessions lead to definite results, not only in the lives of the victims/patients but also in the lives of those who witness the proceedings. When 'the Spirit' and/or ancestor spirits mediate power to the victim/ patient suffering from possession, spirits remove themselves. Ancestors play a role in these matters with many because they continue to take an intense interest in the well-being of their descendants. Such spirit mediumship to their progeny is accepted, but the possession cults referred to extensively above acknowledge possession by alien spirits, not ancestral spirits. The ancestral spirits are mediators but 'the Spirit', implying the Holy Spirit, can enter a person and possess a person in that it strengthens the person. Such Spirit possession occurs mainly among women, without leading to visions, predictions or prophecy. Mediumship results in visions and prophecy, whereas possession of the Spirit implies being elevated to a higher level of spirituality in which the limitations and weaknesses of the flesh have been overcome. It is a sign that "the Spirit" is at work in a church where this happens—such a church has spiritual power. Healing and possession by the "Spirit'" are especially typical of indigenized African pentecostalism. All these activities have a cathartic effect in which the ecstasy reached through dancing is a concrete sign of being under the control of 'the Spirit'. The person is taken hold of by 'the Spirit'. While the ancestor is usually not a possessor but a mediator, Lee maintains that the *"ukuthwasa* possession" by which an ancestral spirit takes hold of and admonishes a person to become a diviner, has been detected among women in the indigenous churches in Zululand (Lee, S.G., "Spirit possession among the Zulu" in Beattie J. and Middleton J.,(eds), *Spirit mediumship and society in Africa*, London, 1969, p. 200). Possession can thus be effected by foreign spirits which are evil forces and have to be removed, or by "the Spirit" which raises a person to a spiritual level in which these forces are overcome. Spirit mediumship, ie. through relaying visions, messages, predictions, etc., is effected by ancestral spirits—they can also mediate the Holy Spirit ie. bring the Holy Spirit to a person.

Healers have a special place in their churches and find great appreciation for their work—a very different situation from that in the established mission churches where healing is a kind of appendix to their church activities. In most of the indigenous churches it is central. All the activities in these churches relate to purification, healing—including immersion in a dam, river or the sea—the driving out of evil spirits through "thrashing" them out, laying on of hands and holy staves to give 'the Spirit' to a person, and many other activities. This elevates religion to the dramatic, and it serves as a catharsis in the chaotic situation that has caused the destruction of old securities and trusted traditions. In this context, the prophet/healer can meet this world of insecurity, often of misfortune, and look into the future in order to be better prepared for what is approaching. The prophets take seriously the world in which their people live. The emphasis is never on "pie in the sky when you die"; the emphasis is on what is needed in the here and now. Theologically, there are issues which need close scrutiny but from a socio-psychological point of view, the prophet's position is firmly established in many AIC and is a tremendous source of security to many.

BIBLIOGRAPHY

Albright, W.F., *Studies in the Old Testament prophecy*, Edinburgh, 1950.

Anderson, E., *Messianic popular movements in the Lower Congo*, Uppsala, 1958.

Baeta, C.G., *Prophetism in Ghana*, London, 1962.

Barrett, D.B., *Schism and renewal in Africa*, Oxford/Nairobi, 1968.

Beattie, J., and J. Middleton, *Spirit mediumship and society in Africa*, London, 1969.

Becken, H.-J., *Theologie der Heilung: Das Heilen in den Afrikanischen unabhängigen Kirchen in Südafrika*, Hermannsburg, Verlag Missionshandlung, 1972.

Benz, E. (ed), *Messianische Kirchen, Sekten und Bewegungen in heutigen Afrika*, Leiden, 1965.

Berglund, A.I., *Zulu thought—the patterns and symbolism*, Cape Town, David Philip, 1976.

Best, E., "Spirit–baptism", *Novum Testamentum*, 1960, pp 236—243.

Brandel-Syrier, L., *Black woman in search of God*, London, Lutterworth, 1962.

Brown, P., *Augustine of Hippo*, London, Faber, 1967.

—, "Sorcery, demons and the rise of Christianity in the Middle Ages", in Douglas, M. (ed), *Witchcraft, confessions and accusations*, London, Tavistock Publications, 1970.

Crehan, J.H., *Early Christian Baptism and the Creed*, London, 1950.

Daneel, M.L., *Old and new in Southern Shona Independent Churches*, Leiden, Mouton, Vol I, 1971; Vol II, 1974; Vol. III, 1988.

—, *Quest for belonging*, Gweru, Mambo Press, 1987.

Dargie, D., *Xhosa Zionist Church music*, Johannesburg, Hodder and Stoughton, 1986.

Dawes, E. and E.H. Baynes, *Three Byzantine Saints*, Oxford, Blackwell, 1948.

Dodds, E.R., *Pagan and Christian in an age of anxiety*, Cambridge, Cambridge University Press, 1965.

Evans-Pritchard, E.E., *Witchcraft, oracles and magic among the Azande*, Oxford, Clarendon Press, 1937; also "Witchcraft", *Africa* 8 (4), 417—22.

Gluckman, M., *The logic of African science and witchcraft*, Lusaka, Rhodes Livingstone Institute for Social Research, 1944.

—, *Custom and conflict in Africa*, Oxford, Blackwell, 1963.

Hammond-Tooke, W.D., "The aetiology of Spirit in Southern Africa", *African Studies*, 1988.

Jeremias, J., *Die Kinder-Taufe in den ersten 4 Jahrhunderten*, Stuttgart, 1958.

Jung, C.G., *Psychology and Religion: West and East*, Vol II, Collective Works, London, 1958. Translation of *Psychologie und Religion*, Basil, 1937.

—, *Symbols of Transformation*, Vol V, Collective Works, London, 1959.

Kiernan, J.P.,"Where Zionists draw the line: a study of religious exclusiveness in an African township", *African Studies* 33 (2), 1974, 79—90.

—, "Prophet and preacher: an essential partnership in the work of Zion", *Man*, 1976, 11 (3), 356—66.

—, "The work of Zion: an analysis of an African Zionist ritual", *Africa*, 46, 1976, 340—56.

—, "Saltwater and ashes: Instruments of curing among some Zulu Zionists", *Journal of Religion in Africa*, Vol IX, fasc.1, Leiden, Brill, 1978.

—, "The weapons of Zion", *Journal of Religion in Africa*, Vol X, fasc. 1, 1979, 13—21.

—, "The 'problem of evil' in the context of ancestral intervention in the affairs of the living in Africa", *Man*, 17, 1982, pp 287—301.

—, *Havens of health in a Zulu City: The production and mangement of therapeutic power in Zionist Churches*, Lewiston/Queenstown/Lampeter, The Edwin Mellen Press, 1990.

Laternari, V., *The religion of the oppressed*, London, 1963.

Lee, S.G., "Spirit possession among Zulu" in Beattie, J. and Middleton, J. (eds), *Spirit mediumship and Society in Africa*, London, Routledge, 1969.

Lewis, I.M., "A structural approach to witchcraft and spirit possession" in Douglas, M., *Witchcraft, Confessions and Accusations*, London, Tavistock, 1970.

—, *Estatic Religion: An anthropological study of spirit possession and shamanism*, Pelican Anthropological Library, Penguin Books, 1971.

Makhatini, D.L., *Ancestor, Umoya, Angels in our approach to the Independent Church Movement in South Africa*, Mapumulo, 1965.

Margull, H.J., *Aufbruch zur Zukunft*, Gutersloh, Kaiser, 1962.

Masambo ma Mpolo, "Kindoki as diagnosis and therapy" in *African Theological Journal*, 13, 1984, 3.

Martin, M.L., *The biblical concept of Mesianism and Messianism in Southern Africa*, Morija (Lesotho), 1965.

—, *Kirche ohne Weisse*, Basel, 1971.

Momigliano, A.D. (ed), *The conflict between paganism and Christianity in the Fourth Century*, London, OUP, 1963.

Mowinckel, S., *Die Erkenntnis Gottes bei den alten testamentischen Propheten*, Oslo, 1941.

Ngubane, H., *Body and mind in Zulu medicine*, London, Academic Press, 1977.

Oosthuizen, G.C., *The theology of a South African Messiah*, London, 1967.

—, *Post Christianity in Africa*, Grand Rapids/London, 1968.

—, *Baptism in the context of the African Indigenous/Independent Churches*, Series F, No 2, University of Zululand, 1985.

—, *Afro-Christian Religions, Iconography of Religions* XXIV, 12, Leiden, Brill, 1979.

—, (ed), *Religion Alive*, Johannesburg, Hodder and Stoughton, 1986.

—, *The birth of Christian Zionism in South Africa*, Publication Series T4, University of Zululand, 1987.

—, *Afro-Christian religion and healing in Southern Africa*, Lewiston/Queenstown/Lampeter, The Edwin Mellen Press, 1989 (co-editors Hexham, I., Edwards S.D., Wessels, W.H.).

—, *Afro-Christian religion at the grassroots in Southern Africa*, Lewiston/Queenstown/Lampeter, The Edwin Mellen Press, 1991 (co-editor Hexham, I.).

Pauw, B.A., *Religion in a Tswana Chiefdom*, OUP, 1960.

—, *Christianity and Xhosa Tradition*, OUP, 1968.

Rendtorff, R., *Prophetenspruch, Religion in Geschichte und Gegenwart*, Tübingen, Mohr, 1961.

Robinson, T.H., *Prophecy and the prophets of ancient Israel*, London, 1923, 1948.

Rowley, H.H. (ed), *Studies in Old Testament prophecy*, London, 1950.

Schlosser, K., *Eingeborene Kirchen in Süd und Südwest-Afrika*, Kiel, Muhlau, 1958.

Shank, D.A., *The Prophet of Modern Times: The thought of William Waddy Harris*, Birmingham, 1985.

Sibisi, H., *Colour symbolism in the treatment of disease among the Zulu*, unpublished, pp 1-18.

Stenzel, A., *Die Taufe: Eine genetische Erklärung der Taufeliturgie*, Hamburg, 1958.

Sundkler, B.G.M., *Bantu Prophets in South Africa*, London, OUP, 1961.

—, *Zulu Zion and some Swazi Zionists*, London, 1976.

Turner, H.W., *African Independent Church (Aladura)*, Vol I and II, Oxford, 1967.

Vilakazi, A., *Zulu Transformations*, Pietermaritzburg, University of Natal Press, 1962.

Vriezen, Th.C., "Prophecy and Eschatology", *Vetus Testamentum* 1, 1953.

—, *An outline of Old Testament Theology*, Oxford, 1962.

Welbourn, F., *East African rebels*, London, 1961.

— and B.A. Ogot, *A place to feel at home*, London, 1962.

Wessels, W.H., *Zulu Folk Healers and Psychiatry: A study of Traditional Healers and Faith Healers of the African Independent Churches in Relation to Psychiatric Disorders*, Final Report supported by NERMIC, 1990, 156 pp.

West, M., *Bishops and Prophets in a black city: African independent Churches in Soweto*, Johannesburg, Cape Town, David Philip, 1975.

—, "The shades come to town: Ancestors and Urban Independent Churches" in M.G. Whisson and M.E. West (eds), *Religion and Social change in Southern Africa— Anthropological essays in honour of Monica Wilson*, Cape Town, 1975.

—, "Propheten", *Die Religion in Geschichte und Gegenwart*, Tübingen, 1961, 610—638.

Zulu, P. and Oosthuizen, G.C., "Religion and World Outlook" in *Afro–Christian Religion at the grassroots in Southern Africa*, Lewiston/Queenstown/Lampeter, 1991, pp 334—363. (Co-editors Oosthuizen, G.C. and Hexham, I.)

INDEX

STUDIES IN
CHRISTIAN MISSION

E.J. BRILL — P.O.B. 9000 — 2300 PA Leiden — The Netherlands